Reclaiming Development Agendas

By the same author

BETWEEN HOPE AND INSECURITY: The Social Consequences of the Cambodian Peace Process, editor (1994)

ECONOMIC REFORM AND THIRD-WORLD SOCIALISM: A Political Economy of Food Policy in Post-Revolutionary Societies (1992)

STATES OF DISARRAY: The Social Effects of Globalization, co-edited with Dharam Ghai, Cynthia Hewitt de Alcántara, Yusuf Bangura, Jessica Vivian and Peter Stalker (1995)

THE GREENING OF BUSINESS IN DEVELOPING COUNTRIES: Rhetoric, Reality and Prospects, editor (2002)

TREES, PEOPLE AND POWER: Social Dimensions of Deforestation and Forest Protection in Central America (1993)

VISIBLE HANDS: Taking Responsibility for Social Development, co-edited with Cynthia Hewitt de Alcántara and Peter Stalker (2000)

Reclaiming Development Agendas

Knowledge, Power and International Policy Making

Edited by

Peter Utting

UNRISD

United Nations
Research Institute
for Social Development

First published 2006 by
PALGRAVE MACMILLAN
Houndmills, Basingstoke, Hampshire RG21 6XS and
175 Fifth Avenue, New York, N.Y. 10010
Companies and representatives throughout the world

PALGRAVE MACMILLAN is the global academic imprint of the Palgrave Macmillan division of St. Martin's Press, LLC and of Palgrave Macmillan Ltd. Macmillan® is a registered trademark in the United States, United Kingdom and other countries. Palgrave is a registered trademark in the European Union and other countries.

ISBN-13: 978–1–4039–9494–3 hardback
ISBN-10: 1–4039–9494–3 hardback

This book is printed on paper suitable for recycling and made from fully managed and sustained forest sources.

A catalogue record for this book is available from the British Library.

Library of Congress Cataloging-in-Publication Data
Reclaiming development agendas : knowledge, power and international
    policy making / edited by Peter Utting.
        p.   cm.
Includes bibliographical references and index.
ISBN 1–4039–9494–3 (cloth)
1. Social policy.   2. Economic development.   3. International
agencies.   4. Knowledge, Sociology of.   5. Power (Social sciences)
I. Utting, Peter.
HN28.R397 2006
320.6—dc22   2005058647

10   9   8   7   6   5   4   3   2   1
15   14   13   12   11   10   09   08   07   06

Printed and bound in Great Britain by
Antony Rowe Ltd, Chippenham and Eastbourne

Contents

Foreword: Some Reflections on the Links Between Social Knowledge and Policy

José Antonio Ocampo
United Nations Under-Secretary General for Economic and Social Affairs

Ideas *do* matter, particularly when they have an institutional backing. However, their interplay with economic and social policy is governed by a wide range of competing factors not related to ideas per se. In particular, knowledge in the economic and social area is deeply affected by ideology and interests, and this factor is critical in understanding the links between knowledge and policy making.

We know all too well from history that the influence of power relations and ideologies on economic and social ideas and policies is often direct and even brutal. However, even when the link is more complex (as we hope it is in democratic societies), it should be recognized that all knowledge systems have what may be called 'blind spots', that is, areas where questions are not admitted or do not make sense within a specific conceptual framework. This affects, in turn, the nature of empirical research and, more generally, the way reality is read. The existence of these 'blind spots' is perhaps the most important channel through which ideology affects knowledge about social conditions in democratic societies, that is, by affecting the questions that are asked and the filters through which reality is read.

Beyond this issue, it is worth bringing into this analysis some concepts derived from the literature on financial markets. These markets are affected not only by 'asymmetric information' among market actors but also by expectations formed about the future, for which factual information will never be available. So, what is called 'information' in financial markets is most of the time just opinions of market actors rather than information in the true sense of the term. Something similar happens with ideas in the social arena. We like to think that knowledge plays a leading role in determining policy, but it is often just opinions partly based on knowledge, which are quite susceptible to the influence of other social factors – that is, again ideology and interests. Furthermore, as in financial markets, these opinions tend to generate 'contagion' – that is, the tendency of the ideas of some actors to be based on those of other actors. The reason is quite simple: it is costly for a specific agent to deviate from the average opinion as, in the case of ideas, it may mean her/his marginalization from access to power and influence.

The great imperfections that characterize our 'knowledge' about social reality and of its links with policy making underscore the import-ance of the liberal principle that recognizes the possibility of error or partial vision, and embraces critical debate among competing schools of economic thought, and among competing ideologies and interests, as the only way to overcome the limitations of any single way of thinking about social reality. Pluralism and critical debate are thus crucial to overcoming the limitations of any individual school of thought in the economic and social area and to better informing policy makers. They are also important to guarantee that different interests that exist in a given society are taken into account in decision making, and to avoid an excessive influence of ideology on practices.

This reflection is essential to understanding the role that the United Nations (UN) has played in the formation of ideas and debates on economic and social conditions since the end of the Second World War. In this regard, a distinct advantage of the UN in the international debates on economic and social issues is that it is a very plural forum. Due to its institutional design, it gives a stronger voice to the views and interests of weaker nations, weaker ministries within governments, civil society actors and schools of thought that do not share mainstream views, including those made up by intellectuals from the developing world. Furthermore, it can be argued that the unparalleled legitimacy of the institution in the international arena is associated with its pluralistic character.

We could go a step further in this analysis. Some of the major achievements of the UN in the realm of ideas have been, precisely, the result of the backing of non-mainstream schools of thought and of 'international civil society'. At the origin of the institution lies the Universal Declaration of Human Rights, which had a profound effect on intellectual thinking in the UN, leading to what has come to be called the 'rights-based approach' to the analyses of social conditions and development. The evolution of this approach, which encompasses not only civil and political rights, but also economic, social and cultural rights, has been deeply influenced by several waves of 'international civil society' movements with both liberal and socialist roots. At the same time, the 'rights-based approach' can hardly be traced to mainstream schools of economic and social thought, which even today find such a framework hard to understand. The influence of non-mainstream schools of thought and of civil society is also reflected in the global summits and conferences of the past decades, through which the UN has opened the space for new thinking and policy decisions on a wide range of critical social and environmental issues: social equity and cohesion, gender equality, sustainable development, and the rights of indigenous peoples, to mention a few.

In the realm of ideas about economic development and the international economic system, the UN played a leading role in the early post-war decades. This was closely associated with the process of decolonization, in which the organization also played a central role. This influence probably reached its peak with the creation of the United Nations Conference on Trade and Development (UNCTAD) and the subsequent dialogue on a new international economic order. As we know, political events have led to significant changes in this regard since the late 1970s. While the UN preserved its place as the central world forum and the source of international policy making for social and environmental issues, the Bretton Woods institutions became the major *economic* forum. This affected in a significant manner the role of the UN in economic development and international economic policy making.

The way development ideas are formed and their links to economic policy making were fundamentally affected during this transition. This can be illustrated first with the experience of Latin America. During the period of state-led industrialization – more commonly but inappropriately known as the period of import substitution industrialization – historians of economic thought have recognized that practice preceded policy and policy preceded theory. Practice was largely driven by the pragmatic response to the unusual circumstances generated by the Great Depression of the 1930s, as well as by the disruption in trade during both World Wars and the collapse of commodity prices after the First World War. Policy, particularly the focus of the attention of authorities on domestic markets and industrialization, came as a late outcome of this empirical response of authorities to external shocks. The theory of industrialization, as developed by the United Nations Economic Commission for Latin America, ECLA (now ECLAC, as it includes the Caribbean) in the 1950s, thus came at the end rather than the start of the process.

In other parts of the developing world the influence of the political struggle against colonialism and of economic planning was more important. Some schools of thought, particularly Marxism, Keynesianism and the social-democratic ideal of the welfare state, influenced economic and social policy making, but in most cases practice was only loosely tied to these schools of thought. Thus, central planning in the Soviet Union was more the result of the application of systems that were initially designed by some belligerent powers to manage their economies during the First World War, particularly Germany, and can hardly be traced to classical Marxist thinking. Planning in general was more the result of distrust in the functioning of markets, which performed very poorly in the inter-war years. This is clearly the reason why planning was such a widespread though variable practice in most industrial and developing countries. However, there was no such a thing as a theory of planning that predated such broad-based practices; rather, theories came as the codification of practices.

Once developed, ideas did influence practice, both at the national and the international level. In the latter case, the ideas developed by ECLA had major world-wide effects, through the influence that ECLA had on UNCTAD when it was created in 1964. However, the history of these ideas indicates that the views of UNCTAD and the debate on the international economic order should be seen not as reflections of theoretical constructs, but of the practice that many developing countries had developed in the light of the economic and political events unleashed by the 'age of catastrophe' (to use the term of the British historian Eric Hobsbawm) and the collapse of colonialism.

The chain of causation has been reversed over the past quarter century, with theory now clearly predating and determining policy. It was the rebirth of neoclassical economics in the 1960s and 1970s, and particularly of its neoliberal versions (that is, those that tend to disregard 'market failures' and to rather emphasize the costs of government intervention), that gradually came to dominate thinking about economic development and international economic policy making. In the 1980s, the debt crisis and a major new collapse of commodity prices created a major opportunity to reshape development policy in those regions adversely affected by these shocks. It can be said, of course, that it was the weakness of the preceding model that led to over-indebtedness and thus to crises. But even if this were partially true, it does not eliminate the major links that we are suggesting, namely, that, unlike the past, theory predated policy.

The 'blind spots' that characterized the new paradigm were crucial, given the dominant role that theory now played in the reshaping of development practice and the international economic order. One major and costly 'blind spot' was found in the analysis of financial markets, despite the significant increase in knowledge about their functioning that came with the theory of 'asymmetric information'. Only the financial collapse of many developing countries that came with the 1997 Asian crisis led to a widespread revision of the virtues of financial liberalization by the Bretton Woods institutions and by many orthodox thinkers.

The way reality is read was also subject to distortions. Two cases illustrate this. The first one is the insistence that success in Asia over the past three decades has been associated with economic practice that followed principles akin to neoliberal economic thinking, thus altogether ignoring the leading role that state interventions played in these success stories. On the opposite side, the attempt to view as 'successful' the economic outcomes of more diligent students of the new paradigm has stood in some cases in sharp contrast with reality, for example the fact that the economic performance of Latin America was much better during the period of state-led industrialization than during the recent neoliberal phase.

Since the risks associated with financial fragility, the role of the state in the rapid growth in Asia and the ambivalent effects of market reforms in Latin America and elsewhere were emphasized by other schools of economic thought, more pluralism in economic debate would have certainly helped to improve the links between economic analysis and policy making. Pluralism in the economic debate has increased as a result of the major disconnect between neoliberal economic analysis and reality in the years following the Asian crisis. Interestingly, this has been accompanied by the return of the UN as a relevant development forum. This is reflected both in the leading role that the United Nations Millennium Development Goals have come to occupy in the global debate on development and also, and very interestingly, with the fact that the International Conference on Financing for Development that took place in Monterrey in 2002 was convened under the umbrella of the UN, although in close cooperation with the Bretton Woods institutions.

A major issue in the application of the new economic paradigm was the inability to understand, at least initially, the crucial role played by *domestic* institutions in the adaptation of any form of knowledge to policy. This has been captured by the dual concepts of 'capacity building' and 'ownership' of economic and social policies, which have come to occupy a central role in development assistance since the issue of the 1996 strategic vision of the Organisation for Economic Co-operation and Development/Development Assistance Committee (OECD/DAC) on development cooperation. These concepts have recognized that a virtuous link between knowledge and policy making in the economic and social fields is dependent upon the stock of human capital and institutions that facilitate the analysis of economic and social reality, the design of policies appropriate to the particular circumstances surrounding a country, and the adaptation of foreign knowledge and, at its best, the creation of autonomous knowledge. Given the leading role of governments in policy making, a central component of such networks must be the accumulation of human capital in the state sector, and the active interaction and participation of the civil service in the intellectual networks.

The development of such virtuous links thus depends on the creation of strong domestic and even local 'knowledge systems', an idea closely related to the need for 'innovation systems' to guarantee the adequate adaptation of technology to the domestic circumstances and the creation of new technical knowledge. A major reason for this is that, due to the inherent imperfections of any form of economic and social knowledge, there is no substitute for a very dynamic interaction between knowledge and practice, which has many context-specific features and thus cannot be merely 'imported' (as institutions in general cannot be purely 'imported'). This is what a deep understanding of 'ownership' and 'institution building' in economic and social policy making implies. So, and contrary to many perceptions, the idea that 'we already know what must be done', although apparently effective in the short run, is an inappropriate approach to achieving a virtuous link between knowledge and policy making in the long run. What is important, in other words, is to develop economic and social analyses at the domestic and local levels, not to import ready-made solutions from abroad.

Such an approach to building a better relationship between economic and social analysis and policy making is less likely in an intellectual world characterized by strong centre-periphery dimensions. In the realm of economic ideas, this is the situation today, in contrast to the experience of the earlier post-war decades. Indeed, in the 1950s and 1960s, some regional institutions in the developing world were able to influence the terms in which policy discussions were couched. The contribution of the ECLA to UNCTAD, mentioned previously, is noteworthy in this regard. Also, in the centre, different schools of thought competed with each other. This meant, in turn, that intellectuals and policy makers from the South that were trained in the North brought to the domestic debates in which they were involved a more pluralistic pool of ideas. This allowed for a diversity of views and approaches to permeate and enliven international economic debates as well as domestic economic debates in developing countries. Today, the centre-periphery character of the system of generation of economic ideas is much stronger, and we could even say that even European economic thinking has become peripheral. A growing pool of students of economics, particularly those likely to be tomorrow's policy analysts and policy makers in the developing world, are growing up in an intellectual universe dominated almost exclusively by United States academia.

The debate on 'ownership' must obviously be tied to that on conditionality. According to the previous arguments, it is local capacity and stronger domestic 'knowledge systems' that will build better links between analysis and policy making in the economic and social fields in the developing world. In this sense, conditionality is not only an inadequate rule to practice: it frequently does *not* work, because it adversely affects the foundations on which better policy making can be built. When conditionality does work, it is not because views are imposed from above, but because it has affected the correlation of forces – intellectual debates as well as power relations – at the domestic level that plays the crucial role in policy making.

In summary, it is not the role of international institutions to promote dominant views on economic and social issues; it is rather to help developing countries build their own institutions for better analysis and policy making. For both, intellectual pluralism is essential. The encouragement of different points of view in all institutional settings, and the willingness to admit that there may be other ways to examine an issue, or new questions to be asked, are crucial to avoid the excessive influence of ideologies and powerful interests in economic and social policy. Thus, the combination of strong 'knowledge systems' for analysis and policy making in the developing countries, and pluralism in international institutions and debates is the best possible mix for building virtuous links between knowledge and policy making in the economic and social field.

List of Abbreviations and Acronyms

ACP	African, Caribbean and Pacific Group of States
ACS	Association of Caribbean States
ADB	Asian Development Bank
AIDS	acquired immunodeficiency syndrome
BWIs	Bretton Woods institutions
CARICOM	Caribbean Community
CBOs	community-based organizations
CCMs	Country Co-ordinating Mechanisms
CDD	Community-Driven Development
CDF	Comprehensive Development Framework
CEO	chief executive officer
CIDA	Canadian International Development Agency
CRNM	Caribbean Regional Negotiating Machinery
CSO	civil society organization
DAC	Development Assistance Committee
Danida	Danish International Development Agency
DAWN	Development Alternatives with Women for a New Era
DBS	direct budget support
DFID	Department for International Development (UK)
EBRD	European Bank for Reconstruction and Development
ECA	United Nations Economic Commission for Africa
ECE	United Nations Economic Commission for Europe
ECLA	United Nations Economic Commission for Latin America
ECLAC	United Nations Economic Commission for Latin America and the Caribbean
ECOSOC	United Nations Economic and Social Council
EFA	Education for All
E-HIPC	enhanced Heavily Indebted Poor Countries
ESCAP	United Nations Economic and Social Commission for Asia and the Pacific
EU	European Union
FTAA	Free Trade Area of the Americas
FTI	Fast Track Initiative
G7	Canada, France, Germany, Italy, Japan, United Kingdom, United States

G8	Canada, France, Germany, Italy, Japan, Russian Federation, United Kingdom, United States
G20	Finance ministers of 19 countries plus the European Union
G77	Group of 77 developing countries (including today 132 countries)
G90	Group of 90 developing countries (including the ACP Group, the African Union and the Least Developed Countries)
GPPNs	Global Public Policy Networks
HDR	*Human Development Report*
HIPC	Heavily Indebted Poor Countries
HIV	human immunodeficiency virus
ICPD	International Conference on Population and Development
IDRC	International Development Research Centre
IDTs	International Development Targets
IFI	international financial institution
ILO	International Labour Organization
IMF	International Monetary Fund
INGO	international non-governmental organization
JICA	Japan International Cooperation Agency
KM	knowledge management
MDD	Millennium Development Declaration
MDGs	Millennium Development Goals
MERCOSUR	Mercado Común del Sur (Latin America's Common Market of the South)
NGO	non-governmental organization
NIEO	New International Economic Order
NT2	Nam Theun 2
ODs	Operational Directives
OECD	Organisation for Economic Co-operation and Development
PDR	People's Democratic Republic (Lao)
PFP	Policy Framework Paper
PRSPs	Poverty Reduction Strategy Papers
SADC	Southern African Development Community
SAPs	structural adjustment programmes
SFA	Schooling for All
Sida	Swedish International Development Cooperation Agency
SPA	Strategic Partnership with Africa
SWAP	sector-wide approach
TSPs	Target Strategy Papers

UK	United Kingdom
UN	United Nations
UNCED	United Nations Conference on Environment and Development
UNCTAD	United Nations Conference on Trade and Development
UNDESA	United Nations Department of Economic and Social Affairs
UNDP	United Nations Development Programme
UNEP	United Nations Environment Programme
UNESCO	United Nations Educational, Scientific and Cultural Organization
UNHCR	Office of the United Nations High Commissioner for Refugees
UNICEF	United Nations Children's Fund
UNIHP	United Nations Intellectual History Project
UNRISD	United Nations Research Institute for Social Development
UPE	universal primary education
US	United States
USSR	Union of Soviet Socialist Republics
WCSDG	World Commission on the Social Dimension of Globalization
WDR	World Development Report
WHO	World Health Organization
WSF	World Social Forum
WTO	World Trade Organization

Notes on the Contributors

Karen Brock is an independent development consultant. She was previously a researcher with the Participation Group at the Institute of Development Studies, University of Sussex.

Andrea Cornwall is a fellow at the Institute of Development Studies at the University of Sussex.

Bob Deacon is Professor of International Social Policy at the University of Sheffield. He is Director of the Globalism and Social Policy Programme (www.gaspp.org) and founding editor of the journal *Global Social Policy*.

Louis Emmerij was President of the OECD Development Centre and Special Advisor to the President, Inter-American Development Bank. Since 1999 he has been Co-Director of the United Nations Intellectual History Project and Senior Research Fellow at the Graduate Center, City University of New York.

Norman Girvan is Professorial Research Fellow at the Institute of International Relations, University of the West Indies, Trinidad. He was previously Secretary General of the Association of Caribbean States.

Shalmali Guttal is Senior Associate at Focus on the Global South (Focus), a non-governmental policy research organization based in Bangkok, where she coordinates the Finance and Development, and Alternatives programmes.

Richard Jolly is Professor at the Institute of Development Studies, University of Sussex, and Co-Director of the United Nations Intellectual History Project. He was formerly Deputy Executive Director, Programmes of UNICEF, and Principal Coordinator of UNDP's *Human Development Report*.

Kenneth King is Professor of International and Comparative Education, and Director of the Centre for African Studies, University of Edinburgh.

José Antonio Ocampo is United Nations Under-Secretary General for Economic and Social Affairs, and was formerly Executive Secretary of the Economic Commission for Latin America and the Caribbean (ECLAC).

Gita Sen is Sir Ratan Tata Chair Professor at the Indian Institute of Management in Bangalore, and Adjunct Professor of Population and International Health at the Faculty of Public Health, Harvard University. She is a founding member of DAWN and a trustee of HealthWatch (India).

John Toye is a Senior Research Associate of Queen Elizabeth House, University of Oxford. He was formerly a Director of UNCTAD and Director of the Institute of Development Studies, University of Sussex.

Richard Toye is Lecturer in History at Homerton College, Cambridge.

Peter Utting is Deputy Director, United Nations Research Institute for Social Development (UNRISD), Geneva.

Thomas G. Weiss is Presidential Professor of Political Science at The CUNY Graduate Center and Director of the Ralph Bunche Institute for International Studies, where he is Co-Director of the United Nations Intellectual History Project and editor of *Global Governance*.

Introduction: Reclaiming Development Agendas

Peter Utting[1]

> The distribution of wealth is closely correlated with social distinctions that stratify people, communities, and nations into groups that dominate and those that are dominated. These patterns of domination persist because economic and social differences are reinforced by the overt and covert use of power (World Bank, 2005).

> ...we find almost everywhere a complicated arrangement of society into various orders, a manifold gradation of social rank.... [E]very form of society has been based...on the antagonism of oppressing and oppressed classes (Marx and Engels, 1848).[2]

About this book

Judging by the similar tone of the above quotes, the language of leading international development organizations appears to have taken a radical turn of late. Such changes in mainstream discourse have, in fact, been evident since the 1990s when various actors and institutions reacted to structural adjustment programmes and other features of economic globalization and 'neoliberalism'. Following a series of civil society mobilizations, institutional initiatives and high profile reports – for example, the '50 Years is Enough' campaign,[3] the World Summit for Social Development[4] and other UN summits, and the annual publication of the *Human Development Report* (HDR)[5] – terms and concepts like 'poverty reduction', 'rights-based development', 'good governance' and 'empowerment' emerged as new mantras. Furthermore, international development agencies began positioning themselves as 'knowledge agencies',[6] attempting to enhance their role as intellectual actors and to be more responsive to 'local knowledge', the 'voices of the poor',[7] and the needs and realities of developing countries.

The World Bank, in particular, has changed its tune, toning down its more orthodox macroeconomic prescriptions and blind faith in market forces, acknowledging the need for more proactive approaches to deal with the social and environmental costs of market liberalization and economic 'reform', upgrading the role of state, and emphasizing the importance of 'social capital'[8] and redistribution[9] in well-functioning markets and societies. As a corrective to forms of technocratic governance and policy conditionality that characterized the design and implementation of structural adjustment programmes, consultation and decision-making processes related to economic and social policy are said to be more participatory, and locally and nationally embedded. Such is the case, it is claimed, with the Poverty Reduction Strategy Papers (PRSPs) promoted by the World Bank.[10]

Why are such changes occurring? Is the uptake of progressive buzzwords reflected in meaningful policy change? Are discursive adaptations and policy and institutional reforms likely to improve the prospects of the world's poorest nations and result in patterns of development that are more inclusive and equitable? This volume addresses these questions by examining the determinants of changes in the discourse and policy of multilateral and bilateral development agencies, and the interrelationships among knowledge, power and policy making. The contributors also assess the potential and limits of what has been called 'the new development agenda', and identify crucial elements of alternative approaches that might enable less powerful countries, actors and institutions to reclaim development agendas. The authors include leading thinkers on development issues, several of whom have played a prominent role in international organizations and social movements. They focus, in particular, on the World Bank, the United Nations (UN) and certain bilateral agencies, as well as specific themes and issues, including poverty reduction strategies, gender equality, education policy, global social policy, and institutional innovations associated with 'knowledge agencies'. What emerges is a powerful critique of contemporary 'development-speak' and policy, as well as important insights into alternative strategies.

Understanding the knowledge–policy nexus

Scholars associated with various liberal, realist, and institutionalist schools of thought have long been engaged in a heated debate about the dynamics of policy change and the relative importance of interests and ideational factors, or of agency and structure (Cooper and English, 2005; Ruggie, 1998). This literature provides numerous pointers to explain the role of ideas, institutions and power in shaping the new development agenda, as well as what we should make of the changing language of development and the emergence of 'knowledge agencies'.

Liberal and more recent 'constructivist' thinking tend to place greater weight on the role of ideas, norms, values, identities, ideology and agency (Weiss and Carayannis, 2001). Reflexivity and 'social learning', and the age-old process of rational problem solving that is a feature of modernization, suggest that policy analysts, technocrats and other decision makers will attempt to understand and respond to complexity, risk and uncertainty, and are eager to learn from best practices, as well as from past mistakes and failures, and to adjust policy accordingly (Hall, 1993; Heclo, 1974). New thinking and particular concepts are thought to stand a better chance of filtering through to policy makers because of institutional developments occurring at national, regional and global levels, such as networking, partnerships, multistakeholder dialogues, and the strengthening of so-called epistemic communities that facilitate links between professionals/scientists, activists and decision makers (Haas, 1989; Ruggie, 2003). Consequently, policy change results increasingly from 'communities of shared knowledge and not simply domestic or transnational interest groups' (Haas, 1989). Furthermore, the technical nature of certain bodies of knowledge increases the influence of new social actors, namely 'experts', in the policy process. Some strands of discourse and institutional analysis suggest that discourses 'do more than just get in the way' of institutional change; they, too, can be reconstituted and facilitate political and institutional change (Dryzek, 1996).

Various schools of thought related to realist and political economy traditions tend to emphasize aspects associated with societal pressures, power relations, structural factors, and the interests of particular actors and institutions, which largely determine the course of events, as well as the ideas they espouse (Cox, 1997). Changes in international development discourse and policy are often seen as a reflection of changes in the balance of social forces. Accordingly, what is needed for world development is not so much a 'rearrangement of knowledge [as] a realignment of power' (Nederveen Pieterse, 2005). From this perspective, contemporary adaptations in discourse and policy are responses to periodic crises (for example, financial), social and political pressures emanating from the perception or reality of the developmental failures of neoliberal policy and 'corporate globalization', as well as from heightened global awareness and activism associated with poverty, human rights and North-South inequality. The potential and limits of policy change are often explained with reference to the ways in which powerful actors and institutions respond to societal pressure, systemic threats and policy failure in order to reassert their dominance, control and legitimacy (Escobar, 1995). And they are likely to mould or 'frame' issues in ways that are compatible with their world view and institutional mandates and cultures[11] (Bøås and McNeill, 2004).

Both post-modernist and certain political economy perspectives have highlighted the political and ideological underpinnings of development 'narratives' and policy prescriptions, and the selective uptake of information and evidence within bureaucracies and policy making circles (Lewis *et al.*, 2005). The social construction of knowledge about development can be viewed as a battlefield[12] between actors and institutions with different world views. Knowledge processes do not simply involve information flows between producers of knowledge, disseminators and utilizers, but complex 'interaction and dialogue between specific actors' with different 'life-worlds' in which 'discontinuity rather than linkage, and transformation not transfer of meaning' are key (Long, 2002: 274). Through such processes, the analysis of development problems is often depoliticized in the sense that it is disconnected from political and structural realities, and alternative or radical ideas are diluted or neutralized. Gramscian analysis introduces an important variant by emphasizing that powerful interests and institutions have the capacity to take up progressive concepts and agendas as part of a hegemonic project that is quite capable of accommodating oppositional views. The relative mix of ideational factors and societal pressures in policy change may also vary considerably depending on what aspect of the policy regime is being challenged or reformed, and the extent to which policy makers 'are armed with a coherent policy paradigm' that, to some extent, can shield them from societal interests (Hall, 1993). In this light, the frequent shifts in international development discourse and policy may be a sign that the dominant neoliberal paradigm is in crisis.

A number of currents and circumstances have come together to explain the depth of contemporary interest in the relationship between knowledge and policy making. In addition to the traditional debate that has preoccupied social scientists as to the relative roles of ideas and interests, or agency and structure, in processes of change, new institutional arrangements and policy contexts associated with globalization and global governance have emerged. We live not only in the 'information age', when the question of knowledge and how it is generated, tapped, managed and used has become paramount, but also in the age of 'good governance' and 'technocratic governance', when policy makers are expected to draw on evidence-based research and 'expert' analysis rather than simply be swayed by conventional power politics and institutional relations. We also live in the era of complexity, risk, and interdependency, which suggest the need for multistakeholder dialogues, partnerships and decision making, as well as networking and new forms of social learning, and forms of activism that place greater emphasis on collaboration and not simply confrontation (Bendell and Murphy, 2002; Utting, 2005a). In a context where the new knowledge culture and industry leads to information overload and 'confusion', 'consultation, coordination and collaboration have quickly become the hand-maidens of knowledge' (Dufour, 2003). And in keeping with principles of new public management, those on the receiving end of international development assistance are expected to demonstrate 'efficiency', partly by being 'results based'. For researchers and their organizations this means having to show their worth by being policy relevant and to craft strategies and relationships to access and influence policy makers (Stone and Maxwell, 2004).

But this raises a complex set of questions. They include not only nuts and bolts issues, such as how research findings are packaged and disseminated, and who in the policy process should be targeted, but also whether research is both credible and relevant as far as policy makers are concerned. More complex still, as suggested above, are other issues related to the uptake of ideas (Carden, 2005; Court *et al.*, 2005; de Vibe *et al.*, 2002; Mosse, 2004a; Weiss, 1977). These include issues of state and institutional capacity, as well as the politics of policy change and the way in which different interests, crisis conditions and perceptions of policy failure exert pressures on the policy-making process. They also include sociological factors, notably the fact that the researcher–policy maker nexus is mediated by a host of formal and informal social and institutional relations involving not only researchers, technocrats and policy makers but also activists, lobbyists, the media and various types of networks. Ideological and bureaucratic realities are particularly important; for example, entrenched ways of thinking and practice, the need to follow the 'party line' within government and development agencies, so-called path dependency and the way ideas 'percolate', as well as the topicality of a particular issue and whether or not policy makers recognize there is a problem that needs fixing. There may be internal resistance to change within bureaucracies, turfs and jobs to defend, economic constraints, and incentive structures that condition the uptake of ideas and policy recommendations based on research.

To reflect on this complex reality, the United Nations Research Institute for Social Development (UNRISD) organized, in 2004, an international conference at the UN in Geneva which brought together scholars from various disciplines, activists and policy makers. The papers presented in this volume were originally drafted for this conference and subsequently revised on the basis of comments received from discussants and participants.[13] As discussed below, they shed light on three sets of issues: first, the relative weight of ideas, institutions and power in explaining contemporary adaptations in international development discourse and policy, and how these elements interact; second, the potential and limits of the discursive and policy shifts occurring within the system of international development agencies; and third, the crucial elements of an alternative political and policy agenda that is needed to promote more inclusive and equitable patterns of development. By way of conclusion, this introductory chapter highlights the importance of such alternative approaches in a context where an apparent convergence is taking place in the discourse and policy of international development organizations. In some respects, this convergence is more worrisome than encouraging, given the failure to rethink the dominant macroeconomic policy framework and to address issues of structure and power.

Ideas, institutions and power

Part of the analysis in this volume examines the determinants of contemporary changes in development language and policy, and reflects on the relationships between knowledge, institutions and power. Such an inquiry is, of course, not only important from an academic perspective, but also as a basis for understanding the potential and limits of discursive, policy and institutional change that claims to be promoting inclusive and equitable development.

In the Foreword, José Antonio Ocampo, United Nations Under-Secretary General for Economic and Social Affairs, sets the scene by reflecting on knowledge-policy linkages. Recognizing the crucial roles of ideology and interests in the interplay of ideas with economic and social policy, he points out that the influence of power relations and ideologies on ideas and policies is not necessarily direct or overt.

Particularly important are the 'blind spots' in knowledge systems that affect 'the questions that are asked and the filters through which reality is read'. Often what passes as knowledge is little more than opinions, which are susceptible to other influences and can spread like wild fire. The scope for 'contagion' is particularly rife in institutional settings where deviation from mainstream opinion and world views restricts 'access to power and influence'. The history of progressive ideas related to development teaches us that they often emerge in settings where individuals and institutions are relatively independent of 'the centre' or mainstream schools of thought, free from the clutches of conditionality and dogmatism, and where intellectual pluralism, critical debate and non-mainstream perspectives can flourish.

Various contributors emphasize the fact that knowledge is not independent of ideology and politics. Shalmali Guttal (Chapter 1) argues that so-called political will is not an objective condition but is shaped by material and economic interests as well as a 'universalization of specific forms of knowledge'. Development theory is not a disinterested body of knowledge but 'speaks both from and to specific positions of class and power'. The upshot is a powerful knowledge industry that justifies the structures that generate inequality and poverty. The capacity to generate information and enshrine it as knowledge is dominated by a small set of academic, donor and international agencies, as well as private interests.

Employing discourse analysis, Andrea Cornwall and Karen Brock (Chapter 2) examine how powerful actors and institutions reinforce their positions and legitimacy through the language of development and the use of specific buzzwords, such as 'participation', 'good governance', 'partnership' and 'poverty reduction'. Ideas and knowledge that are adopted by policy makers need to conform to particular frames of reference, which may vary considerably from one organization to another. The buzzwords they use form part of discourses, defined as 'the ensemble of ideas, concepts and categories through which meaning is given to phenomena' (Hajer, 1993). Today's reformist language of development not only serves to legitimize particular approaches, but also diverts attention from questionable policies and practices that underpin maldevelopment. It is part of a hegemonic project in the Gramscian sense, where powerful actors and institutions attempt to ensure that their policies and practices have broad-based appeal. The authors also remind us that 'struggles over meaning are not just about semantics: they gain a very real material dimension' when terms are put to use in policies.

The limitations of various strands of contemporary development discourse and policy can also be explained with reference to dimensions of academic inquiry and ideology that have deep historical roots. Norman Girvan (Chapter 3) critiques the 'universalistic pretensions'[14] of neoclassical economics, the tendency for 'disciplinary compartmentalization', whereby many economists detach the economic sphere from those of politics, culture and society, as well as 'mathematical formalism', which 'allowed what may have been essentially ideological assumptions...to be cloaked in a scientific garb'. Universalism was further reinforced by Eurocentrism and the colonial mindset that devalued non-European cultures and knowledge systems. Such a tradition partly explains features of contemporary development policy associated with standardized prescriptions and 'additional doses of market-oriented medicine' to correct for failed policies. It also helps explain the inability to acknowledge the importance of policy autonomy to design solutions that are context specific, and that recognise diversity, rather than universality, 'as the principal feature of social reality that provides the intellectual challenge to the analyst and policy maker'.

A major constraint on the ability of international development organizations to act as knowledge agencies that provide intellectual leadership derives from institutional practices and culture. John Toye and Richard Toye (Chapter 4) turn to the sociology of bureaucracy and a modified Weberian theory to show that while there may be some scope for original and critical research from 'defiant bureaucrats' or subordinates within international organizations, particularly in instances when those in authority lack instruments of power, individuals or units engaged in research are subject to a variety of incentives and sanctions to toe the line and reaffirm propositions espoused by senior management or an organization's sponsors.

How knowledge is generated within, and used by, the bureaucracies of multilateral and bilateral development organizations, and its relationship to policy, is also addressed by Kenneth King (Chapter 5). He traces the changes that have occurred in global education policy, arguing that the so-called 'knowledge revolution' within agencies like the World Bank and some of the bilaterals, such as the UK government's Department for International Development (DFID), has been concerned not only with the centrality of knowledge in the aid process and development but also in using and disseminating existing knowledge more effectively within bureaucracies. He shows that the hegemony and influence of one particular strand of research within one particular organization – namely the World Bank – was a crucial determinant of the shift in education policy, from a broader commitment to universal education to the current Millennium Development Goal (MDG) of universal primary education with an emphasis on girls. In a context where development agencies, scholars and activists were searching for alternatives to the traditional approach centred on 'enclave projects', which was seen to have failed, this line of thinking found a receptive terrain, particularly when backed by the dissemination might of the Bank.

The roles of research and activism, and how they interact to influence policy, are examined by Gita Sen (Chapter 6). Focusing on the field of gender and development, she shows not simply that combining research and activism is crucial, but also that building an effective nexus requires managing or overcoming a variety of tensions. These include differences in understanding and perceptions of problems, their determinants and solutions; differences in power related to access to resources and connections; and sociological factors related to differences in the social and economic background of researchers and activists. For the research–activist nexus to be effective in policy change, another complex set of relationships must be managed with actual or potential allies and 'the opposition', recognizing that these are not homogenous categories but require different relations with their constituent actors and organizations. Once sufficient pressure and influence are brought to bear, powerful institutions are likely to respond; but they may do so first and foremost by changing their discourse, and reinterpreting or subverting the meaning of concepts and terms. The process of actually changing policy is likely to be characterized by 'backlashes and foot-dragging', which demands from the movements involved not only ongoing oppositional 'street' politics, but also negotiating power.

Bob Deacon (Chapter 7) also places great store in the role of intellectuals and activists in the construction of a 'counter-hegemonic' project, and draws heavily on Gramscian analysis to understand the relative weight of ideas and power, and their relationship, in processes of policy reform. Referring to the field of social policy, he argues that ideas do matter, but that they need the backing of institutional power to induce policy change. He highlights the role of both 'organic intellectuals' in bridging disparate perspectives and struggles, and of knowledge networks or epistemic communities (Haas, 1992) in both framing issues and debates, and influencing policy agendas. The process of 'framing' (Bøås and McNeill, 2004) continues once ideas are taken up by powerful institutions: 'they exercise their power by "framing" ... which serves to limit the power of potentially radical ideas to achieve change'. For this reason, radical ideas need to be associated with changes in the balance of social forces that derive from various forms of struggle (class, gender, ethnic). In relation to international development policy, transnational social classes (Sklair, 2001) and international struggles have a key role to play, particularly through a counter-hegemonic project where intellectuals and activists influence actors and organizations through a 'war of position' waged in numerous sites and on several scales (local, national, regional, international). Although much of this struggle will be concerned with immediate tasks and projects, it must also be part of a longer term vision and strategy involving the construction of global political alliances and a coherent set of policy principles.

In this latter regard, the UN has a crucial role to play. Louis Emmerij, Richard Jolly and Thomas Weiss (Chapter 8) examine the genesis, trajectory and impact of ideas that have been associated with the UN system. They identify four ways in which such ideas have impacted international policy making: first, ideas – such as human rights and sustainable development – can shape international discourse or change conventional wisdom; second, ideas can shape a particular agenda for policy and action that modifies the dominant approach, as in the case of 'adjustment with a human face';[15] third, ideas can influence the configuration of political and institutional forces and their bargaining power, as has occurred periodically when thinking related to the causes of underdevelopment and North–South inequality has reinforced groupings of developing countries demanding reform; and fourth, ideas can result in the formation or strengthening of institutions or programmes within agencies, for example, those concerned with gender equality or, more recently, the Millennium Project and the UN Global Compact. But why have some ideas, such as human rights and sustainable development, taken off, while others, such as the New International Economic Order (NIEO) have quickly come and gone, or have been extremely slow to surface and gather momentum, as with the critique of neoliberalism. The authors note the broad range and complexity of determinants that include historical context, stifling managerial control, a culture of self-censorship and political correctness, enlightened or visionary leadership, institutional rivalries and coalitions, opposition from powerful states, the participation and influence of civil society organizations in research and consultation processes, and more open or closed networks of researchers and experts.

The potential and limits of mainstream reform

From the above it is evident that considerable caution should be exercised when assessing the pros and cons of recent changes in the language of development and associated policy reforms. While 'poverty reduction' and 'good governance', for example, certainly have a positive and action-oriented ring to them, all is not as it appears. Similarly, to assess the limits of the MDGs and PRSPs we need to go beyond explanations that focus narrowly on resource constraints, lack of political will or the inherent weakness of domestic institutions in developing countries.

The contributors examine the potential and limits of recent discursive and policy shifts associated, in particular, with poverty reduction, good governance and knowledge management. While transnational and local activism, and institutional and policy innovations, have opened up spaces for questioning the negative effects of the neoliberal regime, raising the global profile of poverty and inequality, and building new coalitions, there are some serious faults with current approaches to poverty reduction, targeting and knowledge management, and their ability to promote more inclusive forms of globalization and development. The analysis of what is wrong with mainstream approaches centres largely on five elements: the ways policy and discursive reforms reinforce positions of power; the intellectual, institutional and political constraints that prevent international development organizations from being creative intellectual actors or 'knowledge agencies'; the weakening of research and knowledge institutions supportive of independent and critical thinking; the persistence of the 'one right way' approach and conditionality that constrain development options in developing countries; and the limits of certain poverty reduction approaches, including targeting and PRSPs.

Shalmali Guttal notes the increasing capacity of the mainstream development establishment to respond to market and state failure, and to expand bodies of knowledge relevant for understanding social and environmental dimensions of development. She questions, however, whether the thriving knowledge industry associated with development issues does in fact do anything to change the policies and practices that generate or perpetuate underdevelopment. Particular strands of knowledge that have dominated thinking and policy in recent decades, and the seemingly progressive language of development, can, in fact, marginalize the interests of the disadvantaged, and depoliticize development problems by turning them over to 'experts'. As she and Andrea Cornwall and Karen Brock observe, development problems tend to be taken out of context, and solutions are divorced from local realties and history. When international organizations do take up progressive ideas and terminology, this often has the effect of dumbing down alternative perspectives, as well as diverting attention from certain assumptions, policies and structures that are at the root of inequality, vulnerability and marginalization.

The 'one right way approach' that is often said to characterize the policies of international financial institutions (IFIs) and some bilateral donors comes under fire from several contributors to this volume. Norman Girvan, in particular, questions whether contemporary shifts in mainstream discourse and policy are fundamentally changing this approach. Referring to the IFIs, he notes that 'the standard response [to the failure of neoliberal policy reforms] is that additional doses of market-oriented medicine are required...leading to a practice that some have called "adjustment without end"'. As discussed below, alternative approaches are unlikely to be found within the institutional confines of these organizations, but in the new structural, institutional and political arrangements associated with regionalism and transnational activism.

Examining the case of the World Bank, John Toye and Richard Toye identify some positive responses to criticism and pressure, as well as to economic analysis that emphasized the role of human capital development in promoting economic growth. The upshot was that structural adjustment programmes had to pay far more attention to health, education, environmental protection and poverty reduction, and the policy process had to be more participatory. Nevertheless, the characteristics of large bureaucracies (noted earlier) served to reinforce existing positions and patterns of technocratic governance – to the extent that the authors question whether the PRSP process constitutes a 'better way of securing national commitment to poverty reduction'.

In his assessment of trends associated with knowledge management in international organizations, Kenneth King suggests that it has often been more concerned with the efficient use of existing knowledge than with generating new knowledge. He notes, however, some important differences in approach with some bilateral agencies, such as the Swedish International Development Cooperation Agency (Sida) and DFID, attempting to modify traditional operational work and patterns of aid delivery away from an overemphasis on sectoral knowledge, to a more comprehensive and cross-cutting approach. Of particular concern is the fact that so-called knowledge agencies have done little to promote knowledge development in the South. When attention does turn to sharing knowledge with so-called partners in the South, there is a danger that the priorities regarding research and knowledge for development have already been decided. The recent revival of interest within the World Bank, the United Nations Development Programme

(UNDP) and some other agencies in 'capacity building' in the South is potentially a positive development, but there is still little evidence that either this approach or that of knowledge management and 'sharing' will transform the traditional aid relationship.

Gita Sen examines the constructive role that research-based knowledge has played and can play in transforming international policy related to women and development, when organically linked to civil society activism. A strong research-activist nexus can give the women's movement the analytical and political weight necessary for effective advocacy. She examines three areas where this has happened: the incorporation of gender concerns into macroeconomic policy; sexual and reproductive health and rights; and human rights and violence against women. Analysing the politics of discourse, she recognizes the capacity of powerful institutions to co-opt the language of those seeking change, but argues that the adoption of new terms and approaches by such organizations should been seen in a positive light: 'It makes it possible to fight the opposition on the ground of one's choosing'. She observes that activists and researchers have developed a more symbiotic relationship over time, but three sets of recurring tensions affect their relations: different perceptions and understandings of problems; power relations and control over resources; and control of and credit for knowledge. While the impact of the women's movement in changing mainstream discourse has sometimes been 'monumental', change on the ground at the country level has often been more circumspect. This is largely accounted for by 'the nature of the "opposition"; the positions of the allies; and the internal capacity and self-reflexivity of the protagonists'. At the international level, progress continues to be undermined by the policies of the Bretton Woods institutions (BWIs), which still appear unfavourable to women, as well as by various tensions that continue to divide research and activist communities, and the rise of religious conservatism.

A major concern with contemporary reforms in social policy relates to the retreat from the idea of universal entitlement to social provisioning and welfare, and the shift to targeting particular social groups or 'the poor'. Bob Deacon laments this development, pointing out that the declining financial backing and participation of the middle classes in state services is likely to result in 'poor services for the poor'. He notes, however, some positive advances that have occurred recently in both the discourse and practice of particular multilateral institutions. Shifts in global discourse and particular programmes or activities of some UN agencies and the International Labour Organization (ILO) point to the reassertion of the politics of social solidarity and universalism in social policy. He also notes some signs of a shift in approach in the World Bank with regard to targeting. An important institutional development relates not only to the fact that there are an increasing number of institutions dealing with global social policy issues, but also to the shift in the locus and content of global policy debate and activity from the more established, sometimes more ossified, agencies and secretariats to potentially more dynamic commissions, task forces, networks and partnerships. Such arrangements 'present new possibilities for actually making global change in particular social policy arenas' and for constructing 'longer term global political alliances that might fashion sets of principles of the kind espoused by the [World Commission on the Social Dimension of Globalization]...'.[16] Progress is being stalled, however, by US unilateralism, European Union social protectionism, and opposition to what is perceived by many as a 'Northern' project. Attempts to promote global redistribution and regulation have centred to a large extent on public-private partnerships and an alliance between multilateral agencies and corporate interests, which lack democratic accountability and regulatory clout. And while there is considerable agreement on the need for an international system of global social rights, promulgating and realizing such rights is impeded by weak political and administrative capacity.

What role have UN agencies played as an intellectual actor in contributing to development debates and policy, via the generation, dissemination and legitimization of ideas? In their assessment of this question Lousi Emmerij, Richard Jolly and Thomas Weiss argue that 'the UN has had a more positive and pioneering record in the economic and social arena than is generally recognized', but the record has been very mixed. They note numerous instances where UN agencies have played a pivotal role in changing the way the international community talks and thinks about development: the 1960s and 1970s, when the Economic Commission for Latin America (ECLA) and the United Nations Conference on Trade and Development (UNCTAD) popularized dependency theory and the terms of trade debate; the 1980s, when UNICEF exposed the social costs of structural adjustment; the 1990s, when the idea of sustainable development was promoted. Often, however, innovative and progressive ideas get nowhere, as in the case of the New International Economic Order, or the inability of the Economic Commission for Europe to win the day with its gradualist approach to post-Communist transition. The disconnect between knowledge creation and implementation is partly accounted for by the fact that 'implementation is not in the hands of the ideas-mongers, but of states'. Innovative and critical thinking confronts constraints, not least pressures for UN research to be 'politically correct'. The authors lament the weak reaction throughout much of the UN system to neoliberal thinking, particularly during the 1970s and much of the 1980s, and note that even the current focus on poverty reduction, PRSPs and the MDGs does little to seriously question the prevailing neoliberal economic orthodoxy.

Various contributors concur that there is greater scope for intellectual innovation within the UN than the Bretton Woods institutions. José Antonio Ocampo explains this by referring to the fact that the UN is 'a very plural forum [that] gives a stronger voice to the views and interests of weaker nations, weaker ministries within governments, civil society actors and schools of thought that do not share mainstream views'. Thus the UN is well-placed to reassert its role at a time when neoliberalism shows signs of crisis, and when there has been a revival of interest in the role of domestic institutions in linking knowledge to policy in a virtuous circle. Strengthening local capacity, policy 'ownership' and knowledge systems requires a context that favours intellectual pluralism and a reinvigorated state sector. This cannot be achieved through the approaches that have tended to characterize the policies and operations of the Bretton Woods institutions, involving conditionality and the top-down imposition of ideas.

Alternative approaches

While the changes we are currently seeing in discourse and policy do provide some spaces for progressive reform, the balance of opinion emerging from this volume is that they are unlikely to make a serious dent in the scale of global problems associated with inequality and poverty. At worst, they may divert attention from the real causes of maldevelopment and (re)legitimize conventional approaches and institutions. What needs to be done differently? Here the authors offer up a rich seam of analytical and strategic advice that can be summed up as follows.

First, deconstruct. Shalmali Guttal stresses the need to expose the interests and agendas behind 'the knowledge industry', and the way in which knowledge and theory are used to legitimize mainstream approaches and institutions, dilute alternative agendas and depoliticize development. The crucial challenge is to break 'the knowledge monopoly of the mainstream development establishment... and in order to do this, we must develop a strategic awareness of the political economy of knowledge creation, and actively support alternative ways in which knowledge is generated and shared'. Andrea Cornwall and Karen Brock suggest that deconstruction serves to question taken-for-granted assumptions, and expose worldviews and contradictions: 'no longer shored up by myths, utopias become fragile; no longer underpinned by axiomatic assumptions, they become amenable to being remodelled, or indeed cast aside into dereliction'. Such a task, they suggest, is being facilitated by the current linguistic or hegemonic crisis, where people are becoming more sceptical of development-speak and where 'the different ideological underpinnings that constitute different ways of world-making come into closer view'.

Second, struggle discursively. Do not give up on progressive ideas and concepts whose meanings have been appropriated by mainstream institutions or elite interests. Gita Sen suggests that the uptake of new terms and frameworks is a sign not of failure, but of success: 'if knowledge is power, then changing the terrain of discourse is the first but very important step'. Andrea Cornwall and Karen Brock suggest that strategies for change should attempt to reassert the meanings of progressive terms by relinking them in 'chains of equivalence' to other terms, such as 'solidarity', 'redistribution' and 'social justice', that have transformative connotations. When this is done, it becomes far more difficult to distort meanings.

Third, struggle to reconfigure the correlation of social forces. Various types of coalitions and alliances are emphasized by different authors. Gita Sen stresses the importance of strengthening links between researchers and activists, and building alliances with social movements or sectors of civil society that may share very different views on some questions. All this 'requires clarity, ingenuity, flexibility and, above all, stamina'. Relations with receptive bureaucrats and policy makers also need to be strengthened. This point is emphasized by most of the contributors who stress that international organizations, like states, are not monolithic entities. For Bob Deacon, the keywords are the Gramscian notion of 'counter-hegemony' and 'war of position', where alliances need to involve those within agencies that are supportive of the type of redistributive, regulatory and rights-based global social policy that is needed to promote inclusive globalization. He suggests that the emergence of new sites of decision making and action, and the nature of the intellectuals and experts they involve, may facilitate this task.

Fourth, forge real development partnerships. As Bob Deacon points out, a counter-hegemonic project needs to be sensitive to the diversity of culture and practice at the local, national and regional levels. Norman Girvan's analysis of these issues stresses the importance of exploiting the spaces for participatory policy making and learning that exist within agencies. The goal of such efforts should be to reorient development assistance away from top-down standardized policy prescriptions to 'supporting and facilitating social learning for the attainment of mutually agreed development objectives through a process of continuous interaction, democratic participation and local empowerment'. Kenneth King observes that capacity development has a crucial role to play in the construction of a more inclusive and equitable global development agenda. In the field of education, however, far more attention has to be paid to the role of – and support for – the formal education system in developing countries, including higher education and national research capacity.

Fifth, new policy approaches. Following from their critique of contemporary poverty reduction strategies and aspects of social policy reform that emphasize targeting, several contributors identify elements of alternative policy approaches. John Toye and Richard Toye point out that poverty reduction, historically and today, is less related to adjustments in social expenditure budgets or 'a shopping list' of reforms, than to a coherent set of economic policies that promote broad-based growth and employment. They stress the need to understand the types of macro-micro linkages that make growth more or less effective in reducing poverty, and whether particular patterns of industrial or sectoral development are also key. Regarding the social arena, various contributors emphasize the need to reassert social solidarity and universal welfare provision, not only nationally but globally. This latter approach is developed, in particular, by Bob Deacon who emphasizes three aspects: global redistribution involving international social transfers financed through some sort of global levy; global regulation, particularly of trade, finance, investment and corporations; and global rights – not only promulgation, but realization through strengthening political and administrative capacity.

Sixth, intellectual pluralism and policy space. Various authors call for greater intellectual pluralism and policy space for developing country governments. Norman Girvan insists that developing countries need greater autonomy in relation to the diagnosis of their own problems and the determination of appropriate policy prescriptions. This requires recognizing and validating the role of social knowledge that 'inheres within society and not merely about the society', and taking advantage of the spaces that already exist for participatory policy making and learning. Trends associated with regionalism may offer considerable potential in terms of strengthening the capacity the South 'to shape globalization in its own interest'. Crucial in this regard are, first, the epistemic dimension, which 'relates to the accumulation of local diagnostic and prescriptive capacities for development policy making, linked to democratic participation in decision making at national and regional levels', and second, the instrumental dimension, which involves 'the benefits of intergovernmental functional cooperation and of market integration'. José Antonio Ocampo also stresses the need to promote intellectual pluralism, critical debate within international agencies, and stronger domestic knowledge systems as the only way to counter the imposition of misguided approaches. Rather than conditionality, what is needed is the strengthening of local capacity and national ownership of economic and social policies. This would foster virtuous links between knowledge and policy making by facilitating the analysis of economic and social reality, adapting foreign knowledge, cultivating autonomous knowledge, and designing policies adapted to particular circumstances. The role of international agencies should not be to promote dominant views, but to assist developing countries in building and strengthening their own institutions.

Seventh, strengthen the role of the UN. Several authors suggest that it is necessary to reassert the creative intellectual role of the UN and to correct the current situation where the driving force for economic policy rests with the International Monetary Fund (IMF) and the World Bank. For Louis Emmerij, Richard Jolly and Thomas Weiss this requires correcting the imbalance in funding which has seen resources associated with knowledge generation and management flow away from the UN to the Bretton Woods institutions. They point out that a reading of the history of progressive thought within the UN system suggests that it is not consensus with the Bretton Woods institutions or with Washington that result in useful knowledge and policy change, but rather institutional environments where agencies exercise bold vision and leadership, prioritize the quest for social justice, promote multidisciplinary approaches, pay attention to country-level specifics, and remain relatively free of government and bureaucratic control. In this regard, they note the important role that 'the quasi-university public research institutes' within the UN system, such as UNRISD and the World Institute for Development Economics Research (WIDER), can play in 'reigniting the creative intellectual spark in UN economic and social work', which has waned in recent decades in a context where criticism of neoliberalism has been fairly muted.

Finally, reflexivity. Social science research and civil society advocacy typically challenge the status quo or mainstream reform agendas and then propose alternatives. What often receive short shrift are the possible contradictions, tensions and unintended consequences associated with proposed courses of action. In a reflexive mode, several of the chapters in this volume offer refreshing insights into what might go wrong or backfire. John Toye and Richard Toye note that greater responsiveness on the part of the World Bank to civil society opinion has, on some issues, made that institution more responsive to US non-governmental organizations (NGOs), and US politicians taking up NGO concerns, rather than to its client countries. Gita Sen identifies various difficulties that often beset efforts to forge and sustain alliances between researchers and activists, while Norman Girvan spells out the tensions inherent in alternative approaches based on regionalism. Bob Deacon notes that the challenge of forging a global social policy needs to tackle head on the tensions that currently divide Northern and Southern governments and activists on such issues. And several authors remind us of the dangers of placing too much faith in the role of progressive intellectuals or leaders within mainstream organizations, given the structural and institutional constraints in which they operate, or the absence of powerful coalitions to reinforce their views and policy proposals.

Convergence for development?

Different perspectives on development, which in the past distinguished the Bretton Woods institutions from various UN and bilateral development agencies, appear to have converged significantly during the past decade. In the 1960s and 1970s, UNCTAD, the ILO, the UN General Assembly and other UN agencies and entities promoted a more trans-formative, redistributive and regulatory agenda, emphasizing, for example, the leading role of the 'developmental' state, 'basic needs', agrarian reform, food security, 'popular participation', universal social policy, the New International Economic Order, business regulation, and import substitution industrialization. During these years there was a far clearer division of labour between the UN and Bretton Woods institutions, with the World Bank, for example, heavily engaged in supporting infrastructural development. With the ascendancy of neoliberal thinking and policy in the 1980s, and the decline of the socialist bloc and the non-aligned movement, the UN's more 'radical' turn came to a fairly abrupt end. A context of financial crisis and budget cuts in early

1990s, and even proposals to do away with certain UN agencies, also contributed to an institutional culture where critical thinking was suppressed and self-censorship increased in some organizations that became hypersensitive to the actual or potential criticisms of certain governments. Nevertheless, various reformist perspectives and causes such as 'sustainable development', 'women in development' and 'adjustment with a human face' continued to be actively pursued, particularly through the UN summits of the 1990s. Furthermore, certain flagship publications, notably UNDP's *Human Development Report*, generally projected a message that was different to that espoused by the World Bank in its *World Development Report*.

By the turn of the new millennium, many UN organizations, bilateral agencies and the World Bank seemed to be playing a similar tune. This convergence manifested itself at conceptual, discursive, programmatic and strategic levels. Conceptually there is widespread adherence to 'embedded liberalism', which sees the simultaneous freeing-up of markets and the strengthening of institutions conducive to social protection and stability as the best bet for achieving socially inclusive patterns of globalization and development (Ruggie, 2003). In relation to global governance, there is common agreement that not only 'civil society', but also organized business interests and transnational corporations (TNCs), should play a more active role in development programmes and the policy process.[17] There is also agreement that one of the keys to promoting development is 'good governance', which emphasizes the need for institutions, particularly governmental institutions in developing countries, to be transparent, efficient and accountable. At the discursive level, convergence manifests itself in the fact that agencies are using a similar vocabulary or discourse that has populist or even radical overtones, emphasizing the social, participatory and empowerment dimensions of development. At the programmatic, policy and strategic levels, it is reflected in the term the 'post–Washington Consensus',[18] which implies a more comprehensive range of policies to which most multilateral and bilateral agencies now officially subscribe. It is also seen in the increasing adherence of mainstream development agencies to what can be called target-based development. This involves both the whittling-down of the international development agenda[19] to a narrower set of targets, most notably MDGs, and the weakening of the principle of universalism in relation to the public provision of basic social services and the concomitant strengthening of approaches that attempt to 'target' vulnerable groups or 'the poor' (Mkandawire, 2004).

Implicit in this convergence is a 'grand compromise'[20] that has two main features. First, the World Bank has adopted a more heterodox approach that continues to promote neoliberal basics centred on 'flexibilization' and the freeing-up of markets, foreign direct investment, privatization, export-led growth, and strict fiscal and monetary discipline, but pays more attention to the role of institutions, including the state, as well as to broader development objectives and approaches, such as poverty reduction, participation, gender equity and sustainable development, typically associated with UN agencies and development NGOs.[21] Second, the UN continues to actively promote principles of human, sustainable and rights-based development without fundamentally questioning either the core pillars of the neoliberal project, or the contradictions between these different approaches and objectives. Not only are various UN institutions explicitly or implicitly supporting processes and policies of economic liberalization, stabilization and privatization; they have also transformed their relations with TNCs. Formerly kept at arm's length or seen as objects of regulation, today they are actively engaged as 'partners' in development and poverty reduction efforts, and are expected to give back to society via corporate social responsibility and public-private partnerships part of what they have gained through liberalization and globalization (Utting, 2005b; Zammit, 2003).

Developing country governments and important sectors of civil society and academia in the global South are very much a part of this convergence and compromise. Such support is largely explained by processes related to conditionality and aid dependence, the rise of technocratic governance in developing countries, and the increasing influence in policy making of 'experts' trained in a particular variety of economics in Northern universities. It is also explained by the absorption of Southern intellectuals and NGOs into knowledge, consultancy and consultation networks dominated by bilateral and multilateral agencies, as well as the decline of domestic research capacity.[22]

As the chapters in this volume make clear, such a compromise is extremely problematic from the perspective of forging an agenda that promotes inclusive and equitable development. It ignores not only the perverse effects of certain macroeconomic policies and associated conditionality, but also power relations that underpin maldevelopment, poverty and inequality. It can also foster institutional silence or self-censorship in international organizations on such issues. The compromise, therefore, needs to be challenged both intellectually and politically.

This challenge is gathering force, in a context where there has been an upsurge in activism centred on global justice (trade, tax, environmental and social) and campaigns to 'Make Poverty History', where certain developing countries are flexing their muscles in international negotiating fora, and where the influence of the IMF appears to be declining.[23] And from within the UN system there has been a spate of publications that are highly critical of neoliberal policies, structures of inequality, North–South relations, certain WTO rules, and the dominant discourse and patterns of foreign direct investment, and which propose a very different policy and institutional regime.[24] Such positions, however, still tend to be associated with specific sites within the UN system or particular agencies; sites that enjoy at least some of the prerequisites for critical thinking noted by several of the authors in this volume, namely, autonomy from the intergovernmental process, bold leadership and 'defiant bureaucrats'. It remains to be seen whether this new found radicalism will become a more generalized feature of UN thinking, given the institutional and governmental resistance to some of these perspectives and related publications that has emerged.[25]

Certain adjustments to the compromise are, it seems, being made, reflected not only in the revival of critical opinion in some UN agencies, and in the fact that a number of Asian and Latin American countries are steering a more autonomous policy course, but also in the repositioning of the World Bank and the G8. Through its flagship report on *Equity and Development*, the World Bank acknowledged the important role of 'some forms of redistribution' in both social and economic development (World Bank, 2005). And the G8 leaders approved a series of measures concerned with debt relief and increased levels and quality of aid. They also voiced support for the concept of policy space, calling for 'developing countries themselves and their governments . . . to decide, plan and sequence their economic policies to fit their own development strategies, for which they should be accountable to all their people' (G8 Gleneagles, 2005:27).

As several of the following chapters indicate, however, power structures and institutional culture at the World Bank make it extremely difficult to translate progressive discursive shifts into meaningful policy change related to macroeconomic policy. And with the change in leadership, the question arises as to whether such shifts were a peculiar feature of the Wolfensohn era that may dissipate under Wolfowitz, as a result of changes in priorities and relations with different constituencies.

The limits to change were also apparent when the G8 failed to take concrete action on trade reform, while reforms related to other aspects of macroeconomic policy and to the international financial system and institutions remained off the Gleneagles agenda.[26] The subsequent meeting of the world's leaders at the 2005 World Summit at the United Nations also fell short of expectations. It did, however, reiterate the need 'to enhance the coherence and consistency of the international monetary, financial and trading systems' and also called for greater 'policy space' (see UNDESA, 2005).

These concepts are potentially important for addressing the contradictions between inclusive development and ongoing neoliberal reform, and some of the 'blind spots' within mainstream thinking in international development organizations. If applied in practice, developing countries and a wider range of social interests may stand a better chance of reclaiming development agendas. They might be less constrained by conditionality and certain policy prescriptions, emanating from IFIs and some donor governments, that generate perverse developmental impacts, and they might have greater autonomy to determine policies and strategies better adapted to their own circumstances. However, like so many of the concepts or buzzwords analysed in this volume, the way they are interpreted and applied by elites and powerful institutions, both nationally and internationally, can fudge or contradict their apparent intent. It is for this reason that critical thinking and intellectual pluralism within international organizations and knowledge networks, North and South, are so important, and why progressive ideas need the support of epistemic communities and institutions, as well as the backing of strong coalitions of social and political forces.

1
Challenging the Knowledge Business

Shalmali Guttal

Introduction

For over 50 years, mainstream development discourse has defined acceptable and unacceptable standards of life for the world's peoples. The dominant image of the post-Second World War era of development is one of social and economic transformation through the exercise of economic, technological, scientific, intellectual and institutional expertise. And certainly, such transformations are visible in physical infrastructure, medical science, industry, new technologies and sciences, information and knowledge, new products, legal, financial and administrative systems, and material well-being for many.

At the same time, not all of development's transformations have led to progressive social and economic change. The development era has also been witness to the concentration of wealth and assets in the hands of a relatively small number of commercial entities; increased inequality and unemployment; recurrent famines and hunger; accelerated environmental contamination and destruction; the dislocation of rural societies and economies; shattering debt and economic crises; the growth of unliveable urban environments; chronic health crises; and widespread alienation of millions of people from traditional lands and environments through involuntary displacement and migration.

This has been accompanied by a corresponding increase in wars, social/ethnic conflicts and violence, decreased democratic and political space, and a renewed subservience of former colonies to the industrialized North through contemporary international agreements.

Despite the billions of dollars channelled into the development machinery, development failed in its promise to deliver well-being, prosperity and advancement to the majority of the world's people. On the contrary, it has exacerbated and entrenched the structural foundations of poverty, inequity and injustice. The economic prosperity of some has left disproportionately large numbers in the traditional South in dire poverty. In 2003, the United Nations Development Programme's *Human Development Report* (UNDP, 2003a) noted that the actual number of people living in poverty increased by almost 100 million. The richest 1 per cent of the world's population received as much income as the poorest 57 per cent, while the income of the richest 25 million Americans is the equivalent of that of almost 2 billion of the world's poorest people. At least 54 countries are poorer now than in the 1980s; more than 800 million suffer from malnutrition; more than 13 million children died because of diarrhoeal diseases; and every year, over half a million women die during pregnancy or childbirth. And during this same time, total world income actually increased by an average of 2.5 per cent annually.

Today, the body of knowledge that informs development policy and programme formulation is much larger than 20 years ago. And yet, the development establishment appears unable to address some of the most fundamental crises of our times. Do development planners and policy makers still not know enough to be able to address these crises? Or, is it more that the knowledge base that informs development serves particular class and societal interests, where the voices of the disenfranchized remain just that: voices, but without the political and economic capability to tilt policy making in their favour?

In this chapter, I argue that the repeated inability of mainstream development to adequately address the above crises lies, to a significant extent, in the nature of knowledge creation, dissemination and use. Yes, there is an issue of 'political will' among planners, policy makers and policy executors. But political will is not an objective condition. It is equally shaped by material and economic interests, on the one hand, and a 'universalization' of specific forms of knowledge, on the other hand. There exists today a powerful knowledge industry that justifies the creation of the very conditions that development seeks to address.

Development policies are the bridge between experience, discourse and institutional practice. New policies will not yield anything new unless the discourse from which they are drawn is fundamentally rethought. Knowledge and politics are companion dimensions of the same process of transformation and change. If we want knowledge to lead to progressive social change, we must challenge development's body of knowledge and system of practices, and recognize the central place of politics in the realm of knowledge production and in shaping popular consciousness.

The business of knowledge and knowledge as business

Despite declining aid flows and growing evidence of development's failures, the field of development has continued to flourish financially, professionally, institutionally and epistemologically. Over its half-century history, development has moved inexorably from 'technical' and 'economic' to 'institutional', 'social' and 'sustainable' (Lohmann, 1998a). Today, development is neoliberal and at the service of whichever market forces provide the resources for its sustenance. The mainstream development establishment has vastly expanded to include academics, professional practitioners ('experts'), planners, non-governmental organizations (NGOs), aid bureaucrats and financiers. Private businesses have also joined the team. Most major universities have numerous departments dedicated to creating development expertise, from economics – its founding parent – to sociology, anthropology, nutrition, governance, women's studies, natural resource management and agriculture. Development now has entire armies of experts in every possible field at its disposal, ready and waiting to carry out its bidding. While these actors benefit greatly from grants and contracts through development aid budgets, equally important, they contribute to and hold up the massive corpus of knowledge that legitimizes development's existence and justifies its expansion.

There may not be enough money available for publicly financed clean water systems, basic education, primary health care, workers' compensation, and support for small-scale, family-farm based agriculture. But there is always money available for research on water management, agricultural extension, cost-recovery systems for health and education, and labour mobility. In fact, it would appear that the abundance of theory on the various subjects under development's purview is far in excess of the problems it claims to tackle.

Development theory is not a 'disinterested' body of knowledge. It speaks both, *from* and *to* specific positions of class and power; it re-constructs and re-presents events, phenomena, and material and social conditions in forms that suit the interests of those with access to the tools and institutions of the mainstream knowledge edifice. While theories may not translate perfectly into praxis, imperfections and failures play an important role in strengthening the hegemony of theory over the world outside of theory. Failures are absorbed into the world of theory and models with remarkable ease, and then reproduced as newer and modified versions of the product.

Creating and establishing theory is no small task. Lots of people have great ideas, which they put into practice with astounding results. But these do not become theories. Moving from idea to theory requires a tremendous investment of resources for thinking, research, institutional backing, support and legitimation, and opportunities for application, correction and refinement. These investments have generally come – at various times – from governments, private corporations, political and religious groups, wealthy individuals or families, philanthropic institutions, and the international aid bureaucracy. Each investor brings its own specific interests to the project of theory formulation, which then moves the discourse of development in directions desirable and beneficial to the investor. Material interests are served by knowledge and vice versa.

The capacity to generate information and to enshrine it in social and institutional memory as 'knowledge' is indeed a powerful one. It is also an extremely lucrative one. Today, this capacity is dominated by a handful of academics, 'experts,' universities, think-tanks and institutions of the international aid bureaucracy, including international financial institutions (IFIs), technical agencies of the United Nations (UN) and bilateral donors. Most powerful among these are the World Bank, and to a lesser degree, the International Monetary Fund (IMF) and regional development banks, such as the Asian Development Bank (ADB), who have effectively used their financial and institutional resources to establish dominance in knowledge production and dissemination, thereby seeking to establish hegemony in global and regional policy making.

Knowledge production and distribution are big businesses today, and those involved are keenly aware that not only do ideas matter, but that they also pay. As market forces increasingly replace public support in the arenas of knowledge and learning, university departments, national research institutes and independent think-tanks enter into research partnerships with commercial entities, bilateral donors and IFIs to ensure their survival and perpetuation. More and more, research institutes are taking on the role of research 'managers', whereby, by hiring the talent and skills of independent researchers and consultants, they can produce expert studies on just about any topic, from women's participation to watershed management and food security through hybrid seeds.

The power of finance

The World Bank is an excellent example of an institution that has used its financial clout to entrench its power over international policy making by developing parallel power in the realm of knowledge creation, application and dissemination. Since its inception 60 years ago, the World Bank has successfully situated itself as *the* premier international research institution with 'expertise' in almost every development area, from economic growth, trade, fiscal adjustment and debt to health, education, employment, population and the environment.

The World Bank's generous financial endowments have been instrumental in shoring up its institutional and political capacity, and in establishing it as a 'knowledge institution'. Its mid- to high-level professional staff are trained in the top universities of the world (mostly in the United States and Great Britain) and its consultancy rosters include top-notch sectoral experts who also command top-notch professional fees. Every year, the Bank produces thousands of pages of information in the form of Country Assistance Strategies, social and environmental assessments, poverty assessments, the *World Development Report*, world debt tables, and numerous sector-specific reports pertaining to projects in the pipeline and under review. Because of its position as primary creditor to most countries in Asia, Africa and Latin America, Bank staff have access to a rare, privileged and sensitive cache of country-level information on such diverse subjects as government budgets, public expenditure, household consumption, and forestry and energy resources. Senior Bank staff routinely have the ear of some of the most powerful policy makers in the world, from country presidents, prime ministers and finance ministers to the heads of other multilateral institutions such as the UN technical agencies and the World Trade Organization (WTO).

Although the Bank jealously guards its most coveted data – such as loan, structural adjustment and project finance agreements – under the guise of sovereign, institutional and commercial confidentiality, it also spends an enormous amount of resources in disseminating its knowledge products to establish its hegemony in development discourse and practice. Since the 1990s, the Bank has set up public information centres that often serve as the primary sources of information for government officials and resource strapped researchers in developing countries. The World Bank website is probably one of the most often visited websites by both its supporters and detractors. The Bank's knowledge resources are often the only source of information on the economies of developing countries for much of the world's media and academics. Because of its financial capacity, the Bank is literally everywhere – geographically, financially and substantively. And because of its political access and capacity, its views and analyses are unquestioningly accepted by governments, academics, donors and development institutions as the most authoritative (Wilks and Lefrancoise, 2002).

This powerful research organization, however, also happens to be one of the largest and most powerful financial institutions in the world especially as it always acts in tandem with its 'Bretton Woods twin', the IMF. Together, the World Bank and the IMF have the ability to dictate the terms on which low- and middle-income countries can access development finance and attract private capital and investment.

While the World Bank's importance in global policy making derives largely from the volume of its lending, it has also created a central role for itself as a 'donor co-ordinator' in most developing countries. Without the stamp of approval from the IMF and World Bank, a low-income country can find itself virtually cut off from international aid, trade and finance. The Bank is able to persuade bilateral donors and private financiers to co-finance projects and programmes that it designs and appraises, and has engaged in mutual-assistance partnerships with UN agencies such as the Food and Agriculture Organization of the United Nations (FAO) and the UNDP.

The World Bank's and IMF's powers accrue from the financial and political support they get from the G7 – the seven most advanced, industrialized countries in the world – and other wealthy countries in the Organisation for Economic Co-operation and Development (OECD). Policy thinking and practice in the Bank and Fund are dominated by commercial and financial interests in these countries. Although most of their operations are in the developing world, decision making in the institutions is led by the rich, industrialized nations (Stiglitz, 2002). Together, the United States, United Kingdom, Germany, France and Japan control almost 45 per cent of the voting power in the World Bank, and the United States is the only country on the Bank-Fund Boards with veto power.

There are good reasons why rich countries support the World Bank and the IMF. The Bank influences the fate of more that US\$ 60 billion of official development assistance to the South. Much of this aid comes back to donor countries through the purchase of goods and services from their own companies and consultants. Up to 80 per cent of this aid is spent in donor countries on salaries and fees of staff and consultants (Escobar, 1995). Aid creates business opportunities for Northern companies, and academic and research establishments. Loan programmes disbursed by the Bank are usually accompanied by Technical Assistance (TA) components for project preparation, training and capacity-building, technical studies and other similar activities, most of which are contracted out to universities, consultancy companies and think-tanks from donor countries.

Through its own institutional capacity and through the institutions it gathers in its programmatic fold, the World Bank produces knowledge that justifies its lending practices, project and programme designs and policy prescriptions. Often the Bank is at the same time, programme assessor, designer, evaluator, monitor and financier, with no independent oversight over the inter-locking interests that guide its research and finance operations. The Bank's operations, thus, are routinely situated in a climate of 'moral hazard', but which go unquestioned by donors and most borrowing governments.

Selling large infrastructure

Experience over the years has taught the aid bureaucracy that knowledge not only helps their business of development, but also, it makes for good business in its own right. Large infrastructure projects illustrate this well, especially the dam-building sector. Large dams are notorious for exorbitantly high capital investment costs, displacement of local populations and ecological devastation. In order to make them more acceptable to the public at large and attract the required financing, dam projects are usually accompanied by ambitious resettlement and conservation programmes, schemes for substitute livelihoods and sophisticated financing mechanisms. As more and more negative impacts come to light, new components are added to the project, all of which require new project capacities and more financing, and so on. And this entire chain of events feeds back into the large body of knowledge that props up the dam industry.

While the actual physical fact of a dam remains the same, its rationale can change depending on the nature of opposition or resistance to the project. Irrigation, protection against floods, electricity for export earnings, tourism, poverty reduction and environmental protection, have all been used to justify the same project at various times. Further, from years of bitter battles over watersheds and loan guarantees, dam backers have learned how to engage with their detractors. Dam-builders, promoters and financiers are now able to project themselves on demand as environmental conservationists, populists, human rights buffs, and specialists in participation or local knowledge (Lohmann, 1998b). In a bid to provide ethical and technical justification to the search for dam profits, the hydropower industry has poured huge amounts of money into 'scientific research' on environmental and social impacts, flora and fauna census, conservation options, resettlement plans, reconstructing alternative livelihoods, and so on.

In response to persistent pressure from social movements, civil society organizations and independent researchers, the World Bank – one of the largest institutional backers of physical infrastructure projects – has formulated a wide-ranging set of Operational Directives (ODs) and research requirements to ensure rigorous scientific support for Bank-funded infrastructure projects. These include studies on the social, cultural, environmental, financial and economic dimensions of the proposed project, and often entail financing for additional project components for the mitigation of negative impacts. Although the principle aim of these studies is to establish the Bank's legitimacy in the eyes of an increasingly visible, influential and critical global civil society, it has also provided the World Bank with the opportunity to re-invent itself as an institution committed to environmentalism and sustainable development, backed by scientific research and practice.

Green science

Michael Goldman (Goldman, 2001) has documented the Bank's re-making through the production of 'authoritative green knowledge' in relation to a large hydropower project in the Lao People's Democratic Republic (PDR), the Nam Theun 2 (NT2). According to Goldman, over the past 10 years, the Bank has carved out a 'green agenda', produced policies, financing, tools and data for an applied global environmental science, and trained thousands of professionals in borrowing countries to conduct 'green science' for development. The NT2 is the Bank's flagship green development project, which can showcase its efforts of past years and serve as a model for future infrastructure projects.

But in order for such a project to be successfully field-tested, it must have institutional, administrative and policy support. This, in turn, has triggered a series of policy reforms in sectors such as forestry, the judiciary and commerce. The Bank and Northern aid agencies have financed numerous 'capacity building' initiatives among state agencies on subjects such as Environmental Impact Assessments (EIA), Social Impact Assessments (SIA), Cost-Benefit Analysis (CBA), bio-diversity conservation, Participatory Rural Appraisal (PRA), public consultation and participation, and so on. This research and training has two significant dimensions: first, they lay the ground for institutional and popular acceptance of the Bank's 'green science' (who after all would argue against the findings of scientific research?); and second, they reproduce the country and its people as social and environmental 'facts' in the World Bank's regime of green science, through a programme of largely extractive research.

The World Bank has been a source of inspiration to another powerful regional financial institution, the ADB. The ADB has emulated both the World Bank model of building knowledge competence, as well as its strategy of selling large infrastructure, with remarkable success. The ADB has also positioned itself as a 'knowledge-based institution' and produces thousands of pages of information on a range of subjects from women's education to watershed management and poverty, all of which are available on request electronically, through its website, and in publication form. ADB projects are accompanied by numerous consultancy contracts for research, capacity-building, implementation and evaluation. And like the World Bank, the ADB has also started to develop ODs and policies to provide scientific and ethical backing for its infrastructure projects.

Transforming risks into opportunities

One of the thorniest problems that the development bureaucracy has grappled with over the past five decades is the job of resettling and rehabilitating communities displaced by large infrastructure and extractive industry projects such as dams, highways, ports, mines and oil/gas pipelines. Rehabilitation entails ensuring comparable or better livelihoods for those people whose lands become submerged by a dam reservoir, excavated by a mining project, or paved over by a highway. While it is easy enough for a state to claim the lands in question under the principle of 'eminent domain', it is not quite as easy for the World Bank, the ADB and bilateral donors to provide financing for such projects without paying due attention to mitigating the social, environmental and economic costs that such projects incur. As the disastrous impacts of involuntary relocation and displacement of local communities associated with such projects are brought to public attention by activists, independent researchers and the media, creditors and donors increasingly face harsh criticism for supporting projects that violate the basic rights of communities to life and livelihoods, and which result in domestic strife and unrest.

For multilateral creditors and bilateral donors, the risks associated with such projects are not only reputational. Bad publicity is bad for business: project financing is increasingly difficult to raise for controversial projects, and potential investors and contractors demand higher levels of financial assurances and guarantees because of perceived risks associated with unpredictable project environments. Bad publicity is also bad for politics: policy makers in donor countries are increasingly pressured by their tax payers to uphold standards of democracy, transparency and human rights in aid programmes, and to not support projects in countries where these standards are violated.

Again, the response of institutions such as the World Bank and the ADB to these challenges has been to create new disciplines of social and environmental expertise, which also means new business opportunities for 'green experts'. Sociologists, anthropologists and environmental technicians hired by the banks and donors transform the impending social and ecological impacts of what are sold as beneficial development projects into new 'sustainable development' activities, such as resettlement action plans, environmental action management plans and sustainable livelihoods projects. Only through such transformations can developers cope with the fact that their projects are too often imposed on a reluctant society which would have to be made over to accommodate them (Lohmann, 1998b). Green science then turns out to be useful to the development establishment on several fronts: it helps to sell large infrastructure projects as sustainable development; it provides moral justification for controversial projects and helps to quell unrest among project-affected communities and deflect criticism from civil society, and; it provides employment to the development establishment's loyal professionals.

Establishing hegemony: the politics of knowledge use

In order for development to sustain itself as a discipline, it must create an all-encompassing – hegemonic – discourse that can effectively neutralize challenges to its mission, assumptions and theories. Mainstream development discourse is blind and deaf to realities outside of the world it creates. The world must be composed as a picture that justifies the preferred economic and social models of those that control the discourse and benefit from it. This entails creating and sustaining regimes of truth – or falsehoods, depending on where one is situated. These regimes are backed by research and the establishment of new fields of expertise, and are 'normalized' in popular imagination through conferences, publications, lectures and, of course, through development projects, programmes and policies.

Again, the examples of the World Bank and the IMF are instructive as they repeatedly attempt to apply universal economic 'laws' to the problems of social and economic development in borrowing countries. Whether under the rubric of structural adjustment programmes, debt relief, or the more recent Poverty Reduction Strategy Papers (PRSPs), Bank-Fund solutions to the development challenges faced by their client countries have been non-negotiable market openness and stringent policy prescriptions for macroeconomic, sectoral and institutional reforms. These reforms have sought to remove government intervention in the economy and catapult domestic economies into globalized markets regardless of their specific conditions, characteristics or constraints (Rodrik, 2001). A standard package of reforms includes: unilateral trade and investment liberalization, privatization of property rights, commercialization of agriculture, privatization of public enterprises – including those that have actually been profitable to the state or serve critical public interest functions – public expenditure cuts and deregulation across sectors. The rationale behind these prescriptions is a well-worn story that need not be revisited here. What is remarkable and alarming, however, is the Bank's and Fund's inability – or unwillingness – to tailor their model to the specificities of their client countries.

By any measure of economic or social performance, the last two decades have shown rigid applications of Bank-Fund orthodox economic theory to be a failure (Weisbrot *et al.*, 2001). Most countries at the receiving end of Bank-Fund programmes have not registered the promised economic growth; nor have they been able to come out of their debt crises; and nor have they experienced significant reductions in absolute or relative poverty. Instead, the opposite has happened. No pain, no gain, say the institutions. Well, many in these countries certainly have gained, but at the cost of tremendous pain among the rising number of unemployed, hungry, displaced and poor.

Equally alarming are how the institutions explain failures and how these explanations provide more theories of how a country should be run. When finally compelled to accept the overwhelming evidence of harm that their policies were wreaking, the Bank and Fund concluded that the problem lay not in their own theories, but in corrupt, inefficient, non-transparent, institutionally weak and capacity-poor governments. The problem was not too much market openness, but too little. And the solution lay not in correcting their own theories and policies, but in prescribing even more reforms based on the same assumptions that created the problems to begin with. Thus arrived a new lot of policies on good governance, capacity-building, institutional strengthening, administrative and legal reforms, more privatization and deregulation, and a virtual laundry list of measures to fast track trade and investment liberalization. Similarly, when accused of secrecy, non-transparency and multiplying corruption and authoritarianism, the World Bank decreed that borrowing countries must conduct public consultation exercises before projects and programmes could be considered for approval.

With each failure came new pre-requisites to re-apply to the old model and make it work. And not surprisingly, every new requirement or solution – which the larger development establishment endorsed with little protest – gave rise to yet more disciplines of research and theory-building. At no time, however, did these institutions turn the critical lens on their own operations and procedures. And even if they did, the results of those examinations certainly did not make it to the public realm, nor did they result in any discernable change in their ways of doing business.

For low-income countries today, getting loans from the Bank, Fund, regional development banks and even bilateral donors is a virtual circus act. Governments have to jump through so many hoops that a significant portion of their newly built 'capacity' goes towards satisfying the needs of the development establishment. At the very minimum, governments must prepare 'participatory' poverty reduction assessments and strategies, Medium Term Expenditure Frameworks, debt sustainability analyses, Financial Information Management Systems reports, and so on (Easterly, 2002). For each sector to which loans are applicable, there must also be sectoral analyses, strategies and action plans. And of course, all countries must support greater democratization, which usually means laying the ground for the formation of national NGOs and engaging in 'public consultations' on selected projects with national and international NGOs. And just in case borrowing governments have difficulty in meeting these requirements, the Bank and donors are more than willing to provide professional development experts to 'build national institutional capacity', who more or less write the 'nationally owned' reports, studies, laws and policies.

De-politicizing development

An important outcome of these trends – contradictorily – is the 'de-politicization' of development (Ferguson, 1990). The structural and political roots of poverty, inequality, and social and economic dislocation such as land-grabbing by traditional elites, factory closures, privatization of essential services and the debilitation of subsistence agriculture systems are re-framed as technical problems arising from inefficient land markets, lack of competitive capacity, over-burdened state enterprises and weak agricultural practices. The failure of international debt relief programmes is attributed to national capacity constraints and institutional weakness rather than the imposition of excessive conditionalities. The destruction of traditional coping mechanisms in times of droughts and food crises are attributed to the lack of 'social capital' rather than recognized as the breakdown of the social fabric resulting from hardships caused by misguided and misdirected policy prescriptions. Different class interests that are likely to have divergent views on a proposed project become 'stakeholders', who can be neatly seated at the same table and exhorted to reach a compromise about such contentious issues as loss of lands and livelihood for one group versus higher profit margins for another.

Although the imposition – or willing adoption, as the case might be – of a specific development model is an overtly political act, the outcomes of the application of the model are not viewed through the lens of politics. The world of mainstream development is a self-referential system of assumptions, theories and models, which carries within its humungous body of knowledge the capacity to provide explanations and corrections for faults, while ignoring and thus entrenching the structural flaws in both the system, as well as the reality on which it is imposed. There is simply no place for references from outside the system. Documents of the international development bureaucracy depend on each other for evidence and argumentation, thus producing an incestuous body of knowledge that continues to be protected from the day-to-day reality of workers, peasant farmers, fishers, displaced communities, migrant labour, refugees, the urban poor, street children and trafficked women.

The de-politicization of development is not the precinct of professionals, experts and aid bureaucrats alone. NGOs and academics also frequently fall into the trap. For example, many detractors of the World Bank-IMF development model become so immersed in understanding the minutiae of Bank-Fund policies and operations that they are unable to step outside the Bank-Fund determined framework either in their critique, or in advancing alternatives. Rather than question the larger political system that gives international financial and trade institutions the power to impose externally driven models of development on borrowing countries, they argue for 'tailoring' the PRSP to country contexts and tinkering with growth strategies and international trade policies to make them 'pro-poor'. And of course, very few dare challenge the sacred concepts of economic growth, efficiency and free trade.

Thus, the most powerful institutions of the international aid bureaucracy continue to impose failed and flawed policies repeatedly, without either their competence, or the policies themselves being called into question.

Challenging the discourse: towards a new politics of knowledge

The capacity to generate 'facts' and 'truths' about the world are captured by powerful actors in the development establishment such as the World Bank, the IMF, the ADB, and myriad other think-tanks and academic institutions that serve as ancillary units to the larger industry of knowledge production. Backed as they are by immense financial resources, this entire network of institutions operates as a giant 'knowledge monopoly', edging out competition from alternative perspectives, analyses and ideas. Traditional farming systems and methods for harvesting water are neutralized as 'local knowledge'. Proposals by workers and small-scale producers to manage the economy are set aside as 'useful at the micro-level' but not viable to 'scale up'.

For millions of people across the world, mainstream development's regimes of truth are based on falsehoods. These regimes fail to recognize and respect the realities of peoples' lives and instead, seek to reconstruct these realities through the narrow lens of capitalist development. Resource dependant communities in the highlands of the Lao PDR, Cambodia and India are judged in terms of their 'value' to proposed investment projects rather than as active, thinking actors with evolved and specific knowledge systems and visions. However, the projected benefits of large hydroelectric projects or agro-forestry plantations are not necessarily development 'truths' for many of these communities. More likely, the 'truth' for them is forced relocation, the flooding of lands, homes and entire villages, loss of forests and common pool resources, and alienation from livelihood systems that they have nurtured and depended on for generations.

Development models are not indisputable, objective truths about the world. They are constructions of the world, which appropriate some facts and suppress others. At the same time, applications of these models have material effects and often produce the very realities that the models are intended to address. Poverty reduction programmes based on neoliberal policy prescriptions create the impoverishment that these programmes claim to alleviate (SAPRIN, 2004). Indiscriminate logging of dam reservoir sites and the forced relocation of communities who have tended these areas for generations result in the degradation of natural resource bases and dire poverty that project revenues are ostensibly supposed to alleviate.

The field of development is a field of contestation of ideas. The ideas that win and gain dominance are not necessarily qualitatively better; but rather, are those backed by the power of finance and politics, and specific class and institutional interests. If these ideas were limited to the arena of research, they would not have the ability to wreak the kind of havoc we witness today. But this is not the case. The world has become the testing ground for development models and theories that are removed from the day-to-day realities of the world's peoples, with damaging results that cannot be reversed as easily or efficiently as models are applied.

So where do we go from here? Perhaps the most effective starting point for catalysing progressive social change would be to critically examine the 'truths' projected by the mainstream development establishment and challenge the social, institutional and economic mechanisms by which they are produced, applied and disseminated. This is a political project, not an academic one.

The knowledge monopoly of the mainstream development establishment must be broken and in order to do this, we must develop a strategic awareness of the political economy of knowledge creation, and actively support alternative ways in which knowledge is generated and shared. As already mentioned earlier, the generation and application of knowledge is shaped by class and societal interests. Economic globalization has fragmented national societies into transnational groups bound by specific class and societal interests. Researchers in developing countries can quite often have more in common with their counterparts in developed countries than with the poor or disenfranchized in their own countries.

What is urgently needed is for the research establishment to open itself to alternative traditions by which knowledge is generated and shared. In order to hear and learn from the voices of workers, small farmers and fishers, women, children, rural and urban poor, and those displaced by development and wars, researchers have to change their own research traditions and what they accept as 'empirically valid'. The experiences of those who are marginalized or victimized by development are not 'anecdotes'; they are realities, and researchers must learn how to listen and give political voice to these realities.

Equally important is democratizing access to knowledge and protecting knowledge generation from commoditization through private property regimes. Open access journals and information systems (such as websites and electronic bulletins) that function through both private or public support offer options here. Other options also need to be explored that provide visibility to local research and documentation, and make information and knowledge available to the widest sections of society through local language publications and mass media.

The intellectual dependency of developing countries on a handful of sources in the North for information, analyses and policy directions must be broken. Progressive academics, donors and research institutions, including those in the UN system, must direct financial and substantive support to national and local level knowledge generation and dissemination, so that alternative forms of knowledge can flourish and inform policy making.

The messy realm of reality is the most powerful foe of the mainstream development establishment's tidy world of theory. This world must be tested against the reality it purports to represent, replete with the millions of people who speak different languages, have different aspirations, and who are no longer willing to be the 'cash crops' of the global economy. Theories and models that fail the test must be discarded and new thinking be nurtured and allowed to emerge. Equally important is building new structures for development policies and practice that are grounded in the specific circumstances of peoples and communities, and which support the emergence of theory from the ground of diverse realities.

Tinkering with the knowledge edifice of the development establishment is not going to bring about any fundamental change in the operations or thinking of the establishment's core agencies. Far more useful tasks would be to expose the material interests that shape current development policies and work with those most negatively affected by these policies to establish alternative knowledge bases. Demanding to know why the World Bank, IMF or ADB have not learned from past mistakes is to misread the main purpose of the knowledge components of these institutions. Knowledge production in these institutions is aimed at maintaining the *status quo* beneficial to their core functions and not at facilitating meaningful social or economic change for the majority of the world's people. The core business of development involves high stakes for its principal actors and it is not to the advantage of development officials and consultants to accumulate any knowledge that might compromise these stakes.

Nor is it particularly useful to ask whether development bureaucrats and professionals actually believe in the policies they prescribe, or even the ideology that underpins their practice. In order to be successful, the development establishment needs to maintain a capacity for self-delusion, which is then projected as universal truth. By the same token, it is futile to try and identify individuals in these institutions who 'care', 'can be trusted', and 'are trying to do some good'. The web of development institutions and interests is far larger than the individuals who inhabit its spaces; to confuse personal qualities with institutional mandates is to tie ourselves up in knots and lose sight of the more fundamental question of how to break the hegemony of these institutions on our thinking and actions.

It is crucial that UN agencies assist developing countries to formulate clear positions that challenge the orthodoxy of the mainstream development establishment, and particularly the intellectual hegemony of the Bretton Woods institutions and the regional development banks. The UN system can still provide a platform for genuine multilateralism with one country-one vote. UN agencies have the technical and institutional capacities to steer developmental thinking and practice away from the neoliberal orthodoxy of the World Bank, IMF and regional development banks. It is indeed unfortunate that neoliberal thinking has permeated all major UN conferences over more than a decade.

Bilateral donors need to direct more resources and support to progressive national, regional and international research institutions, and less to IFIs such as the World Bank, the IMF and regional development banks. Bilateral donors are currently assisting in the creation of a powerful and unaccountable aid cartel by contributing the huge amounts they do to the IFIs, and at the same time, by aligning their respective aid programmes with the policy frameworks of these institutions. It is now virtually impossible for developing countries with limited research and knowledge capacities to access policy advice from alternative sources. If donors are genuinely committed to supporting nationally grounded, owned and accountable development policies, they must support the conditions by which such policies can evolve. And this requires channelling more resources towards knowledge intensive work in national research institutions and progressive UN agencies, and de-linking their aid programmes from the World Bank, IMF and regional development banks. Further, donors should conduct independent evaluations of the impacts of the policies that they fund on different communities and population groups.

When faced with criticisms about the policies they promote, many well-meaning donor representatives and development bureaucrats complain that there is no alternative. But there are alternatives, in both ideas and practice. They have simply not been permitted to enter the exalted world of 'high theory' controlled by the mainstream development establishment. To move towards social change that is meaningful for the majority of the people of the world, it is imperative that we turn our attention to that entire body of discontinuous and dispersed knowledge that is systematically suppressed and marginalized from dominant development discourse. It is in this body of knowledge that we will find new directions for social change that are shaped and guided by the aspirations and priorities of peoples, communities and nations.

2
The New Buzzwords

Andrea Cornwall and Karen Brock[1]

Introduction

The last ten years have witnessed the most remarkable apparent conflu-
ence of positions in the international development arena. Barely any
development actor could take serious issue with the way the objectives
of development are currently framed. This new consensus is captured in
a seductive mix of buzzwords. 'Participation' and 'empowerment',
words that are 'warmly persuasive' (Williams, 1976: 76) and fulsomely
positive, promise an entirely different way of doing business; harnessed
in the service of 'poverty reduction' and decorated with the clamours of
'civil society' and 'the voices of the poor', they speak to an agenda for
transformation that combines no-nonsense pragmatism with almost
unimpeachable moral authority. It is easy enough to get caught up in
the emotive calls for action, to be moved by talk of poor people 'crying
out for change' (Narayan *et al.*, 2000a), to feel that in the midst of all
the uncertainties and instabilities of the day international institutions
are working together for the good, and that they have now got the story
right and are really going to make a difference.

Today's development policies capture this sense of purposefulness
and resound with a decisive ring of optimism. They evoke a world
where everyone gets a chance to take part in making the decisions that
affect their lives, where no one goes hungry or is discriminated against,
and where opportunities exist for all to thrive: a governable, regulable,
controllable world in which policies neatly map out a route-map for
implementation. Open the newspaper and the first few pages often
have enough talk of violent death, inequity, deprivation and misery to
make one feel the world we live in is hardly a place where a 'world
without poverty' could ever come to exist. From the delicate tinkle of

43

the fountain in the atrium at the World Bank's H-Street headquarters and the soft-carpeted corridors of the hotels favoured by the development elite on mission, to the sublime confidence which permeates the marketing of solutions by the army of consultants and advisors who occupy these spaces, the trappings of the development industry are part of a world that is ever more removed from the world in which poor people live their everyday lives.

Three words, 'participation', 'empowerment' and 'poverty reduction', have gained considerable purchase in recent years in the language of mainstream development. Carrying the sense of optimism and purpose, as well as properties that endow them with considerable normative power, these words may not have completely permeated the terrain of development policy but their presence in the language of the most influential development agencies would appear, at first sight, to represent a considerable shift in approach. What difference has all this made? Has it led to any meaningful change in the policies pursued by mainstream development? One way to approach this would be a comprehensive look at what is actually being done in the name of 'participation', 'empowerment' and 'poverty reduction', and to ask questions about to what extent this represents real differences in practice – or simply, as some might charge, the appropriation of nice-sounding words to dress up 'business as usual'. This is an important task, one that a number of researchers have turned their attention to in recent years.[2]

But, we suggest here, another tack is to enquire into what these words, *as words*, do for development policy.[3] Georges Sorel (1941), writing in 1908, cautions that comparing statements of intent with what actually happens in practice is to misunderstand their purpose. The fine-sounding words that are used in development policies do more than provide a sense of direction: they lend the legitimacy that development actors need in order to justify their interventions. They are what Raymond Williams (1976) called 'keywords', words that evoke, and come to carry, the cultural and political values of the time. Paying closer attention to the ways in which particular development buzzwords have come to be used, then, sheds interesting light on the normative project that is development. 'The task of deconstructing particular aspects of development discourse', Gardner and Lewis argue, 'can have a directly practical and political outcome, for to reveal what at first sight appears to be objective reality as a construct, the product of particular historical and political contexts, helps problematise dominant paradigms and open the way for alternative discourses' (2000: 19). It is in this vein that this chapter is intended.

Before we begin, a caveat is called for. The published policies of development agencies are often products of successful discourse coalitions, actor-networks that range beyond a particular organization to embrace allies in other spheres (cf. Hajer, 1993), and the way policies work in an organization depends on a host of factors, from organizational culture to the nature of existing bureaucratic fiefdoms. Every development organization is a complex agent, not just an actor whose views and positions can be personified and treated as singular; and in practice, buzzwords produce a multiplicity of contingent, situational and relational meanings that are negotiated in particular settings. An ethnographic study of how buzzwords play out in particular organizational contexts would make these dimensions of their social lives, and attendant implications, apparent.[4] Aware as we are of these complexities, documents remain an important touchstone.

Our analysis proceeds in three steps. First, we investigate the form and function of development buzzwords in the statements of intent of development agencies, exploring their performative effects as well as their semantic qualities. Second, we situate the use of these buzzwords in shifting configurations over time, focusing in some detail on two frames of reference for development intervention that have gained currency in recent years, the Poverty Reduction Strategy Papers (PRSPs) and the Millennium Development Goals (MDGs). Here, 'poverty reduction' and 'participation' come together, with 'empowerment' as an implicit adjunct. Our third step is to situate the shifting configurations of the three buzzwords against a wider backdrop of reflections on the place of such terms in development policy.

Discourses and dissonances

> Nobody trying to be influential can afford to neglect the fine art of buzzwords.... Images conveyed by simple terms are taken as reality, and words are increasingly loaded with ideological symbolism and political correctness. It may seem innocuous. It surely is not. Why make a fuss? The reason is that the terms we use help to shape the policy agenda.... The linguistic crisis is real, and is not going to go away (Standing, 2001: 13).

There is something about today's development language that is quite at odds with the hard-edged linearity of the dominant tropes in development thinking. Many of the terms with which we have become so familiar in recent years evoke a comforting mutuality, a warm and reassuring consensus, ringing with the satisfaction of everyone pulling together to pursue a set of common goals for the well-being of all. Take, for example, the following excerpt from a speech delivered at the plenary meeting of the first, United Nations-hosted, Financing for Development conference in Monterrey in 2002, by James Wolfensohn, a master of the art of feel-good rhetoric:

> What is this new partnership? It is an understanding that leaders of the developing and developed world are united by a global responsi-bility based on ethics, experience and self-interest. It is recognition that opportunity and empowerment – not charity – can benefit us all. It is an acknowledgement that we will not create long-term peace and stability until we acknowledge that we are a common humanity with a common destiny. Our futures are indivisible. And we have the makings of just such a new partnership before us. A new generation of leaders is taking responsibility in developing countries. Many of these leaders are tackling corruption, putting in place good govern-ance, giving priority to investing in their people, and establishing an investment climate to attract private capital. They are doing it in the private sector, in civil society, in government and in communities. *They are doing it not because they have been told to. But because they know it is right* (World Bank, 2002c; available online at www.worldbank.org, our emphasis).

Redolent with purpose, his speech couples terms like 'understanding', 'recognition', 'acknowledgment' with 'together-words' – 'united', 'us all', 'common humanity with a common destiny', 'our futures' – to stake out a normative position as consensus.

'Crucial in all policy practice', Gasper and Apthorpe argue, 'is framing, specifically who and what is actually included, and who and what is ignored and excluded' (1996: 6). In *Ways of Worldmaking* (1978), the philosopher Nelson Goodman argues that how we interpret the world depends on the frame of reference that we use. Different 'ways of worldmaking' use different frames of reference, and can produce very different views of what is true or right. 'A statement is true and a description or representation right', he argues, 'for a world it fits' (1978: 132). Applying Goodman's insights to development is instructive. Policies, speeches and mission statements create versions of the world which fit particular frames of reference. But these frames of reference may be so utterly different that a statement that is true for one way of worldmaking may make no sense for another. For example, the mission statement, 'For a World Free of Poverty' is shared by ActionAid, the World Bank and War on Want. Seen through the frame of their different approaches to the way of worldmaking that is development, three distinctively different possible worlds come into view.

Buzzwords are an ever-present part of the worlds that are made and sustained by development agencies. Making sense of what they do for development calls for closer attention to be paid to the discourses of which they form part. By discourse, we mean the 'ensemble of ideas, concepts, and categories through which meaning is given to phenomena' (Hajer, 1993: 45). The term 'discourse' has become so over-used in development studies it has itself gained the status of a buzzword, and is often taken as monolithic, totalizing: impossible to change. This, we suggest, is far from the case – certainly not in the work of Foucault, whose argument for the 'strategic reversibility' of discourse is central to ours here. As he suggests:

> There is not, on the one side, a discourse of power and opposite it, another discourse that runs counter to it. Discourses are tactical elements or blocks operating in the field of force relations; there can exist different and even contradictory discourses within the same strategy; they can, on the contrary, circulate without changing their form from one strategy to another, opposing strategy (1979: 101–2).

Within and among development agencies, as we go on to suggest, competing ideologies co-exist within the same discourse; despite the apparent uniformity of today's development consensus, which masks dissonance, different actors invest key terms like 'poverty reduction', 'empowerment' and 'participation' with a range of different meanings. 'Discourses frame certain problems' by distinguishing 'some aspects of a situation rather than others', Hajer (1993: 45) argues. In doing so, they define paths of action, containing in their problem-statements certain kinds of solutions. The term 'poverty *reduction*', for example, rings with measurability, and harks to the rationality of policies that can serve to bring poverty into check. Poverty *alleviation* carries quite a different set of meanings, a making-better rather than making less; and to talk of *eradication*, as the United Nations (UN) so fulsomely did some years ago, before being swept up in the discourse of poverty reduction once more, is to evoke another world altogether (Øyen, 1999).

Particular combinations of buzzwords are linked together in development policies through what Laclau (1996) calls 'chains of equivalence': words that work together to evoke a particular set of meanings. In recent years, the 'chains of equivalence' into which 'participation', 'poverty reduction' and 'empowerment' have been brought have included a range of other buzzwords – 'partnership', 'accountability', 'governance', 'ownership', 'transparency', 'rights-based approach' and so on. Configuring 'participation' and 'empowerment' with 'governance', for example, produces a different set of possibilities than would be the case if 'governance' were to be replaced with 'social protection'. As a word comes to be included in a 'chain of equivalence', those meanings that are consistent with other words in the chain come to take precedence over other, more dissonant, meanings. The more words that become part of the chain, the more that meaning resides in the connections between them. Pared down to the elements that would permit coherence, the terms that form part of today's development jargon are reduced to monochrome; while they may be filled with other meanings when deployed in other contexts, by other actors, their appearance as consensus neutralizes dissonant elements that would otherwise jar.

The world that appears through the frame of reference of the international consensus consists of similar objects to previous versions; it is made familiar enough to feel comfortable with elements that work to 'anchor' (Moscovici, 1984) as well as to assuage (cf. Roe 1991). But there is a growing feeling that the words that are used as part of this project of world-making have 'lost their meaning'; a feeling that Standing talks of as veritable 'linguistic crisis' (2001: 12). In what follows, we sketch out some of the discursive shifts that have got us where we are now, exploring shifting and plural meanings of 'participation', 'empowerment' and 'poverty reduction' and the ways in which they have been configured over the last 30 years. Our attention then turns to the MDGs and PRSPs, as it is here that our three buzzwords come together in the service of the consensus; it is here that the increased rhetorical and operational coherence between international development actors is at its most evident. Occupying central positions in supranational governance discourse about what needs to be done in development, and how to go about it, the PRSPs and MDGs encode the declared consensus in linear logic; 'poverty reduction', 'participation' and 'empowerment' are invoked in defining both means and ends.

The narratives of 'poverty reduction', 'participation' and 'empowerment' put forward by PRSPs and MDGs are complementary. Patterns of narrative co-evolution are clear. However there are also essential contrasts between the two, concerning the configurations of actors associated with each discourse, and their imperatives and agency; and the operational elements of the policy instruments associated with the narratives. Each stems from a distinct trajectory, deriving from the UN conferences of the post-Cold War era on the one hand, and from the hegemony of the poverty imperative within international agencies on the other. Both have been shaped by the engagement, demands and pressures of non-governmental actors; and through the enlistment of nation-states, although through very different modes and with different positions of opportunity and power. Examining these contrasts and complementarities foregrounds the processes by which discursive shifts happen and coalesce in changed models for policy.

The art of euphemism in an era of declared consensus

'Participation', 'poverty reduction' and 'empowerment' are 'feel-good' terms: they connote warm and nice things, conferring on their users that goodness and rightness that development agencies need to assert in order to assume the legitimacy to intervene in the lives of others. At times, they come to be used as metonyms: that is, they come to stand for something bigger, signifying the normative project of 'development' or indeed the grander still interpretation of 'rightness' that Wolfensohn is so fond of evoking. Each word has a distinctive history; and each has been, to a greater or lesser extent, 'mainstreamed' across international development agencies, being configured and reconfigured in 'chains of equivalence' with a range of other development buzzwords.

'Poverty reduction' may be the contemporary euphemism for today's development consensus, but the term 'poverty' is bound up with the very notion of 'development' (Escobar, 1995; Rist, 1997). 'Participation' has long associations with social movements, and with the struggle for citizenship rights and voice (cf. ILO, 1978; Pearse and Stiefel, 1979, cited in Stiefel and Wolfe, 1994; Rahman, 1995; Gaventa, 2002). As politically ambivalent as it is definitionally vague, 'participation' has been used for centuries as a means to enable ordinary people to gain political agency and engage in shaping the decisions that affect their lives, but also as a powerful means of maintaining relations of rule (Cohen and Uphoff, 1980). Its uses for neutralizing political opposition (cf. Vengroff, 1974) and taxing the poorest (Chambers, 1974; Salole, 1991) were tried and tested in the colonial era before being deployed in the service of neoliberalism (Ribot, 1996; Rist, 1997). Ideas about its benefits have been part of mainstream development discourse since the early 1970s, appearing, for example, in the United States government's 1973 Foreign Assistance Act (Cohen and Uphoff, 1980), although it is only in the last decade that they have been taken up more widely in attempts to shape the way in which development is done. These competing currents continue to course through discursive representations and practices of participation.

'Empowerment' has a more curious history, having gained the most expansive semantic range of all, with meanings pouring into development from an enormous diversity of sources, which include feminist scholarship, the Christian right, New Age self-help manuals, and business management (Henkel and Stirrat, 2001; Moore, 2001). Its rise and rise in the World Bank in recent years is a story embedded in the harnessing of a range of relational buzzwords by a particular actor-network to create bureaucratic and policy space (Bebbington *et al.*, 2004), as indeed to 'strike a positive chord with those 'progressive' groups on whom the very existence of international aid agencies and programmes increasingly depends' (Moore, 2001: 322–3). Ironically, the feminist emphasis on the politics of the personal has been only too readily taken up in the service of individualism. While 'empowerment' retains a prominent place in agencies' policies concerning 'gender', it often appears in a diluted form, neutralizing its original emphasis on building personal and collective power in the struggle for a more just and equitable world (Rowlands, 1997).

Jan Vandemoortele (2004), of the United Nations Development Programme (UNDP), notes two underlying threads in the construction of the declared consensus:

> The partnership between rich and poor countries takes many forms, including foreign aid or official development assistance. In essence, there are two major dimensions to that partnership: one is concerned with 'money changing hands' the other with 'ideas changing minds' (p. 2).

In the discussion that follows we explore the trajectories of 'participation', 'empowerment' and 'poverty reduction' in the interplay between 'money changing hands' and 'ideas changing minds' that is international development.[5] Our narrative begins in the 1970s and traces threads across the intervening decades to the present. Necessarily brief, superficial and selective, this overview seeks to highlight the moments and movements that we see as critical antecedents to today's policy narratives.

'Poverty reduction', 'participation' and 'empowerment'

A brief consensus about the centrality of 'poverty reduction' as the goal of development was given permission in the early 1970s by the Cold

War geo-political imperative of preventing the poor from seeking solutions in Communism; the World Bank, under the leadership of McNamara, widened the focus of its lending, beginning to embrace rural development for small farmers, and the provision of social services to the rural and urban poor. Beneficiary participation was envisaged as a critical component of development projects and policies even at this juncture (Chambers, 1974; Cohen and Uphoff, 1980), and was articulated with the same mixture of pragmatism and principle that is found in today's calls for 'participation'. What was then termed 'popular participation' had, of course, a much longer history, one that captures some of today's ambivalences but also carries with it some of the radicalism that many bemoan as having been lost in today's participation discourses (Cornwall, 2000).[6]

Contemporaneous with this focus on 'poverty reduction' was the development of the basic needs approach by the UN, which suggested that the focus of aid should shift from investment in capital formation to the development of human resources. 'Popular participation' was positioned as a central pillar of this approach. Statements from UN organizations articulating this relationship are revealing in their similarity to contemporary narratives. In one of the most resonant with the kind of language used in today's consensus, in 1975 the United Nations Economic and Social Council (ECOSOC) urged governments to 'adopt popular participation as a basic policy measure in national development strategy...[and] encourage the widest possible active participation of all individuals and national non-government organisations in the development process, in setting goals, formulating policies and implementing plans' (cited in Cohen and Uphoff, 1980: 213). Almost exactly the same exhortation can be found in the PRSP sourcebook (World Bank, no date).

'Empowerment', in this era, was envisaged as a radical project of social transformation, focused on building countervailing power to enable otherwise excluded social groups to mobilize collectively to define and claim their rights (Fals-Borda and Rahman, 1991; Friedman, 1992). It was also a nascent discourse within the growing movement of second-wave feminism, in which it gained the individual as well as collective dimensions that were to give it such purchase in the mainstream where the message it was associated with in this epoch, of grounding the personal in the political (Rowlands, 1997). These came to be the dissonant elements that fell away as it came to join words like 'social capital', 'assets' and 'capacities' as part of a 'chain of equivalence' that stripped it of any political potency.

For much of the 1970s, as in the preceding decades when social movements carved out political space from which to press their demands, the spheres of officialized beneficiary participation and popular mobilization intersected, but remained largely distinct. It was this interface that was of particular interest to a network convened by Andrew Pearse and others at the United Nations Research Institute for Social Development (UNRISD) in the late 1970s. In 1979, UNRISD's popular participation programme was launched. Its focus was 'the encounter between the pursuit of livelihood by popularly-based groups and the policies being pursued by the state and other "developers"' (Barraclough, in Stiefel and Wolfe, 1994: xii). 'Participation' was, for the UNRISD team, fundamentally about the redistribution of power, and was defined as: 'the organized efforts to increase control over resources and regulative institutions in given social situations, on the part of groups and movements hitherto excluded from such control' (Stiefel and Wolfe, 1994: 5). We will return to the prescience of many of the conclusions from this project, and the continued relevance of the way in which it chose to frame participation.

From grassroots movements to networks of practitioners spanning North and South, participatory approaches became a focus for innovation over the course of the 1970s, and into the 1980s. But whilst grassroots community development work was reframing 'development', with methodologies such as Development Leadership Teams in Action (DELTA) and Participatory Action Research (PAR), what participation had come to mean to the mainstream was less to do with radical shifts in power than engaging communities in sharing the costs, and the burdens, of development – much like today's 'Community-Driven Development' (CDD). The 1970s slogan of self-reliance was fast being transformed into the 'do it for yourself' ethos that was to characterize mainstream development in the 1980s.

Domesticating participation, disciplining the poor

The rising power of neoliberal orthodoxy, triggered by oil crises and the election of right-wing governments in Britain, the United States and other powerful countries, heralded an era of unprecedented power for the international financial institutions (IFIs). Their structural adjustment programmes (SAPs) firmly reinstated technical and economistic policy solutions to underdevelopment. Nonetheless, project funding by donor and creditor agencies spanned the two eras, and continued to create spaces for practices in which new meanings of both 'participation' and 'poverty reduction' were shaped and negotiated.

During the 1980s, earlier people-centred narratives of popular participation met the exigencies arising out of neoliberal reforms, and the realities of the rolled-back state. 'Community participation' became a channel through which 'popular participation' began to be operationalized. In the process, it took a rather different shape than that conveyed by the statements of intent that preceded it. Rather than seeking to involve 'the people' in defining their own development, 1980s 'community participation' largely focused on engaging 'intended beneficiaries' in development projects. Cost-sharing and the co-production of services emerged as dominant modes of participation; the concept of 'ownership' began to be stripped of any association with a transfer of power and control and invoked to describe the need for people to make contributions in cash or kind to support these processes.

What 'participation' meant to mainstream development agencies in the 1980s rarely went beyond cost-sharing and consultation; Paul's (1987) review of World Bank projects highlights how few had 'empowerment' as an explicit objective. What is perhaps most ironic about the entry of the term 'empowerment' into the chain of equivalence that is today's governance-speak is that the very same projects might now be reclassified, and indeed celebrated, as contributing to 'empowerment' goals, much as the label 'Community Driven Development' has served to rebrand otherwise unfashionable interventions.

A decisive impetus for further reconfigurations of meanings came in the last half of the 1980s. Critiques of the negative economic effects of adjustment were an essential stage in catalyzing a broader discursive shift about the nature of poverty, as well as providing a home for the sanitized versions of 'participation' which were a familiar part of the development landscape by the mid-1980s. The publication of *Adjustment with a Human Face* by the United Nations Children's Fund (UNICEF) (Cornia *et al.*, 1987) was pivotal in this regard. In making its critique of SAPs, the report fulfilled several important functions. It served as a singular and morally authoritative voice to transmit the broad concerns of a wide range of development actors, many of them non-governmental organizations (NGOs), making some of these criticisms audible to the IFIs. It presented a hybrid agenda, characterizing the failure of SAPs as one of implementation rather than conceptualization; this lack of foundational critique increased its audibility. The policy coalition it represented was able to exercise influence through translation of a diversity of unhearable opinions into influential language and networks.

In its arguments about enhanced 'participation', it offered the IFIs a vision of a potential route to neutralizing future opposition, one that was more than familiar to the colonial authorities:

> Community participation is an essential ingredient of adjustment with a human face. On the one hand, it can help generating the political support needed to overcome short-term political and bureaucratic opposition. On the other, it is essential for the planning, implementing, and success of the approaches devised, as well as for keeping the cost of the programmes down by means of community contributions (Cornia *et al.*, 1987: 295).

Indeed, some would suggest 'community participation' was subsequently actively fostered by international agencies such as the World Bank precisely because of the opportunities it afforded for countering grassroots resistance to reforms, providing a palliative that served to neutralize popular resistance to SAPs (Rahman, 1995; Leal and Opp, 1998). The practice of 'participation' to which it gave rise served to render technical what were essentially political problems, providing non-challenging support for orthodox development solutions.

A marriage of convenience?

Just as the uptake of 'community participation' in World Bank practice reveals a different normative use of the concept from its historical antecedents, the incorporation of some elements of the basic needs approach into World Bank policy narrative contributed to a subtle reframing of the problems and solutions of 'poverty reduction'. The 1990 *World Development Report* (WDR) (World Bank, 1990a), dedicated to poverty, shows strong traces of the policy agenda put forward in *Adjustment with a Human Face* – advocating investment in human capital and social safety nets. These elements are wedded in a marriage of convenience to the achievement of income poverty reduction through economic growth; but it is growth, and technical prescriptions for attaining it through macroeconomic stability, privatization and liberalization, that dominate the discourse.

Looking forward a decade, from WDR 1990 to WDR 2000/1, several discursive shifts are discernible. Firstly, the World Bank's narrative had acquired a *moral* tone: garnished liberally with quotations from 'poor people', the report attempts to establish moral authority through introducing a new vocabulary (Gaventa, 2001). A second shift concerns the definition of the problem: the nature of poverty, which by 2000/2001, on the surface at least, is presented as a multidimensional phenomenon. Thirdly, the framing of a solution to 'poverty reduction' has shifted: by 2000/2001 the 'two and a half prong' approach of WDR 1990 had given way to PRSPs and the new, coordinated partnership of aid – with the state reinstated as a 'partner' in the enterprise, with whom external development actors conduct 'policy dialogue' in the new language of euphemism.

Events in the 1990s gave rise to the simultaneous co-creation of the three elements of discursive shift, and the changed practice implied by the WDR 2000/1 agenda. With hindsight, this era could be characterized as one where the World Bank reshaped its existing narratives to make them more palatable to an increasingly critical international community; the public reputation of the IFIs needed to be overhauled. Simultaneously, however, the multidimensional nature of poverty needed to be negotiated in order to conform to the 'hegemony of rational choice theory' (Eyben, 2004: 16) and thus be internally palatable; 'participation' needed to be rebranded to connect it to a logic of free market access; and the practices of Southern governments needed to be controlled beyond explicit conditionalities. Several key episodes were important here. Major UN Summits – especially those at Rio (1992), and Copenhagen (1995) – provided spaces for declarations which, while they did not result in structural change, did catalyze influential new discourse coalitions and networks of change agents in development finance institutions, and in bilateral agencies (Bebbington *et al.*, 2004; Eyben, 2004). Rio, for example, offered legitimacy to those who advocated sustainable development, some of whom went on to be key movers and shakers in their advocacy of 'participation'; Copenhagen did the same for those who considered that the state was central to the provision of social services.

One effect of the rediscovery of what was left of the state in the 'poverty reduction' discourse of the later 1990s was to extend advocacy of 'participation' beyond the realm of projects into the broader terrain of economic, social and political life in the context of an attenuated state. Successful examples of 'scaling up' of 'participation' were used by advocates in the mid-1990s to argue for 'mainstreaming' in government agencies (Thompson, 1995; Blackburn *et al.*, 1999). 'Empowerment' was still, by the late 1990s, a term that had a more radical ring to it, and was often invoked by participation practitioners in contrast to the forms of practice associated with the 'scaled-up' activities of bilateral and multilateral agencies (Cornwall *et al.*, 2001; Pratt, 2001). But then, as now, it was a term profoundly associated with local-level processes, and with 'communities'.

A second effect, in the later 1990s, came out of the 'good governance' agenda. 'Participation' came to feature increasingly prominently as providing the mechanisms through which these policy objectives might be realized, recast as consumer involvement in shaping service provision and in accountability mechanisms such as the 'partnership' models that had become a feature of local service provision in the health sector in many countries (Loewenson, 2000; Manor, 2004). Over the course of the decade, decentralized governance sprang into fashion, as the most acceptable route to 'good' governance. Offering the answer to multiple ills, development myths about decentralization regularly invoke the 'participation' of 'the poor'. Conflict and power are as absent from this world as they are from the world we are offered in today's development policies; versions of 'participation' and 'empowerment' invoked in decentralization policies are those that fit the frame, forming part of a chain of equivalence in which the more conflictive elements of both are stripped away in the service of 'poverty reduction'.[7]

Operationalizing the new consensus: the MDGs and PRSPs

The buzzwords associated with different policy episodes and eras – good governance, partnership, scaling-up, multidimensionality – have shaped existing discourses of 'participation' and 'poverty reduction', and of their relationship to each other in development policy. One outcome of the harnessing of 'participation' to 'poverty reduction' is that a set of policy solutions to development, in the shape of over-arching, universalizing models, are now more than ever firmly and explicitly embedded in mainstream discourses of development. The framing of the problem and the solution have become inextricably linked. We view PRSPs and the MDGs as an expression of this linkage, embodying as they do a consensual discourse of collective responsibility for reducing multidimensional poverty.

All three of our buzzwords come together in the PRSPs and MDGs, in which the increased rhetorical and operational coherence between international development actors is at its most evident. Occupying central positions in supranational governance discourses about what needs to be done, and how to go about it, the PRSPs and MDGs encode the declared development consensus in linear logic. While the narratives of 'poverty reduction', 'empowerment' and 'participation' put forward by PRSPs and MDGs are complementary, as befitting their pivotal role in the consensus narrative, there are also essential contrasts between them. These contrasts are the echoes of the dissonance that the consensus submerges; they concern the configurations of actors associated with each discourse, their imperatives and agency; and the operational elements of the policy instruments associated with the PRSPs and the MDGs. While PRSPs are a development instrument, styled out of pragmatism, backed with economic power, MDGs are a normative framework, backed with a moral imperative. Both are championed by supranational institutions, but institutions which contrast significantly in function and modes of leverage, tactics and efficacy. Differing in form, these two frames – an instrument and a statement of aspirations – are familiar objects in the landscape of development, which has always rested on some combination of the two.

In both PRSPs and MDGs, 'poverty reduction' and 'participation' are foundational elements. Each stems from a distinct trajectory – deriving from the UN conferences of the post-Cold War era on the one hand, and from the hegemony of the poverty imperative within international agencies on the other. Both have been shaped by the engagement, demands and pressures of non-governmental actors; and through the enlistment of nation-states, although through very different modes and with different positions of opportunity and power.

The narrative of the PRSP consensus – that 'poverty reduction' can only be achieved through country-driven, result-oriented, comprehensive, partnership-oriented, long-term strategies – chimes with the narrative of the MDG consensus – that international development is a measurable moral goal towards which the governments of all countries should strive. Actors across a broad spectrum have been able to fit their own understandings – whether of the need for a multidimensional approach to poverty, effective aid, structural financial reforms, debt relief, or citizen participation – into the storyline. It is to the MDGs and the PRSPs that we turn in this section, to explore how our buzzwords and the worlds they make translate into targets, instruments and plans.

The MDGs: targets out of buzzwords

The adoption of the Millennium Declaration by the UN General Assembly in September 2000, and the reformulation of the International Development Targets (IDTs)[8] into the MDGs, can be seen as part of a broader consensus with an extraordinarily diverse buy-in. As well as reflecting the evolving, domesticated narratives of 'participation' and poverty reduction discussed above, the MDGs provided a response to several ongoing debates. Designed not only to meet challenges about the effectiveness of aid, and agendas for greater 'coherence' between the IFIs and donors, the MDGs were also a response to the moral authority and effectiveness of the Jubilee 2000 campaign, which caught the imagination of a global development audience and saw the citizens of Northern countries participating around development issues to a previously unprecedented degree.

Although progress towards the MDGs can be monitored at different levels and scales (Vandemoortele, 2004), their primary nature is one of composite measurability. Their narrative is one of measuring change already set in motion, not one of analysis of the forces which produce poverty (Asia Pacific Civil Society Forum, 2003). In doing so, however, the MDGs stimulate new conversations, principally about why they might not be met, and what can be done about it. As a set of time-bound, numerical targets, set within a frame of human development, the MDGs imply, rather than direct, necessary policy change. From one angle, they can be seen as the ultimate in compromise, the lowest common denominators of legitimate change, the price of international coherence and cooperation. From another, they can be seen and used as tools for changing minds, and for holding accountable the powerful. As identifiable discourse markers emerging from a supranational space, the MDGs represent a way of world-making that lacks any sense of place. As 'participation', and now 'empowerment', has become normalized and bureaucratized through exercises in mainstreaming, goals and targets at the global level represent the next step of displacement from the specificities of context. With the mantle of moral credibility that they lend, they are both symbol and product of the new consensus.

While reference to the MDGs appears in many policy documents, usage tends to be decorative; in many advocacy documents, however, they are used to suggest paths of change. Advocacy largely focuses on the behaviour of Northern governments, and has continued both through established networks and constituencies, and through the UN system itself. Jubilee Research, for example, uses the MDGs to advocate debt cancellation, noting that increased aid flows will prove ineffectual in Heavily Indebted Poor Countries (HIPCs), unless there is a 100 per cent debt cancellation (Greenhill, 2002). Meanwhile, paths for Southern civil society organization (CSO) advocacy around the MDGs are considerably less clear. While the UNDP seeks to strengthen CSO capacity in monitoring both MDGs and PRSPs, and to extend beyond 'their narrow role of "social watchdog"' (Vandemoortele, 2004: 2), there is the possibility of further reinforcing experiences of hollow, invited pseudo-participation that have become so prominent a part of the political landscape in many countries, including in bilateral donors' own backyards (see, for example, Taylor *et al.*, 2004).

Civil society actors are not the only ones asking why progress on the MDGs, while apparently feasible, is not 'on track'. There is a tension between changing minds and winning hearts with advocacy, and the realities of changed practices of Southern governance implied by the very notion of 'being on track'. It is worth taking the time to juxtapose two analyses from different sources, because they reveal how some of the implicit assumptions of the MDG narrative play out. The first, from within the UN, addresses the question 'why are promises not being kept?', and suggests a way forward, including stronger partnership, and deeper participation. What meaning do such recommendations have when they are applied to a particular place, a particular context? This is the subject of the second extract, from an empirical study of the domestic politics of the Tanzanian PRSP, which discusses the meanings which emerge when buzzwords like 'partnership' and 'participation' are applied to an existing context.

Why are the promises not being kept? Why are hundreds of millions of people struggling to overcome the daily grind of hunger, disease and ignorance when the global economy is experiencing unprecedented prosperity? . . . Two reasons stand out in virtually all countries: (i) underinvestment in basic social services, and (ii) public action that frequently fails to take advantage of cross-sectoral synergies. . . . While the MDGs remain unfulfilled, they also remain feasible and affordable. Committed leadership, stronger partnership, extra money, and deeper participation by the poor can bring the world back on track towards the MDGs (Vandemoortele, 2004: 16).

The Strategy privileges allocations to social sector spending at the expense of the longer-term structural issues like factor productivity, employment, the viability of smallholder agriculture and agro-industrial linkages. The Government's responsibility for promoting economic transformation is largely restricted to budgetary instruments for the management of aid-sponsored public expenditure. . . . The trend of co-ordination and harmonization cements the bonds between the parties to the partnership and contributes to the lowering of the transaction costs of aid management. At the same time, these arrangements also streamline the negotiation and disbursement of new lending from the International Financial Institutions. Since democratic public oversight of foreign lending is virtually non-existent, there is a serious risk that the streamlining of new credits will lead to the rapid accumulation of new debt for social sector investments.... In sum, the lack of a strategy for economic transformation in concert with the removal of bureaucratic obstacles to new credits is likely to deepen Tanzania's already crippling long-term aid dependency (Gould and Ojanen, 2003: 7–8).

Read side by side, these two extracts show a worrying set of consequences that are not part of the explicit intentions of the MDG narrative. As both a product and a tool of a supranational arena of governance, the MDGs encapsulate considerable assumptions about how change happens in different arenas: closer 'partnership', for example, facilitates new debt as well as lowering transaction costs; focusing on social spending detracts from other issues. Beyond this, it has also been argued that the MDGs make considerable assumptions about the benign nature of the IFIs to create equitable change (Alexander and Kessler, 2003), and about the efficacy of PRSPs as the principal route to mobilize national actors to achieve the MDGs (Bullard, 2003).

Policies in practice

Thus far, we have paid particular attention to the dynamics by which discourses of development are transformed among international institutions. But what have the discursive shifts represented by the PRSPs meant in practice?

As PRSPs, these discourses translate into a policy model which is projected towards existing national level policy processes. These involve a diverse set of actors – some from the supranational level, but also certain agents of national governments, development-oriented CSOs, international NGOs, and bilaterals. Beyond this is a third level, where the projected model is transformed anew, through implementation, involving a different set of actors again – agents of decentralized government, service delivery CSOs, citizens, and (ostensibly at least) – the poor. The meanings of buzzwords are transmitted and transformed by actors and networks, which overlap across these different domains and levels. The sanitized, consensual meanings from the centre of the discourse are refracted again and again.

The application of discourses of 'poverty reduction' and participation to national processes via the PRSP model refracts into the key binary adjuncts of 'ownership' and 'partnership'. In this instance, the pair are entirely inseparable: co-dependent. Gould and Ojanen's (2003) study of the Tanzanian PRSP discusses the meanings of ownership and partnership which emerge from implementation:

[In Tanzania,] the international aid agencies have convinced state representatives to remake their multilateral aid relationships into a new breed of 'partnership'. Under the terms of this partnership, the donor community promises African governments greater 'ownership' of their social policies. For the elected leadership, the main perk was the increased leeway for political manouevre that the (partial) relief of foreign debt can provide. In return, recipient/partner governments are required to commit themselves to a multi-tethered program of state reform (2003: 30).

Framed as a necessity for 'poverty reduction', country or national ownership is closely related to the narratives of coherence, cooperation and harmonization that are encapsulated by the consensus that emerged from the same conference in Monterrey, where James Wolfensohn evoked the 'rightness' of contemporary approaches to 'poverty reduction'. Under the logic of the Monterrey Consensus, the MDGs can only be achieved by harmonization of the operational procedures of donors, 'ensuring that development assistance is delivered in accordance with partner country priorities, including 'poverty reduction' strategies and similar approaches' (OECD, 2003). The implicit assumption, that 'poverty reduction' strategies deliver national priorities owned by partner countries, is acted on regardless of ongoing negotiations of meaning, such as those outlined by Gould and Ojanen. Examined in context, rather than in the displaced world of the consensus, the meanings of ownership, partnership and harmonization circumscribe and bound the legitimate terrains of agency for a range of different actors, located in government, civil society and 'the donor community'.

The nature of ownership actually created through PRSP partnership inheres, at least initially, among a small group of actors (Eyben, 2004; Gould and Ojanen, 2003), among whom the totalizing nature of the policy model that forms the foundation of the partnership has become deeply ingrained so that 'they are no longer capable of imagining other kinds of policy approaches' (Eyben, 2004).[9] The new vocabularies of this model, suggests Kakande (2004), can 'reinforce status and widen the gap between expert and novice', creating an 'inner circle' of people who share a common language. The master buzzwords of the PRSP – 'ownership' and 'partnership' – may create an overarching embrace, but the new vocabularies that arise from them as they are operationalized spread out beneath and create patterns of exclusion in implementation. The processes of establishing joint meanings for language that signals a united goal require negotiation (Hinton, 2004); the dynamics of who is allowed to participate in that conversation of negotiation are part of the pattern of determinants upon which the transformation of model into practice depends.

The dynamics of ownership in this 'inner circle' are at odds with the PRSP narrative, which purports that a broader, social ownership can and should be created through 'participation'. In PRSP implementation, the consultative processes which are designed to create this social ownership have relied on a narrow conceptualization of 'participation', and often run to externally dictated timetables which seldom regard the rhythm of the domestic policy process (Knoke and Morazan, 2002; Stewart and Wang, 2003; Booth, 2004). They have usually offered limited spaces for engagement to invited CSOs, whose views beyond the consensus, if they are expressed at all, seldom find their way into final documents (Whitehead, 2003). Craig and Porter label this phenomenon 'surrogate political participation', noting also that the politics of PRSPs themselves 'have hardly been a matter for debate' (2003: 58). The framing of CSO 'participation' in PRSPs creates 'roles' for CSOs that are not necessarily congruent with their existing form or function (Lister and Nyamugasira, 2003) and presents considerable contradictions. International NGOs, proactive in the realm of policy advocacy around PRSPs, and have gained new levels of access to the 'inner circles of the policy elite' (Gould and Ojanen, 2003: 8). In some cases, this has created a crowding out of national NGOs.

In both the bureaucracy and the polity, the implementation of the PRSP model has infused the partnership and ownership binary with meaning; in doing so, it has also demonstrated what partnership and ownership do not mean. Creation of meaning circumscribes versions of change; policy change is as much about what is *not* said and done as about what is said and done. Country ownership, for example, has seldom meant the 'participation' of democratically elected actors in a PRSP process. Further, the poverty analysis presented in PRSPs is not structural; the distribution of resources, income, human capital and power are not analysed or understood. Nor do they offer an understanding of the national distribution of resources, income, human capital and power (Whitehead, 2003). Many commentators note that PRSPs seldom vary, usually prescribing the three or four 'basic' prongs which mirror the WDR 2000/1 framework.[10] Craig and Porter (2003) note:

> PRSPs' silence in the face of rising concern about the pervasiveness of unequal market power, consolidating corporate power, restricted migration and access to rich economies, and local political realities

(elite capture, underregulated monopolies, rising global and local inequalities) has fuelled critics. Promoting universal global integration, while remaining silent about power issues, PRSPs heighten critics' fears that they serve as an instrument of hegemonic economic interests.

The mutually reinforcing dynamics of ownership and partnership mean the perpetuation of the dominant narrative, almost regardless of what is going on either behind the façade of participating institutions, or at the level of national policy. Potential change here is circumscribed, hemmed in, boundaried, by the discursive shifts that have already taken place upstream in time and space, in the centres of global power.

Little attention, then, is paid to the actual dynamics of the national policy level, the interface where the policy model may be expected to create change with a downward orientation. Even less attention has been given to what happens in the contexts where this downward orientation plays out, the level of decentralized governance. Here, where the PRSP is little more than another policy of a distant central government, existing meanings of 'participation' and 'poverty reduction' have been constructed not only through exposure to international development discourses, but through lived experiences of local planning and the structures of the state. These experiences are often at odds not only with the world of the national PRSP, but with the positive visions of ownership and partnership encapsulated by the supranational consensus narrative. A snapshot image of a sub-county planning meeting in Uganda illustrates some of disjunctures of meaning to which the disconnection between worlds gives rise.

While a single snapshot such as this obscures the complexity of local political dynamics, it does serve to illustrate the refractions of meaning discussed above. Participatory, demand-driven, poverty alleviation and ownership are all invested with meanings that differ radically from the imagined, decontextualized world of the consensus narrative. A participatory process is one in which participants cannot ask questions, and are told what to do. The demands that drive local development are made in the form of material contributions. Ownership is created through listening to an inaudible rendition of problems, and an illegible rendering of solutions.

PRSPs and the consensus narrative they represent are, as we argue above, seductive; but they are also profoundly decontextualized from the kind of scenario described in the snapshot. They focus the gaze of development's civic audience on the centre of the state, where the PRSP

Box 1: Implementing the PRSP in Uganda: participatory local planning for 'poverty reduction'?

The sub-county administration is holding a four-day planning meeting as part of its planning process. The District Planner proudly tells us that this is a 'participatory, bottom-up planning process'. It is supposed to contribute to a locally-owned development plan, which will dictate how resources from debt relief, secured by the government through the elaboration of a PRSP, will be spent on poverty reduction. Elected councillors from village, parish and sub-county, and representatives of civil society, have been invited to attend the meeting.

One of the meeting facilitators informs us that the purpose of the gathering is 'to tell the sub-county representatives what government policies are so that they can correct their sub-county plans according to these guidelines'.

Attending the meeting are about 120 people, of whom perhaps 10 are women. They sit in classroom-like rows facing a raised platform on which several officials – all men – were seated. 'Situation analyses' of the water and health sectors are made from the platform. For each sector, the relevant civil servant from the District stands on the platform and addresses the audience, writing key points on flip-charts in writing so small it cannot possibly be legible from the second row of the audience, even if the audience were literate. The presentation is hardly audible from the front row, let alone the back; and it is in English, not the local language.

During the presentation, one of the civil servants notes that 'there is a part the community is supposed to play – mobilized community participation – contributing labour and materials to government programmes.' He observes that 'the community has to express their demands by making some contribution'.

At the end of the water sector presentation, questions are invited, and one man stands up to enquire about the status of two boreholes in his village which are in disrepair, and what the sub-county might be able to do about this situation. In response, he is asked abruptly and aggressively, 'Have you made any contribution? Do you really want this water?' He is unable to reply to this, and sits down again.

Someone attempts another question from the audience, but is ignored by those on the platform.

In closing the meeting, the planner addresses the audience. 'The main purpose of us being here', he says, 'is to own these problems.

After owning it, you ask yourself why. How do we share the responsibilities? Who should do it? How do you get that person to do it? Exposing ourselves arouses our answers.'

Some weeks after the meeting, we meet a civil servant from the sub-county, waiting for a bus to go to the District capital. He is going to present the sub-county plan, which is the product of the planning meeting we attended. This hand-written plan is organized by sector – health, production, education, administration, and so on. Each sectoral plan was in the form of a flip-chart, with columns for problems, objectives, strategy, activity and source of funding.

The objective of the production sector is 'poverty alleviation and improved livelihood of the local population'. Only the health sector plan has anything written in the 'source of funding' column.

The civil servant tells us that he has not been told by the District about any sources of funding, or about how much was available. 'Not all secrets can be revealed to us down here.'

Source: Karen Brock, fieldnotes.

---

consultation circus is being enacted in the services of a benign set of goals, firmly framed in an assimilated, yet foreign, language of moral imperative. Watching this show – speculating on what the PRSPs might offer development via their intended and unintended consequences – helps us forget the street outside the theatre, the world outside; and the action backstage.

This has several consequences. It diverts and directs our attention within a single country, away not only from spaces of decentralized governance, but from non-consultative spaces at the centre where important decisions and negotiations take place. Secondly, beyond national borders, it takes our attention away from countries and regions of the world that are less dependent on the aid industry, but where mass poverty and inequality are issues with a different political resonance.

While PRSPs are notionally 'country owned', global targets – to non-HIPC and HIPC countries, Northern and Southern governments alike – represent attempts to tackle poverty as a *global* phenomenon, one in which every nation is implicated. As such, the MDGs have a potential to galvanize concerted action to tackle the causes as well as symptoms of poverty which is, in many respects, unparalleled; and the terrain on which they are able to do so is in a universal moral debate about progress. As such they could provide a significant counterbalance to the narrow focus of the PRSPs, harnessing the good intentions of the Millennium Development Declaration (MDD) to urge routes to policy change that depart from the 'business as usual' solutions peddled from Washington. Donors may have latched onto targets, forms that fit more neatly into the linearity of development planning, and are more amenable to the kind of reductionism so evident in the kind of one-size-fits-all 'solutions' that we see emerging from PRSPs. But the statement of principle they signed up to with the MDD promises something else altogether.

Contrast Wolfensohn's 'global responsibility based on ethics, experience and self-interest' with what the MDD has to say:

> We recognise that, in addition to our separate responsibilities to our individual societies, we have a collective responsibility to uphold the principles of human dignity, equality and equity at the global level. As leaders we have a duty therefore to all the world's people, especially the most vulnerable and, in particular, the children of the world, to whom the future belongs (United Nations, 2000: 55/2, para. 2).

By locating the world's leaders as duty-holders, the MDD situates the commitment they made within a frame of reference set some 14 years before with the declaration of the Right to Development, a right emerging from the successful mobilization of countries in the global South and long sidelined by Northern governments.[11] The MDD goes on to name a series of fundamental values: freedom, equality, solidarity, tolerance, respect for nature and shared responsibility. Used alone, these terms can be as easily manipulated as any other: think, for example, of the fate of 'freedom' in the hands of George W. Bush. But, put together in a 'chain of equivalence', they come to capture something that could serve as a moral underpinning for a way of approaching the MDGs that would give them the bite that so many feel that they currently lack.

Of myths and utopias

'Humanity requires 'myths' – inspiring images of battle and triumph – for any substantial forward movement', wrote Albert Hirschmann (1967: 31), drawing on the work of the one-time anarchist Georges Sorel. Citing Sorel's caution not to confuse such promises with any actually existing reality, he contends that 'extravagance in promising future benefits' (1967: 31) is a necessary part of what makes the development enterprise tick.[12] The MDGs might be understood in this vein, as grand, evocative, calls to action. The part policy statements play in discourses of development is, in many respects, *performative*: their 'extravagance in promising future benefits' is coupled with modelling the very controllability that they wish to bring about (Wood, 1985). If policy statements encode these promises, development buzzwords lend them the normative basis they require, swathing development agencies with the mantle of rightness, and conferring on them the legitimacy to intervene on behalf of 'the poor' and needy.

We argue in this chapter that 'participation' and 'empowerment', words that speak to the laudable aim of enabling poor people to have voice and choice, have now come to symbolize the legitimacy to pursue today's generation of development blueprints, under the rubric of 'poverty reduction'. In the texts of mainstream development agencies, this triad of Good Things is used to purvey a story-line that situates these agencies as guardians of rightness and champions of progress. This story-line is more than utopian, in Sorel's sense: more than an exercise in intellectual construction. It comes imbued with powerful myths about the desirability of 'donor co-ordination', 'policy coherence' and a series of embedded assumptions about the doing of development that place the entrenched ideas and practices that undergird the development industry entirely beyond question. Sorel (1941: 33) contends:

> ... myths are not descriptions of things, but expressions of a determination to act.... A myth cannot be refuted since it is, at bottom, identical with the convictions of a group.

Myths safeguard utopias, Sorel argues. The statements of intent that constitute the policies and prescriptions of international development agencies gain the qualities of myth precisely because they are born of convictions: and they seek to call us to action, name what we can do, give us a sense of the possible, and make us into agents of the possible. Like all successful ideologies (cf. Althusser, 1971), they work because they do more than convey a good argument; they compel people to listen because they themselves are the main protagonists of the story. Development myths work through emotional identification, not through rationality (cf. Laclau, 1996); they build and sustain the feeling of conviction that people need in order to be able to act. Good argument has its place here, but is secondary to something that is of quite a different order: a feeling of rightness, backed by the creation of normative instruments, like the MDGs, which serve an almost ceremonial function in bolstering a feeling of togetherness, purposefulness, of a visionary goal towards which to strive.

But buzzwords are more than pep-words. Their use in development discourse is not just to promote a 'we-can-do-it' feel-good boost. The utopias that are shored up by development myths and bolstered by buzzwords are profoundly ideological constructions (cf. Rist, 1997). International development organizations may appear to have appropriated concepts once used by radical alternative movements, but they have not necessarily swallowed them whole. Efforts to promote particular concepts within these institutions have produced partial 'victories', as actor-networks linked to broader, overlapping networks of advocates and activists in 'civil society' organizations have sought to gain ground in their efforts to expand room for manoeuvre within their own institutions, large parts of which may remain entirely unresponsive to new ideas (cf. Bebbington *et al.*, 2004; Cornwall and Pratt, 2004).[13] And to talk of terms being 'co-opted' is to assume that buzzwords have singular meanings. But buzzwords are useful in policy statements because they are fuzz-words. Their propensity to shelter multiple meanings with little apparent dissonance makes them politically expedient, shielding those who use them from attack by lending the possibility of common meaning to extremely disparate actors.

The downside of all this is discursive closure: it becomes more difficult to disagree with the use of 'warmly persuasive' words like 'empowerment' than it would with the ideas that underpin the way of world-making that frame their use by particular institutions. Nice-sounding words are, after all, there for the taking, and the nicer they sound, the more useful they might prove to be for those seeking to establish their moral authority. As Gita Sen argues, what makes a concept valuable is precisely that which gives it broad-based appeal.[14] To have that appeal, it needs to 'speak' – in Althusser's terms – to those who work in development and speak about their preoccupations, their hopes, their values. To become *hegemonic*, in Gramsci's (1971) terms, is to move beyond contests over meaning to unquestioned acceptance. What is perhaps most interesting about the 'linguistic crisis' is that the use of euphemism has become so extreme that more and more people are coming to regard words that were once taken for granted as something about which to be a little more circumspect. Hegemony is dissolving into mere ideology; and with it the different ideological underpinnings that constitute different ways of world-making come into closer view.

Conclusion

In this chapter, we have considered what our buzzwords have done for mainstream development policy. What might they do for alternatives to the current orthodoxy? To consider this, we return to a definition of 'participation' in which all three buzzwords are implicitly present. It was put forward 25 years ago, as part of UNRISD's ambitious programme of work on popular participation, and spoke of 'participation' as:

> ...the organized efforts to increase control over resources and regulative institutions in given social situations, on the part of groups and movements hitherto excluded from such control (cited in Stiefel and Wolfe, 1994: 5).

Let us take a closer look at this definition. It is packed with presuppositions, no less partial than any other. But what it does offer is an example where our buzzwords are put to a rather different kind of work, and where a deliberate choice of words reduces ambiguity and signals, with greater clarity as to what is meant than we find in any contemporary statements on participation. 'Participation' in this definition does not speak simply of being given information, being asked opinions, being invited to join committees and the like – the lower 'rungs' on the ladders used to assess degrees of involvement (cf. Arnstein, 1971; Pretty, 1995), which account for most of what passes as 'participation' today. It speaks of '*organized efforts*... on the part of *groups and movements hitherto excluded from such control*'. This is not the 'voices and choices' variety of participation that one might find in a Participatory Poverty Assessment (Narayan *et al.*, 2000a; Brock and McGee, 2002); nor the 'users-as-choosers' variety favoured in sectoral decentralization policies (Manor, 2004). Rather, 'participation' is about '*control over* resources and regulative institutions'. 'After all, everyone 'participates' in society, whether as an effective actor or a passive victim' (1994: 5), Stiefel and Wolfe argue, 'By specifying "control"', they point out, 'the definition aimed to rule out evasion of the central issue of power. It excluded certain technocratic or paternalistic approaches that aim to provide access to resources and institutions while withholding control' (1994: 5). Talking of '*given social situations*', they go on to explain, 'was intended to ward off over-generalizations and the quest for universalized prescriptions characteristic of some criticisms of development during the 1970s' (1994: 5).

Twenty-five years on, the 'encounter between the pursuit of livelihood by popularly based groups and the policies being pursued by the state and other "developers"' (Stiefel and Wolfe, 1994: xii) remains perhaps the greatest challenge for 'inclusive' development. As 'over-generalizations' and 'universalized prescriptions' have become the norm, and as 'participatory' initiatives have come to colonize the landscape of development, hard questions need to be asked about the failure of the uses to which mainstream ways of world-making have put our three buzzwords (cf. Leal and Opp, 1998; Cornwall, 2004). Are they being used to create opportunities for the 'hitherto excluded', or to 'gain control over resources and regulative institutions'? Or for the domestication of potential dissent in arenas far removed from those in which real power lies (cf. Taylor, 1998)? Does the 'decentration' of power, 'the shifting of governance away from the national level, upwards to supra-national levels and downwards to regional or local levels' (Standing, 2001: 21) simply turn nice talk about 'empowerment' into what Moore (2001) calls 'cheap talk'? For all the pressure to hold the consensus together, through talk of 'donor co-ordination' and 'policy coherence', few could seriously maintain that the neoliberal way of world-making is doing anything more than making the world most of us live in more unequal, conflictual and miserable.

Reckoning with the paradox that the words that 'work' in projects of world-making are those that lend themselves most to being filled with multiple meanings, we suggest that it is high time more attention was paid to language in development. If words make worlds, struggles over meaning are not just about semantics: they gain a very real material dimension. But if – as some would charge – our three buzzwords have become implacably emptied of meaning, what can be done? One option is to invent new words, or to pilfer from other vocabularies – much as development tends to do with regularity. 'Participation' and 'empowerment' might be abandoned to the dust of history, left for erstwhile radicals to reminisce about and replaced with a sexy, urgent, new term. But what is to stop the next new word sharing the fate of the buzzwords we have discussed here? The World Bank has such propensity to appropriate and rework terms that it is possible to imagine even stubborn old words like 'class' being filled with new, self-referential, meanings, threaded into a chain of equivalence with 'social capital' and 'opportunity', and put to work.

Giving up on 'participation' and 'empowerment' as irrevocably contaminated by their mainstreaming would be to lose concepts that have been critical, for decades, in animating struggles for equality, rights and social justice. It would, as Gita Sen puts it (Chapter 6), not only be giving up the battle but losing the war. What, then, remains to be done? Let us look at what Sorel, Goodman and Laclau might offer in the way of resources. 'Participation', 'empowerment' and 'poverty reduction' come together in mainstream development discourse in a 'chain of equivalence' with 'ownership', 'accountability', 'governance', 'partnership' to make the world that the neoliberal model would have us all inhabit. Dissident meanings are stripped away to ensure coherence. But some of these meanings might be recuperated through a similar strategy of using 'chains of equivalence' that link these terms with *other* words to reassert the meanings that have gone into abeyance. In configuration with words like 'social justice', 'redistribution' and 'solidarity', there is little place for talk about 'participation' as involving 'users' as 'consumers', nor about poor people being 'empowered' through the marketization of services that were once their basic right. Nor is there a place for development solutions that fail to recognize how embedded richer countries are in the fortunes of others. Recognizing the 'strategic reversibility' of discourse is important (cf. Foucault, 1979), as it helps us to recognize that alternative ways of world-making can take shape even out of the most apparently closed discursive spaces.

While a well-honed critique can chip away at the intellectual edifices built to promote and defend the neoliberal way of world-making, we need – with Sorel – to recognize the powerful grip that myths have on people, placing certain assumptions beyond question. Far from being a game of destructive and ultimately indulgent semantics, the practice of deconstruction and of making strange what is ordinarily taken for granted can serve, in Goodman's terms, to reveal the frames of references used in different ways of world-making, and with this, the different worlds they would make. No longer shored up by myths, utopias become fragile; no longer underpinned by axiomatic assumptions, they become amenable to being remodelled, or indeed cast aside into dereliction.

What are the implications of all this, a policy maker might ask, for the real world challenges of addressing poverty? What has language got to do with development? Our argument in this chapter has been that the terms we use are never neutral. They come to be given meaning as they are put to use in policies. And these policies, in turn, influence how those who work in development come to think about what they are doing. The way words come to be combined allows certain meanings to flourish, and others to become barely possible to think with. Consider, for example, how differently the MDGs would sound if they were animated not with targets but with some of the language of the

Millennium Declaration. Think of what uses they might then be put, by progressive governments contending in the international arena with foot-draggers, as well as how much more vital and relevant they would become to the struggles pursued by advocates and activists. Consider, too, what a difference might be made by more 'clarity through specificity' that Cohen and Uphoff (1980) called for at the end of the decade in which 'participation' came of age, to avoid, as Cernea put it in 1985, a 'cloud of cosmetic rhetoric' from settling permanently over our heads.[15]

To do so would require taking apart the existing chain that connects 'participation', 'empowerment' and 'poverty reduction' with other development buzzwords, and naming the differences between the ways these terms can be understood. Such a move would make visible the different frames of reference that co-exist within the fuzz of current development rhetoric, and expose different ways of world-making they imply. It would allow us to recognize that there are many possible worlds to be made with these words, something which consensus thinking calls on us to pretend to ignore. Most of all, it would under-score the lesson of history that development actors ignore at their peril: that any way of world-making that gives us one-size-fits-all development recipes stripped of any recognition of, or engagement with, context or culture, politics, power or difference, does violence to the very hope of a world without poverty.

3
The Search for Policy Autonomy in the Global South

Norman Girvan[1]

Introduction

This chapter is about the need to secure greater autonomy for the South in development policy making and greater space for its 'own' diagnosis and prescription. For this to happen, the claims to universal validity of neoclassical economics and of neoliberal policies need to be refuted, drawing inspiration from the legacy of development economics. Social learning in development policy making is a crucial element in improving its effectiveness. A valuable supporting role can be played by development partnerships based on equality, interdependence and mutuality of interest. The chapter ends by discussing the role of regionalism and points to some of the challenges faced in making it effective.

Development economics and policy autonomy

In the 1950s the new sub-discipline of development economics provided a set of analytical and policy tools that responded to the political need for the development of the 'underdeveloped' countries, in the context of political decolonization and the Cold War. A characteristic feature of development economics was its assertion of the existence of pervasive market failure in the poor countries and of the necessity for government intervention to ensure development. To that extent it has been characterized as neo-Keynesian, but it went significantly beyond Keynes, who focused mainly on short-term macroeconomic equilibrium in the closed economy. One branch of development economics modelled the world economy as a centre-periphery system (Prebisch, 1950) and led to Latin American structuralism. Another stream investigated the factors responsible for long-term growth and non-linear

73

development, including cultural and institutional variables (for example, Lewis, 1955). Some went as far as to argue that a special economic theory, or the adaptation of existing theory, was needed for the poor countries (Seers, 1963; Myrdal, 1969).

For the West, development economics served the political function of providing a non-communist recipe for poor countries to use in the 'catch up' game. Nonetheless it made a significant contribution to the Global South in at least two respects. It legitimized the principle that their economies should be understood on their own terms. Secondly, it supplemented the leverage available to the South as a result of Cold War competition by providing the intellectual justification for policies of state intervention and protection of the domestic market that succeeded in building up industrial capabilities in many countries over several decades. Although development economics has been the subject of many critiques and policy mistakes were inevitably made, the period of its predominance in the 1950s–1970s laid the basis of an intellectual tradition and a stock of policy experience that could and should have become the basis for further policy innovation.

This period also coincided with the proliferation of national universities and academic centres in the South. The United Nations (UN) system was strongly development-oriented and provided additional institutional supports, notably through the United Nations Department of Economic and Social Affairs (UNDESA), the United Nations Conference on Trade and Development (UNCTAD), and the regional commissions. Southern self-confidence was high, infused with the expectations accompanying decolonization and the spirit of Bandung.[2] These developments provided the impetus for a great wave of indigenous empirical research and theorizing on the economic realities of the developing world. United Nations Economic Commission for Latin America and the Caribbean (ECLAC) thinking, together with Latin American and Caribbean structuralism and dependency, as well as the Indian industrialization school and Chinese socialism, were notable expressions of Southern development perspectives at this time. In retrospect, the UNCTAD conferences of the 1960s and 1970s and the United Nations Declaration on the New International Economic Order were high points of Southern impact on the official discourse on international development.[3]

Neoliberalism and its dissidents

The neoliberal backlash came in the Reagan–Thatcher era of the 1980s. The attack was equally against Keynesianism in the North as against its presumptive intellectual offspring, developmentalism in the South. The softening up process of the South began from the late 1970s when the Organization of the Petroleum Exporting Countries (OPEC) oil shocks, the growth of international lending and world recessions led to a debt crisis in the energy-importing, primary commodity exporting countries. The Washington-based international financial institutions (IFIs) stepped in and new forms of conditionality lending were invented to discipline countries with unsustainable deficits. The interest-rate shocks and protracted global economic downturn of the early 1980s led to a generalized Third World debt crisis. This further strengthened the IFIs, whose role in Southern policy-making became widespread and pervasive.

Developmentalist theories and policies were discredited, marginalized and dismissed. As a result, there was a marked discontinuity in the accumulation of policy experience in the South. The baby of extra-market intervention was thrown out with the bathwater of government failure. As a caveat, this generalization may be more applicable to Latin America, the Caribbean and Africa than to much of Asia.

During the decade of the 1980s governments came to power in the South convinced of 'the magic of the marketplace'. Northern universities and their imitators in the South trained a new generation of Southern economists in the theorems of neoclassical economics and the practice of neoliberal policies. The new dispensation ruled out the notion of an economics *sui generis* for the developing countries. Such a category was defined as invalid, and therefore unnecessary and irrelevant. At worst, it was dangerously misleading since it could lead to erroneous policies. Much of the South suffered a reversal of the previous gains associated with a tradition of autonomous theorizing and policy making.

In related developments, the North-South dialogue collapsed and UNCTAD was marginalized. The World Trade Organization (WTO) came to occupy centre stage, with a scope and coverage extended to embrace services, intellectual property rights and investment measures. The new rules of the game centred on reciprocal market liberalization, which would lead to trade expansion and economic growth. Where development was mentioned at all, it was assumed that this would fall into place. By the end of the decade, the collapse of the Union of Soviet Socialist Republics (USSR) and of Eastern European socialism removed one of the last sources of leverage available to the South in their relations with the North.

In the 1990s neoliberal globalization was universally proclaimed as the 'Only Way'. China, India and a small number of Southeast Asian countries retained a degree of policy autonomy, the first two because of size and the existing level of industrial development and the latter because of the success of previous export-oriented industrialization. They too embraced market-oriented reforms, although in the case of China and India both the pace and the content were shaped by local policy makers rather than dictated by IFI conditionalities. In the case of Southeast Asia the IFI role was more decisive and focused on the (in)famous capital account liberalizations. In the rest of the South the triumph of the new orthodoxy was virtually complete; the combined result of IFI conditionalities and internal ideological and political change. Where coercion stopped and conviction started varied from country to country, but the effect was largely the same. The underlying factor was the shift in the constellation of global political and ideological forces. The shift was held to be permanent and irreversible by contemporary acolytes who proclaimed 'The End of History' (Fukuyama, 1992).

This triumphalism, of course, was to be significantly qualified by subsequent developments. First, there was the emergence of global civil society as a new political force capable of resisting elements of neoliberal globalization and of asserting the possibility of an alternative. Events surrounding the abortive Multilateral Agreement on Investment (MAI), the Jubilee Campaign, protests in Seattle, and the World Social Forum, attest to the considerable capacity of global civil society for organization and mobilization, not least as a result of its use of the new communications technologies associated with globalization itself. The movement has also drawn together hitherto disparate activist organizations concerned with issues related to gender, the environment, ethnic and cultural minorities, farmers and workers. Perhaps most importantly, it has shown the potential for global, people-based political alliances that transcend the South-North divide.

A second development was the 1997–98 financial crises that spread from Asia to Latin American and Russia. This was directly associated with one of the extreme forms of globalization, namely capital account liberalization, but it was politically decisive in discrediting the entire ideological edifice, since the policies that led to the crises had been presented as part of a complete package that was considered foolproof. The crises threw tens of millions into poverty, served as an instrument of economic recolonization of previously 'successful' developing countries, and eventually exposed the technical deficiencies of the IFIs, not unrelated to their geopolitical role. The episode served to embolden the intellectual and political critics of the Washington orthodoxy while undermining the self-confidence of some of its leading exponents.

One should point here to the key supportive role of the UN system in facilitating alternative thinking during the 1990s, through the critical research of agencies such as the International Labour Organization (ILO), the United Nations Children's Fund (UNICEF), the United Nations Development Programme (UNDP), the United Nations Research Institute for Social Development (UNRISD) and the regional commissions, as well a through a series of global conferences on social and environmental issues. The UNICEF report, *Adjustment with a Human Face* (Cornia *et al.*, 1987) influenced the human development approach of UNDP in the 1990s, which provided some continuity with the basic needs approach of the 1970s. Although the *Human Development Reports* could not launch an explicit, frontal assault on neoliberal globalization, they relentlessly documented the growth of global inequalities and critiqued the underlying assumption of market-led global growth. These and other reports provided invaluable reference documents for civil society in their public education and advocacy activities, for governments in their efforts to prioritize spending related to human development, and for researchers and teachers on the human costs of neoliberal globalization. Further evidence that these organizations provided an outlet for critical thinking informed by the perspectives of the South is shown by the fact that the two principal intellectual god-fathers of Human Development, namely Amartya Sen and Mahboub Ul Haq, were products of that part of the world.

Since the turn of the 1990s decade there has been a noticeable shift in the political climate, as shown by political developments in Venezuela, Argentina, Brazil and other parts of Latin America and in India, at the WTO Ministerials in Seattle and Cancun, where the South was a force to be reckoned with, in the impasse over the Free Trade Area of the Americas (FTAA) and rise of anti-FTAA sentiment in Latin America, at Porto Alegre and Mumbai. While neoliberal policies continue to be prevalent, this may be attributable as much to the constraints derived from existing international trade and financial arrangements – WTO rules, IFI conditionalities, the operation of financial markets – as it is to intellectual conviction and genuine political support. Furthermore, coherent altern-ative models of macroeconomic management, trade and industrial policies that countries might pursue in the current environment are yet to be clearly articulated. Nonetheless – and this is the point we wish to emphasize here – further space has been opened for academic enquiry and policy experimentation outside of the neoliberal box by elements both in the South and North. In the academic sphere, for example, UNRISD has helped to catalyse an important initiative for the rethinking of development economics (UNRISD, 2003). It is in that spirit that the reflections in the rest of this chapter are offered.

In celebration of diversity

It is instructive to briefly revisit issues raised by development economics regarding the particular versus the universal as applied to the Global South, beginning with an interrogation of the epistemic basis of the claims to universal applicability of neoclassical economics. Related to this is the question of the political function of these claims in the dynamic of North–South relations.

It may be recalled that economics as a discipline, along with the other branches of the Social Sciences, had its epistemic roots in the Enlightenment and the scientific revolution in Western Europe in the sixteenth to eighteenth centuries; and that its emergence and subsequent development were directly associated with the European Industrial Revolution and the worldwide spread of Western industrial capitalism. The universalistic pretensions of neoclassical economics can be attributed to these two features of its 'original sin'. As physical scientists studied the laws governing the behaviour of nature and the universe, economists sought to discover the laws that govern the functioning of the economic system. Adam Smith's 'invisible hand' appeared as the equivalent of an unseen force in the Newtonian universe. To explain the material behaviour of individuals, the mythical figure of *homo economicus* was invented, a totally self-serving entity whose every action, even when apparently altruistic, could be analysed in terms of a utility-maximizing calculus. Writing in 1969, Myrdal observed that conventional economic theory 'is still far from having liberated itself from the metaphysical assumptions it inherited from the moral philosophies of natural law and utilitarianism' (Myrdal, 1969: 109).

The quest for logical precision also led to a process of analytical detachment of the economic sphere from the sphere of politics, culture and society; which became the subject areas of other social science disciplines (Sankatsing, 1998). This disciplinary compartmentalization paralleled the commodification of all spheres of human activity accompanying the development of capitalism – the economy was disembedded from society (Polanyi, 1957). Mathematical formalism was a further means of elevating the status of economic theory to a level on par with that of the physical sciences, in the process becoming increasingly devoid of empirical content.[4] Hence formalism allowed what may have been essentially ideological assumptions about the way the real world operates, to be cloaked in a scientific garb.

In its concrete historical context, the tendency to universalism was buttressed by the Eurocentric assumptions that were integral to European imperialist expansion from the fifteenth century onwards (Amin, 1989). Sankatsing has aptly summarized this process as the 500-year 'globalisation of the local experience in the Occident', proposing that

> Eurocentrism, the underlying discourse, was derived from the premise that out of the experience of the West all universals for humanity were bound to be born, since what was good for the West is best for the rest (Sankatsing, 1998: 1).

Hence, the degree of advancement ('civilization', 'development') of other societies came to be rated according to a Eurocentric scale; non-European cultures and knowledge systems were, by definition, devalued.[5] As expressed in economics, this worldview meant that the neoclassical schema came to assume the role of the normative framework by which the social and cultural realities of the non-European 'other' are judged, notwithstanding the fact that the ideal neoclassical world of perfectly functioning markets and optimizing economic agents is a highly unreal abstraction from the real world, even in the North. The paradigm holds that economies everywhere either *actually* operate like the ideal, or *should be made to do so* by means of enlightened policies. Diversity is allowed in the real world, but it is defined as a shortfall from the ideal. The main interest in diversity is in understanding how it can be 'corrected' and ultimately eliminated.

A good example of this kind of thinking is the responses of the IFIs to the failure of neoliberal policy reforms to produce the results that they had confidently predicted for much of the South; and even to have 'perverse' outcomes in the form of worsening income distribution, increased poverty, mounting debt burdens and stagnant growth. The standard response of the IFIs is that *additional* doses of market-oriented medicine are required.[6] Hence, the discourse shifted to a focus on the need to follow 'first-generation reforms', with 'second-generation reforms' and to move towards the 'Post-Washington consensus'. In this Alice in Wonderland world, the failures of neoliberalism provide a justification for even more neoliberalism, leading to a practice that some have characterized as 'adjustment without end'.[7]

Development economics had the merit of insisting that an effort should be made to understand the specific characteristics of the 'underdeveloped' countries and to use these as the point of departure for the formulation of policies. Further intellectual justification for this approach comes from the considerable body of non-mainstream economic literature in the subject areas of economic history, economic anthropology and institutional economics. Scholars in this tradition generally view the economic processes of a given society as being embedded in its specific historical, sociocultural and institutional context. This context conditions the behaviour of individuals, households and other social units in the material sphere of their existence. It has a bearing on the character of entrepreneurship such as preferred areas of investment, attitudes to risk-taking, the time horizon for expected returns and employee relations. It influences the economic role of the state in its management and planning capabilities, propensities to patronage and corruption, and its ability to promote social partnership.

These factors condition the responses of entities in the society to economic policy instruments. They need to be taken into account in determining the appropriate role of market instruments and state intervention in achieving desired outcomes. In other words, what works for one country at one time may work differently in another country at the same time or in the same country at a different time. There is no universally applicable prescriptive principle regarding what ought to be the role of market and state: the appropriate solution is highly context-specific.

An example is provided by the experience of different centrally planned economies in implementing market-oriented reforms. In Russia the reforms were virtually directed by the IFIs and took the form of neoliberal shock treatment. The results were catastrophic; and believers in the faith then made the belated discovery that the institutions did not exist for markets to function properly. In contrast the market-oriented reforms of China, Viet Nam, and Cuba have been internally driven and carefully managed with regard to the content, scope, timing and pace. This is not to suggest that these processes have been free of errors and contradictions; but the enormous human and social costs of the Russian debacle have, in the main, been avoided.

The context-specific approach asserts that *diversity*, rather than universality, is the principal feature of social reality that provides the intellectual challenge to the analyst and policy maker. Intellectually, the approach is open to the objection that it does not permit rigorous analysis by means of mathematical formalization and statistical testing, and that it leaves unacceptably wide room for subjective interpretation. The idea that it is not subject to formalization and testing is debatable. More importantly, there is the question whether the acceptability of a given approach should be contingent on its susceptibility to formalization. As suggested before, the importance attributed to formalism may be due as much to the need to preserve existing power relations in the production and reproduction of knowledge as it is to a concern with rigour.

The relevant issue is that of identifying the appropriate criteria of validation for propositions related to the functioning of the human economy. In other words, there needs to be open debate as to what constitutes acceptable procedures for investigation, the generation and validation of propositions, the derivation of policy prescriptions, and the monitoring and evaluation of their application. Formalism will probably be part of the answer; but should be qualified by the necessary caveats, especially when propositions are the basis of policy interventions in the real world. In this respect, one is reminded of Sen's observation to the effect that it is better to be partially right than to be exactly wrong.

It is here that universalism probably has a role to play. If transparadigm intercourse is to go beyond a dialogue of the deaf, then there should be common agreement on rules of procedure. If analysis of the specific is to minimize the room for subjective judgement and interpretation, then there ought to be commonly accepted methods of investigation and verification. But there cannot be any final word on this. What is universally accepted will itself be the subject of continued experimentation, debate and enrichment. Universalization, therefore, may be seen as a continuous process of *expansion of consensus on method*. Basic to the process are recognition of diversity, mutual cross-cultural respect, and rejection of dogma.

There is also the question of the relationship between policy autonomy and the universalization of norms of human justice.[8] These norms are represented by the provisions of the UN Charter, declarations by the General Assembly and by international conventions and agreements to which the world community as a whole has subscribed. Recently these include the Millennium Development Goals and commitments made at the various world summits. Policy autonomy, however, is more about the *means* that are employed to achieve agreed ends of development and justice, than about the ends themselves. It relates to the right of a society to work out the combination of state intervention, market organization and civil society participation that is appropriate to its reality, for the achievement of goals that may incorporate norms that are elements of a global consensus. In that sense it helps to give meaning to the right to self-determination and of states to choose their own social and economic systems, rights which are enshrined in the Universal Declaration of Human Rights and the Charter on Economic Rights and Duties of States (see United Nations, 1974: Chapter II, Article 1).

Difficulties arise where there is a real or apparent overlap between means and ends. An example is provided by the assertion that 'economic freedom', defined as a regime of private property and of freely functioning markets, is an essential component of political freedom and democracy and constitutes a universal norm – an end in itself. The proper method of resolving this dilemma is by accepting that the universalization of norms of justice and of development goals should be freely negotiated among states to arrive at continuous enlargement of the content of global consensus; not imposed by one or other combination of Eurocentric epistemological arrogance, economic conditionalities and the exercise of military force.

Social learning as a resource

Social knowledge, in the sense of knowledge that inheres *within* the society and not merely knowledge *about* the society or of its social aspects, has a crucial role to play in the derivation of appropriate policies. Social knowledge resides at various levels of the society; in its history, culture, and institutions; in the society's collective consciousness; in the accumulated knowledge, experience and wisdom of the population. This resource needs to be recognized and validated. To take fullest advantage of it there needs to be open, transparent and participatory processes permitting vertical and horizontal information flows at all levels; lubricated by a culture of consultation and cooperation. An integral part of this is the existence of feedback loops by which the results of policy interventions are constantly evaluated by social actors so that adjustments can be made. Ideally, there should be a continuous accretion of knowledge and understanding of how the system works and how policy interventions can be made to achieve desired outcomes.

What we are proposing here is a kind of synthesis of the elements of the 'policy cycle' with those of firm level 'learning and technical change' in the literature on technology transfer. The policy cycle begins with Problem Definition and Identification and proceeds through the elements of Research, Policy Generation, Policy Implementation, Evaluation and Feedback, and Policy Modification. The process is normally assumed to be agency-based, but there is no inherent reason why it could not embrace entire areas of national life or even the society as a whole.

The literature on learning and technical change originated with the concept of the 'learning curve' as applied to the problem of technology transfer. The learning curve represents the observation that the time necessary for an individual to complete a given task declines at an increasing rate from the moment when the task is first performed, and then levels off as mastery over the task reaches the maximum achievable. The same observation applies to production teams. Alternatively, the relationship can be expressed as a curve showing productivity per unit of time as a function of previous aggregate production; the curve rises at an increasing rate and eventually levels off. However, researchers on firm-level technology transfers to developing country enterprises concluded that learning is not limited to the performance of specific tasks and in any case is not an automatic process (Hoffman, 1990). A firm can learn to adapt and modify acquired technology and to innovate; but to do so it must consciously organize itself for this purpose and pursue appropriate strategies.

The same idea can be applied to a country's policy making to achieve development objectives. A country can have as one of its objectives the accumulation of experience, distilled knowledge and intervention capacities in development policy making. It can seek to consciously organize itself to this end by broadening participation in the policy cycle to the whole society and by designating specialized institutions to be the repositories and transmission agents of this knowledge. Many developed countries show features of such a system in the mechanisms of their political process and the role of their state bureaucracies and elite universities.

It will be observed that this is a rather utopian model of development and change that abstracts from the real world of power relationships. Internally, societies have interest groups that fight for their own advantage and that frequently dominate state policy making in a dictatorial or quasi-dictatorial manner. International institutions are, on the whole, dominated by the Northern countries, which obviously use them to pursue their own agendas. But spaces for participatory policy making and learning do exist within countries, as well as internationally, for example, in some agencies in the UN system and International non-governmental organizations (INGOs). My purpose here is to suggest an ideal that may be useful as an instrument in exploiting this space; opposing it to the universalistic claims of policy prescriptions advanced by the IFIs and other Northern-dominated agencies. It suggests an alternative approach to the structuring of development 'partnerships' between the north and the south to that which characterizes, for example, the World Bank-sponsored Poverty Reduction Strategy Papers (PRSPs).[9] In this alternative approach, the overarching goal of development partnerships is seen as that of *supporting and facilitating social learning* for the attainment of mutually agreed development objectives through a process of continuous interaction, democratic participation and local empowerment through the accumulation of knowledge and experience.[10]

Regionalism and policy autonomy

In the past two decades the proliferation of regional economic integration groupings such as free trade areas and common markets, as well as of other kinds of regional organizations and networks, has occurred side by side with globalization. Often referred to by scholars as the 'new regionalism', this development is characterized '... by [the] increasing scope, diversity, fluidity and non-conformity' of regional processes, involving a variety of non-state actors (Padrigu, 2004). Considerable analysis has been undertaken of the new regionalism in its different forms, levels and dimensions; with discussion of its theoretical implications, its relationship with globalization and with national sovereignty; and its implications for security and for global governance (Hettne *et al.*, 1999, 2001; Schulz *et al.*, 2001).

Much of the early discussion of the economic dimension of the new regionalism centred on whether it is complementary to, or competitive with, the broader thrust towards globalization (Mittelman, 1999: 25). Scholars now tend to agree that the two processes are interrelated (Mittelman, 1999: 25; Byron, 2003: 71; Padrigu, 2004). Thus, a distinction may be made between *regionalization*, as an economic process accompanying the internationalization of trade and finance, and an aspect of globalization; and *regionalism*, as a set of intergovernmental arrangements that is part of the political response to the centrifugal tendencies of globalization. Less attention appears to have been paid to how far regionalism can enhance the policy autonomy of the South and can strengthen the South's capacity to shape globalization in its own interest.[11] Here, both the epistemic and the instrumental dimensions of regionalism have a role to play.

The epistemic dimension relates to the accumulation of local diagnostic and prescriptive capacities for development policy making, linked to democratic participation in decision making at the national and regional levels. Special mention should be made of the merit of *regional epistemic communities*[12] in this context. Such communities can be constituted with the regional units of the UN system as their institutional base or focal point. As noted previously, ECLAC, under the leadership of Raul Prebisch, was a pioneer in the indigenization of development thinking that gave rise to UNCTAD. ECLAC continued to be a source of heterodox thinking from a Latin American perspective during the 1980s and 1990s, as shown by a number of seminal publications (for example, ECLAC, 1990, 1992, 2002; Ocampo and Martin, 2004). Similar examples are found in the work of other regional commissions, for example that of the United Nations Economic and Social Commission for Asia and the Pacific (UNESCAP, 1990).[13] Regional epistemic communities are also constituted by cooperation among academic institutes and independent think-tanks, non-governmental organizations (NGOs), advocacy organizations and regional professional bodies. The Council for the Development of Social Science Research in Africa (CODESRIA), the Consejo Latinoamericano de Ciencias Sociales (Latin American Council of the Social Sciences/CLACSO), the Coordinadora Regional de Investigaciones Económicas y Sociales (Regional Coordination for Economic and Social Research/CRIES), the Association of Caribbean Economists (ACE) and the Caribbean Policy Development Centre (CPDC) are only a few of the examples of such regional networks that have opened up space for alternative viewpoints to be formulated and expressed; often linking such processes to popular education and grassroots mobilization.

There is an organic link between the epistemic dimension of regionalism and its instrumental dimension, which refers to the benefits of intergovernmental functional cooperation and of market integration. Regarding functional cooperation, regionalism offers the potential to modify the power relations in the negotiation of international economic agreements through the pooling of bargaining power and of negotiating skills among developing countries with the objective of expanding their 'national policy space'. As noted at the UNCTAD XI conference, held in São Paulo, Brazil, in June 2004, the scope for domestic policies in the areas of trade, investment and industrial development is being framed by the emergence of rules-based regimes of international economic agreements, but it is particularly important for developing countries to maintain an 'appropriate balance between national policy space and (their) international disciplines and commitments', bearing in mind 'development goals and objectives' (UNCTAD, 2004: para. 8). Making this operational involves the strengthening of provisions for Special and Differential Treatment to allow greater flexibility in the implementation of provisions such as those relating to market access, industrial protection, export promotion, performance requirements for foreign companies and the promotion of technology transfer. These are matters for negotiation and the bargaining power of developing countries in such negotiations can be bolstered by regional cooperation as well as by cross-regional alliances.

This benefit of regionalism is of especial interest to the smaller developing countries (WICOM, 1992; UNDP, 1999: 11). Here the experience of the Caribbean Community (CARICOM) is instructive. CARICOM's members are 15 small countries with a combined population of 14 million. CARICOM's Regional Negotiating Machinery (CRNM) conducts negotiations on behalf of the membership in the WTO, the FTAA, and with the European Union (EU) as part of the African, Caribbean and Pacific Group of States (ACP). It commissions technical studies on issue areas and convenes seminars and workshops in preparation for negotiations.[14] The existence of the CRNM has had a notable impact on the quality, professionalism and effectiveness of the region's external negotiations in the various fora. For example in the FTAA, where the CRNM speaks on behalf of 14 of the 34 participating countries (although CARICOM has less than 2 per cent of the population), the region's united stance has succeeded in drawing attention to the special circumstances and needs of the smaller economies.

Regionalism can also strengthen the bargaining position of larger developing countries, as shown by the experience of Latin America's Southern Common Market (MERCOSUR). Its four members account for 26 and 13 per cent, respectively, of the population and gross domestic product (GDP) of the FTAA countries. Led by Brazil, MERCOSUR has had a marked influence on the pace and content of the FTAA negotiations. It has also become a major player in relations with the EU, with which it has concluded a trade and economic partnership agreement, and indirectly in the WTO. Moreover, the WTO process also provides compelling evidence of the power of cross-regional alliances within the South. Coalitions represented by the G20 (agricultural exporters) and the G90 (the ACP Group, the Africa Group and the Land-Locked Developing Countries/LLDCs) played a decisive role in the outcome of the Fifth WTO Ministerial meeting in Cancun in 2003 and the 'July Package' agreement of 2004 on the Doha Agenda work programme.

In the internal sphere, regionalism provides scope for efficiency gains through market integration and for synergistic benefits through crossborder investment and joint ventures by local enterprises, strengthening the competitive capabilities of local firms on regional and international markets. However, intraregional functional cooperation at the governmental level is an important, if sometimes neglected, aspect of regionalism. This is especially relevant for small countries in those sectors and activities in which economies of scale, critical mass requirements and the scope for synergies are significant (Girvan, 2003: 536–7); for example, science and technology, research and development, higher education and the promotion of industrial clusters. Notably, CARICOM's functional cooperation provides support for a wide range of regional institutions including the University of the West Indies, the Caribbean Agricultural Research and Development Institute and the Caribbean Court of Justice, which will adjudicate disputes under CARICOM Single Market and Economy arrangements.

Here Mittelman's proposed distinction between 'neo-liberal integration' and 'development integration' is of relevance (Mittelman, 1999: 32). Whereas neoliberal integration emphasizes the role of efficiency gains through the operation of market forces, in development integration a significant role is played by state intervention for investment in physical infrastructure and for the coordination of production. Mittelman's exemplar of development integration is the Southern African Development Community (SADC). In fact, the original arrangements for CARICOM integration in 1973 provided for a substantial role by state enterprises and production coordination; but like SADC progress in implementation was limited. Indeed, the now defunct Council for Mutual Economic Assistance (CMEA or COMECON) of the former USSR and socialist countries of Eastern European could be regarded as a mode of development integration through central planning.

Perhaps the most far-reaching proposals for regionalism are those advanced by Amin, who sees it as a basic building block for the construction of a polycentric world characterized by equitable development among its constituent regions and by respect for cultural diversity:

In today's conditions, then, a multipolar world is first and foremost a regionalized world. Regional interdependence, negotiated and organized in a way that permits nations and dominated classes to improve the terms of their participation in production and their access to better living conditions, constitute the framework for this building of a polycentric world . . . the regions that one can imagine participating in such changes would not only be economic areas with preferential tariffs; they would also have to be built as political areas that helped to strengthen the collective social position of underprivileged classes and subregions (Amin, 2003: 131, 133).

Amin lists six issues for regions to address: (i) renegotiation of market shares and the rules governing their allocation (challenge to WTO rules); (ii) renegotiation of capital market systems to replace the dominance of financial speculation with productive investment in the North and the South; (iii) renegotiation of monetary systems to establish regional arrangements that provide relative exchange rate stability; (iv) moves towards a global tax system; (v) global demilitarization; and (vi) democratization of the UN.

Regionalism, however, is not a panacea, and the experience of attempts at regionalism in the South shows the formidable obstacles that need to be overcome in order to make it effective. At the root of most of the difficulties experienced is the contradiction between the maintenance of national sovereignty on the one hand and the requirements of collective regional action on the other hand. This contradiction is inherent in most, if not all, of the regional groupings in the South. For example, as noted by Mittelman, neither SADC nor the Association of Southeast Asian Nations (ASEAN) have legally-binding instruments similar to those of the EU (Mittelman, 1999: 31–2). The same is true for CARICOM. This feature underlies the recurring 'problem of implementation' – that is, the failure of member states to implement decisions taken at the regional intergovernmental level. Brewster has called this a mode of integration through 'discretionary intergovernmental cooperation', arguing that it was tried in Europe and eventually abandoned in favour of the arrangements that contain the limited supranationality that are feature of the EU. He proposes a model of 'customised transfer of sovereignty' for CARICOM (Brewster, 2003a, 2003b). I have pointed out that the method of discretionary intergovernmental cooperation makes substantial demands on the administrative, technical and political resources of member states in their attempts to implement regional decisions, demands which fall relatively more heavily on the smaller members (Girvan, 2004). Furthermore it maximizes the opportunities for counter-mobilization at the national level by negatively affected interest groups. In effect, the decision whether or not to implement each regional agreement becomes the subject of a separate cost/benefit calculus by the national government of each member state.

Another problem area has been the adequacy of the institutional infrastructure and the related issue of funding for regional institutions. In the case of Europe, this issue has been resolved by means of the mechanism of 'own resources' – funding generated by the EU's own duties and levies that accrue directly to Brussels for the financing of Community institutions. Absence of such a mechanism in other regional arrangements has meant that each regional institution is the subject of separate budgetary appropriations and contributions at the national level. Hence, funding is vulnerable to fiscal problems experienced by member states or to national political considerations. Thus, for example, CARICOM'S CRNM has experienced cash flow problems from time to time due to the discretionary nature of contributions and to dependence on donor funding.

A third problem area is the absence of provision for financing for disadvantaged and less developed countries or regions in integration arrangements in the South. Such provisions have been a notable feature in the case of the EU and have served as a means of accelerating the development of its poorer members. In their absence, trade liberalization and market integration tend to yield disproportionate benefits for the more industrialized partners, weakening political support for the integration arrangement among the disadvantaged members.

Regionalism in the South also has to contend with the diversity of interests among member countries that result from differences in size, levels of development and economic structure. A case in point is the experience of the Association of Caribbean States (ACS), an intergovernmental organization of 28 countries located in and around the Caribbean Sea, whose objectives are cooperation for economic and social development. To the extent that shared geographic space is the criterion of membership of the ACS, cooperation has advanced in such areas as tourism, transport and managing natural disasters. On the other hand cooperation in trade has been problematic, especially where the coordination of external negotiating positions is concerned, due to wide disparities among the membership in size, trade structure, export market orientation and level of industrialization (Girvan, 2003).

These disparities are reproduced within the Global South as a whole. They are reflected in the diversity of coalitions that exist among developing countries in negotiations on international trade and finance. Their existence does not negate the value of regionalism or of wider South-South cooperation. Rather, they underline the need to address the concrete challenges of regional solidarity and the building and maintenance of coalitions that are an integral part of the search for policy autonomy in the South.

4
The World Bank as a Knowledge Agency

John Toye and Richard Toye

In considering the manner in which social knowledge is used in policy making in international financial institutions (IFIs), it is necessary to maintain a broad and comparative approach. It is altogether too easy to start from the conviction that certain international organizations have a negative (or positive) impact on developing countries, and then proceed to show how their use of social knowledge contributes to the type of impact that was assumed in the first place. Demonizing some international organizations while idealizing others is undoubtedly a very popular pastime, but it is one that generates more heat than light. This chapter claims that the production of social knowledge in all international organizations is problematic, because of their nature as a form of public bureaucracy. This general claim, advanced as a modification of Weber's theory of bureaucracy, is argued in the first section.

Turning to the World Bank as a case study of the problems of managing social research inside an international public bureaucracy, it is argued in the second section not only that managerial constraints exist on what the Bank is willing to publish, but that the binding constraints on publication change over time, depending on managerial objectives and managerial competence in exercising editorial control over research output. We then examine the evolution in managerial objectives at the Bank in recent years, and the factors that have influenced shifts in its rhetoric and policy. In the last decade, the Bank has had to adjust to a variety of pressures from its major sponsors, arising both from geopolitical events and from opposition to particular institutional modes of operation. This leads on to the underlying question of the final section, which is whether these pressures have brought about a fundamental transformation of attitudes at the Bank. Are we seeing signs of change, or only a change of signs? Recent research on the issues of poverty reduction, governance and conditionality (policy-based and process-based) are discussed in an effort to gauge how far the Bank has moved.

Social knowledge and international policy making

That public organizations operate at times as intellectual actors is startling. The role of an international bureaucracy may extend to the collection and dissemination of available knowledge, if this helps it in the discharge of its functional responsibilities. That the production of novel ideas should be one of its functions would come as a surprise to most people. An organization that does such a thing could well be viewed as going into competition with universities, institutes, think-tanks and consultancy firms, but without having the necessary advantages, either of human and physical infrastructure or, perhaps more importantly, in terms of the structure of institutional incentives. 'Universities and think-tanks can out-perform the UN in research', according to Michael Edwards, because they are 'without the combination of high costs and low levels of innovation that characterises organisations lacking both market discipline and social pressures to reform' (Edwards, 1999: 180).

In the twentieth century, national governments increasingly became the locus of the creation of economic knowledge. This went beyond the gathering and presentation of economic statistics. Statistics, as the word implies, had long been the province of the state. In the years between the two World Wars, by contrast, some statisticians became unusually inventive, creating new empirical representations of novel economic concepts. In Germany, Ernst Wagemann's theoretical work inspired the Statistical Office to use census data to produce an input-output table, quite independently of Wassily Leontief (Tooze, 2001). In the United States (US), Lauchlin Currie and Martin Krost, while on the research staff of the Federal Reserve Board, made pioneering estimates of the effects of government fiscal changes on the national income – as early as 1937–38 (Barber, 1990). These examples could be multiplied. In step with national governments, international organizations moved from statistical collection to the quantification of new economic concepts. The League of Nations moved on from collecting balance of payments statistics in the early 1920s to producing innovative studies of trade and the business cycle in the late 1930s. This transition was undoubtedly hastened after the Great Crash, when it seemed to many that academic economists had little that was useful to contribute to the formation of economic policy.

Yet the economic justification for the state becoming an intellectual actor was, and is, problematic. Admittedly, knowledge is a public good, and the market, if left to itself, will tend to supply too little of it to achieve maximum welfare. The force of this argument is to justify public intervention to boost investment in new knowledge. However, it does not entail that the new knowledge must be produced in a public sector institution. If individuals tend to underinvest in their health and education, this is not a sufficient justification for setting up public hospitals and state schools, because a better outcome might result from giving private schools and private hospitals a public subsidy. Similarly, if knowledge is undersupplied, it might be better for public sector institutions to subsidize its private production, rather than to produce it themselves.

Some international public institutions have, nevertheless, wanted to be intellectual actors, rather than just investors in the production of knowledge. In the field of economic and social development, perhaps the foremost contemporary repository of this ambition is the World Bank. The Bank advances the economic justification that only by producing knowledge in-house can its benefits for the institutions' functional operations be secured (Squire, 2000). Partly, it is argued, this is a matter of being able to ensure that outside researchers undertake the research agenda that the institution in question wants them to undertake. Partly it is that, in the absence of in-house champions of specific pieces of research, potentially useful research will not get noticed and will not in fact be used. While there is doubtless some merit in these arguments, they look only to the advantages of doing research in-house, and these advantages always need to be balanced against the potential difficulties.

What, then, are the drawbacks? To answer this question, one must turn from the economics of public goods to the sociology of bureaucracy. Max Weber argued that modern bureaucratic organizations would increasingly replace patrimonial ones. He claimed that they are formally the most rational means of exercising control over human beings, because their goals are set by their sponsors and are implemented by bureaucrats who remain politically neutral. In making this claim for the efficiency of modern bureaucracy, Weber simply assumed that the formal roles assigned to bureaucrats are always congruent with their actual motives and orientations. However, this is not necessarily so: officials may don their organizational masks, but they do not easily or frequently become them (Rudolph and Rudolph, 1979). Weber's ideal type needs to be modified to take account of the fact that people inside bureaucracies can rebel against the machine-like expectations of formal rationality.[1] Experience forces us to confront the fact that 'defiant bureaucrats' exist, and that they do 'engage in behavior that is from the perspective of organizational goals and procedures irrational and dysfunctional' (Rudolph and Rudolph, 1979: 209).

We propose a modified Weberian theory of bureaucracy. It asserts that, inside all public organizations, authority stands in potential tension with power. Authority is hierarchical, and is formally delegated from the pinnacle of the President (or other like role) downwards in a very precise manner. Power – the ability to make others act as one requires – may be distributed differently. It will be exercised from above only to the extent that those in authority at the top have the resources of power – personal leadership skills, access to information, incentives and sanctions – with which to motivate, control and appropriate the efforts of those below them in the hierarchy. This potential tension sets the scene for the outbreak of power struggles between superiors and subordinates, as the former seek to conjure up from the latter the activity that will support the goals of the organization (which are derived from those of its sponsors), and as from time to time they meet resistance (Ansari, 1986). Maintaining the congruence of power with authority is a quite onerous task that heads of bureaucracies often fail to perform.

This is especially so in international bureaucracies. Here control by sponsors is weaker than in the national case, because the conflicting interests of the multitude of country sponsors permanently dilute it. This is partly a matter of a lesser ability to determine clear and consistent objectives. It is also because divergent interests of sponsors can reduce the resources of power available to those in high authority in international organizations; requirements of geographical balance in recruitment, or the diplomatic consequences of disciplining officials of particular nationalities, deplete the normal armoury of sanctions that high officials can deploy against subordinates who engage in dysfunctional behaviour.

Within an international bureaucracy, the in-house research function presents a special case. Intellectual originality and creativity are achievements that, almost by definition, cannot be commanded, sometimes not even by their authors. Original research, when produced, may turn out to be congruent with the objectives that an international bureaucracy and its sponsors are seeking to fulfil. Yet it also has the potential to be dissonant with those objectives. In that case, therefore, its authors, because of the peculiar nature of their specialized expertise, run a particularly large risk of becoming, in the course of defending their research procedures and results, 'defiant' bureaucrats. The political neutrality required of a Weberian bureaucrat may turn out to be at odds with the intellectual disinterestedness that must discipline the good researcher. Ideally, researchers should have no personal stake in the results of their enquiries. If they are researching, for example, whether trade liberalization does or does not stimulate economic growth, or whether commodity prices are set to rise or fall, they should have no vested interest in reaching a particular conclusion.[2] When the organization that employs them aims to persuade external agents of the truth of certain propositions, and researchers willy-nilly have such a personal stake, this threatens to damage the integrity and quality of their work. Thus in-house intellectual activity will be constantly in danger of being distorted, to some degree, by the attempts of managers to impose their organizational goals.

International bureaucracies still wield some incentives and sanctions, even if to a lesser degree than national bureaucracies. International officials who are researchers on political economy resemble their colleagues in that all are wholly dependent on their organization's managers for their material rewards, so they may face disincentives to coming up with results that top managers find unhelpful to their goals, even if the results that they produce are intellectually sound. Similarly, they may face incentives to certify propositions as valid knowledge, even if they are not, when their top managers find it helpful to their goals that that be done. The independence that is the only safeguard for intellectual honesty will be lacking, when the internal power struggle favours the top management. This does not of course imply that intellectual honesty must always be lacking: it may or may not turn out to be consistent with an international organization's goals.

However, the significance of this potential drawback is amplified as soon as we recognize that international public institutions do indeed at times identify with, and defend, certain doctrines of political economy. They are often required to do so by the governments that are their members and their main financial sponsors. The defence of an organization's core doctrines can be managed in several different ways. One is to design the research agenda in a way likely to support the consensus, for example, by not devoting resources to researching topics that are regarded as marginal, or potentially antagonistic to it. Another is for top managers to vet carefully high-profile research output, and to edit out unwanted messages.[3] Another is the self-censorship of the researchers, who can usually guess where the limits of acceptability lie. Even when top managers try to avoid shooting the messengers that bear bad, but accurate, tidings, it will not be every staff member who will venture to put that restraint to the test.

Institutional constraints on creative research

In its early years, the World Bank defended the doctrine of sound finance and had little use for its few economists.[4] Even this commitment to a limited doctrine elicited some assertion of editorial control, however. An early example of the Bank's tendency to control occurred in 1955, when it held up the publication of Jan Tinbergen's *The Design of Development* (which it had commissioned) for three years because the then President objected to Tinbergen's support for a mixed private and public economy.[5]

The breaking of the Latin American debt crisis in 1982 marked the adoption by the Bank of a much stronger and more elaborated doctrinal stance. At the behest of the new conservative government of the United States, West Germany and Britain, the Bank propagated to developing countries a set of neoliberal economic policies that became characterized as the 'Washington Consensus' (see Williamson, 1990). This policy set was supposed to represent the 'sensible economic policies' that developing countries would have to implement in order to restart the flow of commercial lending that had so abruptly ceased. It established the more extensive doctrinal boundaries that were defended by the Bank through the 1980s.

That the Bank's research was very clearly subservient to its management's objectives was illustrated by its research on the sustainability of debt levels and the debt crisis. Compared with the academic literature of the day (see Eaton and Gersovitz, 1981), World Bank researchers made more optimistic predictions in 1981 about the future availability of private capital flows to already indebted developing countries. In this, they supported the view of the Bank's then President, Robert McNamara, that the debt problem was manageable and would not obstruct economic growth. Moreover, as the debt crisis worsened, the Bank fell well behind academic opinion on the need for debt relief. The Bank's chief economist, Stanley Fischer, candidly acknowledged the reasons for this.

> It was clear to the participants in this . . . conference at the beginning of 1989, as it had been clear to many much earlier, that growth in the debtor countries would not return without debt relief. But the official agencies operate on the basis of an agreed upon strategy, and none of them could openly confront the existing strategy without having an alternative to put in place. And to propose such an alternative would have required agreement among the major shareholders

of the institutions. So long as the United States was not willing to move, the I[international] F[inancial] I[nstitution]'s were not free to speak... (Diwan and Husain, 1989, cited in Armendariz and Ferreira, 1995: 226).

An anecdote from the 1980s confirms both the existence of this constraint, and how 'defiant bureaucrats' tried to circumvent its effects. Gerald K. Helleiner has recalled how

a UN professional group, the one on African finance and debt, was put together with the full cooperation of a vice-president of the World Bank, precisely because he could not, within his constraints, get from the Bank a strong public declaration of the need to act on African debt.... We decided that...an expert group [of the UN] including a private banker or two, was the way to go. And the World Bank man, Kim Jaycox, was really supportive and told us that he could not do this and that he could not get a Bank study done that would say what an independent group could say that needed to be said.[6]

The short and controversial career of Joseph Stiglitz as Chief Economist of the World Bank from 1997 to January 2000 provides further evidence of the constraints on Bank research.[7] To his credit, Stiglitz wanted to broaden the original Washington Consensus of ten policy thrusts (fiscal and exchange rate reform, trade and financial liberalization, privatization and deregulation, among others), by adding improved financial sector regulation, competition policy and technology transfer policies. He also suggested multiplying the objectives of development policy, by adding a sustainable environment, democratization and a more egalitarian income and asset distribution (Stiglitz, 2001). However, he did not then question the idea that it was the Bank's job to promote a consensus of some kind on development policy; he merely wanted to move away from a narrow version of neoliberalism. He also began an internal campaign against the deflationary policies recommended by the International Monetary Fund (IMF) during the Asian financial crisis.

The US Treasury Department under Laurence Summers was unhappy about these intellectual ambitions. He made Stiglitz's departure from the Bank a condition of US support for James Wolfensohn's second term as President. Stiglitz duly submitted his resignation in November 1999.[8] After leaving the Bank, however, Stiglitz moved from modifying the Washington Consensus to rejecting outright the Bank's drive to promulgate any package of development policy doctrines.

Opposition to globalisation in many parts of the world is not to globalisation per se...but to the particular set of doctrines, the Washington Consensus policies that the international financial institutions have imposed. *And it is not just opposition to the policies themselves, but to the notion that there is a single set of policies that is right.* This notion flies in the face of both economics, which emphasizes the notion of trade-offs, and of ordinary common sense (Stiglitz, 2002: 221, with emphasis added).

Stiglitz's post-resignation reversal suggests that, while in the Bank, he was constrained to agree that the role of the Bank is to provide the developing world with 'the single set of policies that is right'. It seems that even defiant bureaucrats, or 'rebels within', cannot escape from the Bank's institutional imperative to preach a doctrine, and that the United States will act to reinforce this imperative when it thinks it is under threat. Kaushik Basu, reviewing Stiglitz's recent book, confessed to being persuaded that in subtle ways the big powers do indeed take control of the major international organizations, using them to defend ideas and policies compatible with their interests. As he went on to explain:

This is not hard because... [while] economics has had some major successes [it] remains woefully inadequate on many of the most important issues that confront policy makers. In these latter areas, it is easy for myths to develop. By repeating certain propositions sufficiently often, they can be made to sound like facts, and given the credibility of economics in other areas, most people treat them as facts. This creates scope for subversion, feeding people with 'facts' that are convenient to some (Basu, 2003: 892–3).

Thus to insights from the sociology of bureaucracy, one should also add insights from the sociology of knowledge. We need also to understand how powerful institutions are able to establish and sustain the hegemony of dominant ideas. As well as modifying Weber, we need to absorb the teachings of Gramsci.

In circumstances of such tight editorial control linked to strategic objectives, it is not surprising that, when the World Bank's role as an intellectual actor was evaluated, little evidence was found for the originality of the ideas directly emanating from it. Even in the area of economics that concerns its own operations most closely, namely the economic appraisal of projects, the Bank did not pioneer new methods.[9]

However, despite failure to originate key ideas or methods in development economics, the Bank's power to propagate ideas is well attested in the media and in university graduate-level syllabi. The Bank has also become 'the single most important external source of ideas and advice to developing-country policymakers' (Gavin and Rodrik, 1995; see also Stern and Ferreira, 1997). The example of the World Bank seems to show that international public organizations can become powerful propagators of ideas, if they invest sufficiently in the mechanisms of intellectual propagation. Yet it is almost impossible for them, especially when those in high authority in the organization can command the resources of power, also to operate successfully as creative intellectual actors in areas where their managers are already committed to maintaining an economic doctrine.

In this connection, it has been observed that criticisms of the Bank's economic doctrines and policies that academics and non-governmental organizations (NGOs) voice in the borrowing countries are often dismissed by the government there. This is because it likes to go along with the Bank's requirements, because of the political material dividends for cooperation. However, these same criticisms are subsequently 'discovered' by Bank representatives, and used to make policy corrections. What is demotivating for the local critics is that the Bank cites its 'discovery' as evidence of its own ability to produce new ideas and respond creatively to changing circumstances![10]

Comparing economic research in the World Bank with economic research in the United Nations (UN) provides contrasting experiences of the relation between the creation of economic knowledge and managerial control. UN managers also recruited economists directly into the organization and yet, contrary to the ideal-typical view of bureaucracy, they had greater difficulty than the Bank in establishing managerial control over economic research. The UN's looser editorial control over economic research allowed its economists on occasion to produce creative new ideas that were dysfunctional in terms of the organization's bureaucratic objectives (as in the Prebisch-Singer case, or that of Michal Kalecki) (see Toye and Toye, 2004: Chapters 3 and 5). When, after 1980, the industrial countries built up the World Bank as a counterweight to the UN, the power exercised by its sponsors was related to their capital contributions, which gave a few industrial countries a heavy leverage. The Bank succeeded in pleasing these sponsors and maintained a tight editorial control, but its economic work has not been judged as particularly creative.

The paradox that dysfunctional organizations can be creative in the field of political economy and functional ones can be sterile need not, perhaps, be too disturbing. What is good for organizations (including international ones) cannot be assumed to be good for those who work for them, or for the wider society in which they operate. What is dysfunctional for them may be functional on a broader view. To achieve the compliance of participants with the goals of their organization is not necessarily an unmitigated good. Sometimes conflict within organizations may promote desirable values and legitimate interests on a grander scale. There may be more to life than the triumph of a particular bureaucracy, however elevated.

The new development agenda

Why have the IFIs shifted the focus of their attention to poverty reduction and the role of the state and other institutions?

'Reduce poverty' was never one of the ten precepts of the Washington Consensus. Yet it would be a mistake, if one wants to understand its persuasive force, to ignore the fact that it called for improvements in income distribution as an argument to justify the shrinking of the state. The claim was that a smaller state would be good for growth, and growth would be good for poverty reduction. Also, since poverty is severer in rural areas, and since state economic production and regulation disadvantaged agriculturists and privileged industrialists, a smaller state would tend to reduce inequality in the distribution of income and wealth. The manifesto of the counter-revolution in development was not simply about greater efficiency: it contained a promise of poverty reduction through growth and greater equity as well.[11]

Nevertheless, by the end of the 1980s, the very considerable effort expended on structural adjustment seemed to have distracted attention from the tasks of reducing poverty, let alone income inequality. The willingness to let poverty reduction wait upon increased growth eroded as the growth record of structural adjustment policies was shown to be rather unimpressive. Greater credence was given to the idea that growth itself depended on poverty reduction. It was argued (once again) that better health and education services for the poor would permit the formation of socially desirable human capital that would not otherwise take place, and thus make the economy more productive. These claims could be rationalized by reference to new theories that installed human capital accumulation as the engine of endogenous growth (see Scott, 1989; and Lucas, 1988).

The World Bank (1990a) acknowledged the new interest in poverty reduction in its *World Development Report 1990*, which stressed the need to ensure that growth was labour-intensive, and that basic social services were better funded. Enthusiasm for specific social safety nets was markedly less evident. The programme of structural adjustment was by no means abandoned, but it now had to be pursued with a much greater concern for its effects on the level and intensity of poverty. How was this renewed concern for poverty reduction made operational? An IMF-World Bank 'concordat' (1989) established effective (though not formal) cross-conditionality of these institutions' loans. Bank adjustment lending became conditional on a pre-existing IMF programme, and a statement of economic policy for the borrowing country had to be agreed by both institutions. In usual practice, apart from one country government representative on the drafting team, they jointly drafted the Policy Framework Paper (PFP) and the country government would then agree to sign it. This general statement of agreed policies – the PFP – was transformed at the end of the century into a new type of document, the 'Poverty Reduction Strategy Paper' or PRSP. This change of title signalled that the recipient country government was now expected to make a national poverty reduction strategy the centrepiece of its overall development strategy.

The Bank, in promoting this extended version of economic reform in developing countries, still relied on large programme loans carrying conditions about policy changes, conditions reflected in the PFPs, and after 1999 (though to a lesser extent) in the PRSPs. However, as well as using loan conditions, the Bank sought the power to persuade on issues of development policy. Hence, it has continued to invest heavily in an intellectual infrastructure. By the end of the 1980s, the Bank employed no less than 800 economists, and had a research budget of $25 million a year, resources that dwarf those of any university department (Stern and Ferreira, 1997). Although the production of publishable research is only one of the functions of its research department, the Bank now conducts what is almost certainly the largest single publication programme on development issues in the world. The Bank's influential flagship report, the annual *World Development Report*, inaugurated in 1978, has been credibly claimed as the most widely read document in development economics. In the 1980s the Bank began to publish more research through two new house journals, *The World Bank Economic Review* and *The World Bank Research Observer*. The Bank has also become a major provider of statistical data, including regular published series such as the *World Debt Tables*, and data from household and firm surveys.

From the early 1980s, the Bank has used this augmented intellectual armoury to minimize any doubts in client countries about how 'sensible' the West's approach to the debt crisis really was, and about the neoliberal content of its loan policy conditions. Inside the Bank, greater pressure for doctrinal conformity caused mixed reactions, and key figures on the research staff disagreed on the merits of research being subordinated to the operational requirements of structural adjustment.

> The early 1980s was full of the excitement of structural adjustment, but it was not here that the research side of the Bank led the way. A switch of interest towards markets and prices was welcomed by many. However, some spoke of a decline in the research atmosphere, of a degree of intolerance and of a requirement to tow (sic) the party line. Others saw a rescue from intellectual tiredness and dead-ends (Stern and Ferreira, 1997: 87, 102).

Since 1980, the pressure of operational needs has had the inevitable effect of dampening in-house intellectual creativity and boosting research that serves the Bank's current persuasive purposes. Attempts to evaluate the quality of the Bank's research and publication activities have noted that their extensive influence on policy makers and educators has been matched by the modest extent of their intellectual innovation. Even Bank insiders do not claim to have played a major role in the economics profession, and many are frustrated by the lack of a good atmosphere for serious research. Some of them do, however, claim to have 'produced more high quality research than other UN agencies' (Stern and Ferreira, 1997: 83, n.51). This claim may seem plausible, but the more interesting question is how the comparison would look on the basis of equality of research resource endowment.

The Bank's lending portfolio has been increasingly diversified in the 1990s to support a new development agenda that includes not only poverty reduction but also gender equality, popular participation, stronger civil society, improved governance and environmental conservation (see Miller-Adams, 1999). One important conditioning factor was major geopolitical change, namely the collapse of the socialist regimes in Eastern Europe and Russia in the early 1990s. The new European Bank for Reconstruction and Development (EBRD) made an explicit political condition for its lending – that borrowing countries should not revert to socialism. Bilateral aid agencies began to insist that developing countries abandon one-party rule, and institute multiparty elections. Although formally the requirement that the World Bank should operate in a non-political manner never changed, the arrival of the EBRD's explicit political conditionality, plus the political pressures applied by the bilateral donors, encouraged the World Bank to move into quasi-political areas of operations. It introduced loan conditionality to a range of quaintly named 'governance issues', in addition to its general neoliberal requirement that the state be 'rolled back'. These included new institutions of state accountability and decentralization, as well as new institutions of civil society to check and balance the power of the state. Behind the old Middle English word of 'governance', there clearly lurked very modern dreams of liberal constitution making.

Against this general *zeitgeist* of transition from socialism, a more specific pressure weighed on the Bank. It had already begun to get into political difficulties in the United States in the middle of the 1980s, when several US environmental NGOs attacked Bank-financed projects in Brazil for encouraging environmental damage. They claimed the Bank's procedures for making environmental impact assessments of its projects were inadequate. The Bank gave in under pressure from the US Congress and Treasury and set up an Environment Department in 1987. Then in 1992, an independent review charged that the Bank had breached its own guidelines for the conditions on which the people displaced by the Narmada dams in India were to be resettled.

In the course of these controversies, the US NGOs demonstrated their ability to harass the Bank by means of well-organized lobbying of the US Congress.[12] The Bank has since put in place new measures of accountability, including an independent inspection panel to make public reports on contentious cases. The ironies of this campaign were that the US NGOs themselves are, for the most part, not publicly accountable; and that the Bank has become more accountable to US politicians, rather than to the politicians of its client countries (Woods, 2003).

The power of NGOs to move the US Congress brought about a fundamental change of political stance at the Bank. Since 1996, when James Wolfensohn became President, the Bank has been proactively reaching out to its NGO critics, and shaping its policies to reflect their concerns. Wolfensohn, not wanting the Bank to be so badly wrong-footed again, pursued this populist approach both in his public rhetoric and in a managerial style that placed him at odds with the pre-existing bureaucratic culture of the institution. He tried to deflect NGO criticism of the Bank by promoting his brainchild, the Comprehensive Development Framework (CDF), a matrix for coordinating all the development activities of a country. Being the guardian of the CDF allows the Bank to adopt a central position in the development process. It is able to provide a diverse range of services (loans, technical assistance, advice) to the entire development community, and yet to identify itself as a development partner and facilitator, instead of as a bunch of arrogant bankers.

Moreover, his choice of new issues for the Bank tried to pre-empt the opposition of the NGOs. As well as declaring poverty reduction to be the Bank's overriding objective, efforts have been directed to a range of other aims that will find favour with US NGOs – including the strengthening of civil society and the reform of public institutions.

The Bank's concern with governance was strengthened further as evidence built up that its favourite instrument to induce economic reform, policy-conditioned programme lending, was not being as effective as originally believed. The first independent evaluation of the Bank's structural adjustment lending of the 1980s indicated that, owing to incentive problems in its design, compliance with policy change conditions was far from universal; and that compliance was rewarded with pretty small improvements to growth, exports and the trade balance (Mosley *et al.*, 1995). Subsequently, other independent studies using alternative methodologies came to similar conclusions (Killick, 1998). By the end of the 1990s, these results had been digested inside the Bank, whose staff followed up with their own studies. David Dollar and Jakob Svensson argued that exogenous political economy factors were crucial in determining the success of adjustment loans, and not any of the variables that the Bank was able to alter by its own efforts. They recommended a strategy of 'selectivity' in programme lending. The Bank should abandon policy conditions in loans, they advised, and concentrate instead on developing political economy criteria to identify countries willing to implement the kind of reform policies of which the Bank approves (Dollar and Svensson, 2000; see also Collier, 2000). The strategy of loan selectivity is an unattractive one for the Bank's management. The alternative strategy, of not merely responding to but trying actively to influence the political economy variables, remained alluring.

The Bank's liberal political aspirations, its willingness to accommodate pressure from NGOs and its search for policy leverage set the scene when a consortium of NGOs launched the Jubilee 2000 campaign for enhanced debt relief for Heavily Indebted Poor Countries (HIPCs). This was something that President Wolfensohn could only support, so the Bank and the IMF devised the enhanced Heavily Indebted Poor Countries (E-HIPC) initiative. Its terms were more liberal than its predecessor's and it carried an implicit target of getting 20 new HIPC countries over the hurdle to benefit by the end of 2000. Since debt relief was intended to be additional to existing aid flows, and since the E-HIPC beneficiaries were countries that had not managed their debt well in the past, the

Bank and IMF felt that they had to insert extra safeguards. This concern was the origin of the PRSPs. Production of an interim PRSP was part of the E-HIPC qualification procedure. The overall aim was to ensure that the additional HIPC resources were used for poverty reduction purposes, and that this could be verified.

Operational changes

It was intended that the introduction, in late 1999, of PRSPs for HIPC countries, and the subsequent replacement of PFPs by PRSPs in other countries, would improve the institutions of poverty reduction policy-making in developing countries. It was assumed that the indirect effect would be to improve actual poverty reduction policies. The aim was a new, more inclusive national process of poverty policy formation, which would create a greater national ownership of, and commitment to, the anti-poverty policies that emerge from the process. This was recognition by the Bank that lack of ownership and commitment had been an obstacle to economic reform in the past, and that the device of policy-based lending had not overcome this obstacle. PRSPs shifted the locus of conditionality away from specific policies, toward processes of policy formation and the public institutions that sustain them. What has been the result?

The most substantial evaluation to date, done for the Strategic Partnership with Africa (SPA), covers the seven African countries of Benin, Kenya, Malawi, Mali, Mozambique, Rwanda and Tanzania (Booth, 2004). It finds that compliance with the required PRSP process was prompt and cooperative and not entirely driven by the prospect of the anticipated E-HIPC resources windfall. It notes that primary responsibility for the national poverty reduction strategy shifted to the Ministry of Finance, bringing it closer to central decision making on the budget. Consultations with actors from civil society have taken place, although public understanding of the PRSP process remains narrow and shallow. The realism of countries' national poverty reduction strategies was found to be greater where more progress had already been made in establishing a comprehensive, transparent and outcome-oriented medium-term expenditure plan. Without such progress, the PRSP process could easily run into the sand.

Whether all of the above adds up to a vindication of the PRSP process as a better way of securing national commitment to poverty reduction is not yet clear. On the whole, the degree of national political commitment has been less than the degree of technocratic commitment. This will be problematic if complementary reforms in public financial management are vital to the success of the PRSP process (Booth, 2004). Consultations with citizens have not been merely formal, but have generated significant changes to the full PRSPs. Nevertheless, the hope that consultation of this kind will become institutionalized, and will deepen high-level political commitment to poverty reduction remains no more than a hope in the seven countries that the SPA report surveyed.

At the same time, the hope that the IFIs and other aid donors would reduce their demands for consultations with the government, as country-led reviews of performance developed, has so far not been realized. If anything, the problem of process overload has grown, as joint reviews of the PRSP process are added to existing uncoordinated donor review requirements. Very little, if any, pooling or streamlining of reporting and evaluation requirements has been achieved.

While the development of a new process is vital for local institution building and for re-invigorating the aid relationship, poverty reduction depends not just on a better planning process, but also on a sound causal analysis of how poverty can be reduced. Unfortunately, it is not clear that this is yet forthcoming, from either side of the aid partnership. On the recipient side, taking the views of civil society seriously may lead to the compilation of a shopping list of demands rather than a credible plan for reducing poverty (Booth, 2004). At the same time, prior and possibly also non-transparent IFI loan conditions may limit the scope for arriving at an integrated poverty reduction strategy (Hewitt, 2003).

On the donor side, pressure from NGOs has led the Bank to propagate the idea that poverty reduction is a matter of expanding public expenditure on social services, to the neglect of wider growth and development priorities (Killick, 2004). While well-functioning education and health care services will reduce poverty if the poor have access to them, changing budget allocations is hardly sufficient to make social services function well, or to open them to the poor. Moreover, the most dramatic reductions in poverty have been associated with broad-based economic growth. Some aid donors, including the World Bank, are now promoting work on the issue of pro-poor growth. Why are certain growth episodes more successful in reducing poverty per unit of growth? What are the macro-micro linkages that make growth more or less effective in reducing poverty? Is it the particular sector in which most of the growth occurs (agriculture), or the particular functional beneficiary of growth (labour)? What is the contribution of public expenditure, and of the political economy factors that influence public spending decisions? Research is currently being undertaken on these questions, in an attempt to provide a better understanding of policies that will generate pro-poor growth. However, there must be a real doubt about how results from this research will be received, and how much they will influence policy, should they go against the conventional wisdom that the NGOs have persuaded the members and staff of the Bank and IMF to endorse.

Has the advent of PRSPs been part of a larger change in aid modalities? Has the IFI's desire to enhance the local ownership of reform programmes led them to reduce their use of policy conditionality, especially in the light of the studies cited earlier that concluded that it is a weak instrument?

This would not seem to be the case. First, as noted, the E-HIPC countries are faced with process conditionality that does not fully substitute for the policy change conditions that may be in their other loan agreements with the IFIs. Although the potential for such a substitution is there, it is unclear how far it has actually been realized. Second, some assiduous bean counting shows that the average number of policy change conditions has fallen in Bank agreements – from 58 (1988–92) to 36 (1998–2000) for the Bank. Also, it is likely that the average number of 'structural' conditions in IMF agreements, which rose from 2 (1987) to 14 (1997–99), has since fallen. Logic tells us, however, that fewer conditions make policy conditionality more effective, not less, and it is the non-binding conditions where the reduction is greatest. The probability that some of the dropped IMF conditions have been picked up and adopted by the Bank also suggests that the design of conditionality is being rationalized, rather than slowly abandoned. So do the indicators that show some improvement in compliance with conditions in the 1990s compared with the 1980s (Killick, 2004).

What does the debate about conditionality tell us about the use of knowledge in the IFIs? Killick sees 'a large apparent gap between what the balance of available evidence tells us about the efficacy of conditionality as a way of securing desired policies and the continuing policies and practices' of the IFIs (Killick, 2004: 17). He attributes this gap to the representatives of major shareholders remaining unaware of, or unconvinced by the evidence, and to the managers of the institutions therefore being unwilling to change. This conclusion would sit very conveniently with the earlier history, summarized above, of the Bank being in the rearguard of academic opinion because of constraining institutional objectives. This would, however, be rather too neat a conclusion.

What the academic evidence showed was that the initial design of the policy conditionality mechanism was flawed, and it explained the reasons for the flaws. Some of them were remediable. Much later, the Bank insiders claimed to have shown econometrically that policy conditionality was a total failure. They concluded that it should be wholly abandoned and replaced by selectivity based on political economy variables. That conclusion and policy implication can, however, be academically challenged. The Dollar and Svensson paper, for example, finesses the whole question of compliance with policy conditions by using as its explicandum an indicator that does not distinguish between compliance and programme success (Dollar and Svensson, 2000). It also treats political economy variables as wholly exogenous, rather than as factors that differ depending on initial macroeconomic conditions, the design quality of the adjustment programme and its initial short-run impact (Mosley *et al.*, 2003). Thus although it is certainly true that institutional imperatives would make the adoption of selectivity a practical challenge for the Bank, they are not the only source of inhibition. On this occasion, there are also intellectual matters that should make the Bank pause, in particular, the need for more thought about the analytical rationale of the proposed policy change.

Returning to the question of how far the Bank has moved in the last decade, one may conclude that, not very surprisingly, the rhetoric of change has moved faster than the reality. Nevertheless, the Bank has taken significant new policy initiatives, in an attempt to respond to shortcomings in past attempts to instigate economic reform policies. The requirement that borrowers develop a national poverty reduction strategy, and do so in consultation with civil society was a bold move, which has met with limited success so far. At the same time, the advent of process conditionality does not seem to have replaced, or even much reduced, the use of policy-based conditionality.

However, the question remains: should it do so? The case that the instrument of conditionality cannot be reformed is far from being proven, despite the claims of Bank insiders. Yet one would hesitate to argue for using a more effective conditionality unless the policies to which it would be attached gave credible hope of succeeding. For all the talk of the Bank becoming a knowledge bank, much still has to be discovered about appropriate poverty reduction policies. An optimist would say that the Bank is fully engaged on the search for more appropriate policies. A pessimist might fear that the Bank's populist turn and its greater responsiveness to sections of civil society have not improved the intellectual quality of this debate, and may, in fact, have worsened it.

5
Knowledge Management and the Global Agenda for Education[1]

Kenneth King

Arguably, aid or development cooperation have always had an intimate connection with knowledge. From the time of the Truman Inaugural in January 1949, with its emphasis on humanity for the first time having the knowledge and skill to relieve the suffering of half of the world's population (Rist, 1997: 71; King, 2002) to the present day with agencies identifying knowledge as the key driver in development (for example, World Bank, 2002b), knowledge has been central to the aid enterprise. Knowledge has had many different faces in development cooperation, from technical assistance in the South, to technical cooperation training awards in the North, and from despatch of experts, to support of research institutions and networks in the South. The aid modalities have changed a good deal in the last fifty and more years, and especially at the beginning of the 1990s from the agencies' own projects to support of appropriate national policies; and the language has changed to reflect this, with less emphasis now on Northern knowledge transfer and more on joint knowledge and capacity development with the South. But knowledge asymmetries remain one of the key differences between the developing and industrialized worlds, and inequalities and contrasts in access to higher education, research funding, patents and numbers of scientists continue to grow (World Bank, 2002b).

This chapter addresses one particular aspect of the development community's ongoing preoccupation with knowledge, namely the role of knowledge in the construction of both agency policy and what can be termed the global development agenda. As bilateral and multilateral donors have increasingly come to see themselves as 'knowledge agencies' and as institutions involved in 'knowledge-based aid' (King, 2000), so it becomes important to identify the sources of these claims, and to examine the role of knowledge in the global development agenda. In terms of the older debate about how external research could influence agency policy, it may well appear that the new knowledge discourse conceptualizes a great deal of knowledge as being already embedded within agencies. Hence the new knowledge challenge for agencies is sometimes presented as the need for them to capture more effectively and explicitly what they already, in some sense, know (King, 2000). In other words, the knowledge sources for their development policies are felt to be potentially within agencies or at least within their reach. James Wolfensohn expressed this famously in the autumn 1996 Annual Meetings' Address in the World Bank:

> We have been in the business of researching and disseminating the lessons of development for a long time. But the revolution in information technology increased the potential value of these efforts by vastly extending their reach. To capture this potential, we need to invest in the necessary systems, in Washington and worldwide, that will enhance our ability to gather development information and experience, and share it with our clients. We need to become, in effect, the Knowledge Bank (Wolfensohn, 1996: 7).

I will examine, accordingly, the role of knowledge in the formation of agency agendas, including, where appropriate, the United Nations (UN) family, and particularly in the elaboration of the global development agenda. In the process I will question whether in many of the economically weaker states, these global priorities and initiatives have begun to replace some of their essential national planning cycles. It will be somewhat paradoxical if this does appear to be the case since today, several donors – but most notably Japan – emphasize the crucial importance of self-reliance in development policy at the recipient country level (King and McGrath, 2004: 156–9).[2] This notion suggests not only that the recipient government should own the aid agenda and thus be in the driver's seat – a grossly over-used current aid metaphor – but also, and more rarely, that the country should be able to make a substantial contribution towards the financing of the reform agenda, and to its longer term sustainability. In other words, ownership should imply a serious degree of responsibility for implementing and maintaining the agenda.

I will illustrate this interplay of agency knowledge, country ownership and financing with examples drawn from the global reform agenda for education, although the donor modalities which have facilitated its development and implementation are common to the delivery of aid in other sectors as well. While the main argument concerns the country level, there are parallels with the setting of research priorities in higher education in institutions that are highly dependent on external financing.

Global agenda-setting

The role of the world conferences

With the elimination of the bi-polar world in 1989, there followed a decade of World Conferences, which focused on themes such as education (Jomtien, 1990), the rights of the child (New York, 1990), environment (Rio, 1992), human rights (Vienna, 1993), population (Cairo, 1994), social development (Copenhagen, 1995) and women (Beijing, 1995). The impact and visibility of these conferences in the first half of the 1990s were greatly increased by the decision of the Development Assistance Committee (DAC) of the Organisation for Economic Co-operation and Development (OECD) to base their new development strategy – *Shaping the 21st Century: the Contribution of Development Co-operation* (OECD/DAC, 1996) – on a selection of their main themes. Selection is used advisedly since what appeared in the DAC's six International Development Targets (IDTs) was very much a sub-set of what had actually been proposed by the conferences. Thus, in place of the expanded and deliberately tentative vision of basic education laid out in Jomtien,[3] the DAC version focused on just two of the most easily quantifiable education targets – universal primary education (UPE) by 2015, and the elimination of gender disparity in primary and secondary education by 2005.

Considerable research would need to be undertaken to understand how the World Conferences themselves and the OECD/DAC process translated knowledge into policy. In the case of the World Conference on Education for All, however, there can be little doubt that it was the World Bank's much earlier research on the crucially important developmental impact of primary schooling that was one of the main themes that was reinforced in Jomtien.[4] At this conference there was a near-to-final draft of the Bank's new primary education policy available, and the research that informed this document was merely asserted and taken for granted in the *World Declaration* and *Framework for Action* at Jomtien:

> Primary education has direct and positive effects on earnings, farm productivity, and human fertility, as well as intergenerational effects on

child health, nutrition, and education. In considering the effects of education on economic productivity, a wide number of studies conclude that investments in primary education yield returns that are typically well above the opportunity costs of capital (World Bank, 1990b: 10).

This process, whereby a series of World Bank research studies that were originally country and context specific[5] become generalized and eventually so widely disseminated that they no longer need to be sourced to particular countries and research environments, is certainly evident in the history of World Bank findings on the multiple developmental aspects of primary education.[6] Equally, although the World Conference covered multiple facets of basic education – from early childhood education and adult literacy to primary schooling and skills development, it was already clear even before the Conference was over that its two most influential agency sponsors, the World Bank and the United Nations Children's Fund (UNICEF), had made public that they would principally be supporting primary schooling (King, 1990: 16–17; Colclough and Lewin, 1993).[7]

This narrowing of the original Jomtien agenda of Education for All (EFA) to Schooling for All (SFA) was one of the first steps in the donor determination of the global education agenda. It is not difficult to see how primary EFA children became a more compelling aid objective than adult literacy, early childhood education or non-formal skills development – not to mention post-primary or tertiary education. Access to and completion of primary education – especially by girls – was rapidly to become the core element of the external agenda on education. Primary education was apparently more measurable than non-formal skills development and adult literacy, and it coincided with an increasingly powerful global campaign by non-governmental organizations (NGOs) to secure the rights of all children to be in schools (Oxfam, 1999). Whether the prioritizing of schooling and of girls' schooling in particular was due to the apparently powerful World Bank research evidence or to the fact that UPE could be made a more compelling time-bound target than the other elements of basic education is not yet clear.[8]

But the other crucial element, which would recur in the 1996 OECD/ DAC meeting and also in the 10-year follow-up to Jomtien, held in Dakar, was the notion that the international development community would stand ready to support those poorer countries that could not reach the agreed goals. These pledges were not restricted to primary education, but they were most explicit about the commitment to support this goal of UPE:

> International funding agencies should consider negotiating arrangements to provide long-term support, on a case-by-case basis, to help countries move toward universal primary education according to their timetable. The external agencies should examine current assistance practices in order to find ways of effectively assisting basic education programmes which do not require capital- and technology-intensive assistance, but often need longer-term budgetary support (WCEFA, 1990: 17–18).

The words were out in the open – 'longer-term budgetary support' to help the poorest countries reach SFA. Thus, at the very time that donors were allegedly beginning to retreat from 'their' projects and move towards policies and programmes 'owned' by their partners in the South, the Northern agency discourse was laying down what those policies should consist of. Equally, the emphasis on the ownership and responsibility of the South for their own priority-setting coincided with a new imperative that the North should assist particular sub-sectors in the weakest countries through budget support. Along with the new ideas about national capacity, sustainability, autonomy and self-reliance there was appearing, then, a rather different logic about the poorest countries receiving substantial amounts of external funding in order to reach the key Jomtien goal (of the agencies) of SFA. In 10 to 15 years' time, direct budget support (DBS) would be even more salient.

What was not made clear in Jomtien was the crucially important relationship between national financial capacity to provide SFA and the obligations upon donors and the world community to make this possible, especially in the poorest countries. It was not clear whether external aid would be needed just to speed up a process that the country could then take over; or was it being suggested by the use of phrases such as 'long-term' and 'budgetary support' that there were some countries which would not be able to achieve SFA, and which would be on the donor books for the foreseeable future? We shall return to this tension between national autonomy and financial sustainability on the one hand and the implementation of the global agenda with its overtones of aid dependency – if its targets are to be met – on the other.

National self-reliance and the IDTs

By the mid-1990s, as noted above, the global agenda on education had been somewhat redefined within the framework of the IDTs of the

OECD/DAC's *Shaping the 21st Century* (OECD/DAC, 1996). The IDTs reinforce the narrowing of the education agenda that had already become evident in Jomtien and they focus on just two aspects of education: UPE by 2015 and the elimination of gender disparity in primary and secondary education by 2005. Realistically, the UPE target was re-set 15 years later than the Jomtien goal of 2000, but, illogically, the goal for the elimination of gender disparities in education was set for 2005.[9] The wider set of four other economic, social and environmental targets are all time-bound for the identical date, 2015.

But more important for our purpose here, the OECD/DAC report presents itself as an exercise in the 'lessons learned' about what works in development cooperation. What takes place in this synthesizing of research about development success and failure into a concise policy document is very revealing for understanding what happens to knowledge in the process of international policy-making. Intriguingly, in terms of the donor discourse, this short report makes it absolutely clear, from the record of 50 years of aid, that 'the efforts of countries and societies to help themselves have been the main ingredients in their success' (OECD/DAC, 1996: 1). Development assistance has been only a complementary factor. The argument is all about countries and their peoples being 'ultimately responsible for their own development', about 'locally-owned country development strategies and targets', about development only being possible 'if developing countries drive the action, with full participation by all of their societies' stakeholders' (OECD/DAC, 1996: 11, 14).

And yet, the report can be interpreted very differently. It is not just the title that suggests that the DAC donors see themselves as playing a key role in 'shaping the 21st century'. But the whole process of identifying these particular six targets, and setting them within a new aid approach that would be much less project-based, and more to do with donor coordination and harmonization, suggests that the donors continue to have a crucial part in the IDT strategy.

As happens so often in the setting of international policy objectives, the more measurable, quantitative goals have taken precedence over the other factors that the OECD/DAC report also emphasized very strongly. Indeed, the report had stressed the need for a highly context-dependent approach which gives a very different feel from the one-size-fits-all shape of the IDTs: '... these goals must be pursued country by country through individual approaches that reflect local conditions and locally-owned strategies'. It argued, in addition, that there were a whole series of 'qualitative factors' that were 'essential to the attainment of these measurable goals' (OECD/DAC, 1996: 2). These included capacity development for democratic governance, human rights and the rule of law.

These critical qualifications of the quantitative targets get completely side-lined in the presentation of the new 'global development partnership effort' around the six 'realisable' goals (OECD/DAC, 1996: 2). OECD/DAC's concern to have just a limited number of indicators of success by which their efforts could be judged removed these necessary preconditions, and distanced the whole exercise from the complex country priorities of the developing world. The global development agenda essentially was fashioned in Paris.

Yet, side by side with the rhetoric of national self-reliance and country ownership goes a vision of partnership that, potentially, has the donors deeply involved in the economies of their Southern partners:

> One way to reinforce locally-owned strategies may be for donors increasingly to finance those aspects of the strategy calling for public expenditure through the budget of the developing country. This approach is being tested in a number of pilot efforts with a view to ensuring both effectiveness and accountability by the developing country (OECD/DAC, 1996: 15).

Interestingly, this expression is not restricted to the poorest developing countries. Quite frequently in the report, and reminding us of the Jomtien Declaration, is the view that there are many countries where longer term concessional aid will need to be the flip-side of national self-help.

We are left with a paradox in *Shaping the 21st Century*: it is one of the main expressions of the necessary policy self-reliance of developing countries, and yet it is also one of the clearest expressions of a set of donor-driven and donor-selected policies, strategies and targets that have been agreed by the OECD member states on behalf of the developing world.[10]

Within a little more than a year of its publication, the new United Kingdom (UK) Labour government had made them the centrepiece of its *White Paper on International Development* (DFID, 1997) and by December 2000, Clare Short, the then International Development Secretary, was able to claim that there was an unprecedented consensus across the UN system, the International Monetary Fund (IMF), Regional Development Banks, the G8 and the OECD – that the achievement of the Targets should be the focus of their joint endeavours (Short, 2000: 7). Interestingly, there was no reference to their being owned by the South.

Before leaving the IDTs, it is worth noting that the UK's Department for International Development (DFID) which, arguably, took the IDTs more seriously than other agencies,[11] actually worked out a series of Target Strategy Papers (TSPs) that would allow it – and the wider development community – to be judged against the delivery of these Targets. Across these TSPs the use of knowledge and research is illuminating. Elsewhere we have reviewed whose knowledge and research were used to support the Targets, and reached the following conclusion – first about the Education paper, and then more generally across the TSPs:

> Here the notion appears to be very much one of telling Southern governments what 'international best practice' says on issues that DFID has already identified as central to the education policy debate. There is no place in this vision for Southern knowledge or for issues of context. Across the TSPs, Southern knowledge deficits are far more in evidence than concerns about the development of Southern knowledge economies or societies (King and McGrath, 2004: 102).[12]

Reinforcing financial commitments

In April 2000, the world community concerned with EFA reconvened, in Dakar, to examine a decade of attempted implementation of the Jomtien agenda. Two issues are pertinent for our current concerns with knowledge and policy. First, the collective consensus on education goals went back to the expanded Jomtien Declaration with its six goals and not just the two OECD/DAC education targets. In so doing, it would appear that the huge amount of evaluative data produced for Dakar by the developing world had little influence. But, more important, the financing commitment of the international community went beyond what was stated in Jomtien. It was no longer just some or the poorest countries that were mentioned. The famous financial pledge on EFA at Dakar made it clear that there were a substantial number of countries that were potentially involved:

> The international community acknowledges that many countries currently lack the resources to achieve education for all *within an acceptable time-frame*. New financial resources, preferably in the form of grants and concessional assistance, must therefore be mobilised by bilateral and multilateral funding agencies, including the World Bank and regional development banks, and the private sector. *We affirm that no countries seriously committed to education for all will be thwarted in their achievement of this goal by a lack of resources* (World Education Forum, 2000: 9, emphasis added).

A clear linkage, then, had been laid down between the so-called global agenda for education and the future pattern of donor funding. But what was not said in Dakar was anything about the time-frame over which such aid would be made available, or anything about the possible trade-offs between reaching the international goals and increased aid dependency. Nor was there any evidence readily available in the *Dakar Framework* that would give any sense of the existing aid dependency of developing countries, at a point immediately before the famous pledge was enunciated. But, arguably, this could have been important if there had been a genuine concern to balance self-reliance, sustainability and aid dependence.

The Millennium Development Goals (MDGs)

A few months after Dakar, at the September 2000 Millennium Summit, the process for reaching eight MDGs was elaborated and agreed.[13] Containing 18 targets and 48 indicators, the MDGs are more complex than the six IDTs. It is not at all clear, however, how this latest component of the international architecture relates to the much proclaimed importance of national planning, national priorities or country ownership. Now that there is also a Millennium Project, and a three year research process in place to demonstrate how all countries will be able to reach the MDGs, we seem to have moved a long way from the tentativeness of Jomtien, or from the much earlier and highly differentiated regional strategies of the great United Nations Educational, Scientific and Cultural Organization (UNESCO) education conferences in Karachi, Addis Ababa and Santiago (IJED, 1981). In some situations, for example, in the United Kingdom, the MDGs have actually become the centrepiece of the government's development policy, and, in terms of public accountability, DFID has declared it will be judged by its contribution towards the achievement of these Goals.

When the minimalist target-setting of the MDGs – with their identical time-lines for all countries, rich and poor – is compared with the holistic and necessarily sector-wide planning of Ministries of Health, Education, Industry etc, it would be surprising if some countries did not identify the MDGs as the donors' agenda rather than their own.[14] What is intriguing is that donors seem able to combine a discourse that suggests their aid policy is to support country priorities with a conviction that the MDGs should be supported. Here is a not untypical example from the Danish International Development Agency (Danida):

> Development co-operation must support the national policies for poverty reduction on the basis of partnership. Through a series of

UN conferences international agreement has been reached on the following major goals for poverty reduction: [a statement of the 8 MDGs]. . . . These are ambitious goals and their fulfilment will require a comprehensive international effort. Denmark subscribes to these goals (Danida, 2000: 22–3).

The new aid agenda and modalities

Having sketched one version of the way that research knowledge and convictions about primary education and the schooling of girls became a key part of the global development agenda – to the exclusion of even agency research about skills development or higher education[15] – it would appear that these new development priorities were then reinforced by changes in aid modalities. Arguably, this has led to the new agenda of the MDGs having a potentially greater impact, especially in the economically weaker countries, than might have been the case in earlier years. These new modalities have begun to work their way through several donor agencies during the 1990s, and they have latterly been affected by a knowledge revolution within the agencies themselves. Interestingly, it has been suggested that the new approaches are more likely to build ownership, capacity and self-reliance in the South.

These aid delivery mechanisms are often presented as moving agencies away from the multiple disadvantages of their traditional project approaches. The latter have often been said to have resulted in unsustainable project enclaves where the aid initiatives were protected from the mainline ministries by project implementation units, and frequently staffed by former ministry personnel now on higher salaries. By contrast, the new sector-wide approach (SWAP) was thought to be able to coordinate a whole range of donor moneys around an agreed set of nationally owned policies for a particular sector such as health or education. Similarly, DBS has been seen to be moving aid money away from projects and technical assistance. For example, the UK's 2000 *White Paper on International Development*, which encouraged 'nationally owned poverty reduction strategies', committed the government, where circumstances were right, to 'moving towards providing financial support directly to recipient government budgets using their own systems' (DFID, 2000a: 93).

The Poverty Reduction Strategy Paper (PRSP) has been the most recent part of the new aid architecture to be required for the poorer countries of the world. Taken as a whole, these new approaches demand much greater ownership of the policy process than heretofore. They are almost certainly an improvement upon the myriad of uncoordinated projects, when they are adopted by a government which, however poor, has elaborated a strongly focused development policy. But the challenge is precisely that in so many of the poorer countries which are the very candidates for these new approaches, the national policy terrain has been eroded by a combination of low salaries, brain drain, and decades of orientation to external donor priorities.[16] In these circumstances, the very complexity and coordination requirements of the new aid modalities almost certainly end up being more invasive than the older project approaches, and allow donors to come closer to the heart of governments' financial planning and decision making. In this sense, these mechanisms may now be substituting for national planning processes, since they have indeed become synonymous with the national planning activity. They may in this way also contribute to the by-passing of democratic processes through the coordinated high-level donor discussions with the finance ministry.

Here, then, is the link to the new aid agenda just described: that for the basket-funding requirements from many donors of massive programmes like free primary education in several of the countries of Eastern Africa, these new ways offer a vehicle to move very large amounts of external money. This is not to suggest country complicity in proposing fee-free primary education. But such an initiative, which may involve 2–3 million new entrants to schools, and tens of thousands of teachers, and massive needs for textbooks and buildings, is exactly the priority that is now on many donors' agendas, thanks to the IDT/MDG process. Securing coordinated donor support for secondary, technical or higher education would be hugely more difficult. Yet what has been learned in research over the last 40 years about the successful implementation of large-scale reform projects in education seems not to be being applied widely in the adoption of these new modalities (Smith, 2003).[17]

New 'welfare states'?

Before looking at how the so-called knowledge revolution in agencies has connected with these trends, it may be worth noting what has, arguably, been happening to our other theme of country ownership and national self-reliance in the face of the growing international donor consensus over the contents of the development agenda. In the sphere of education, this connects particularly to the Dakar pledge that 'no countries seriously committed to education for all will be thwarted in their achievement of this goal by a lack of resources' (World Education Forum, 2000: 9).

Rather than coinciding with greater national ownership, these new modalities appear to be contributing to the formation of what might be termed new 'welfare states', not in the usual sense of a state that has taken responsibility for the health, education and even living allowance for all its people but rather a state that is dependent on welfare from the world community.[18]

Whatever the precise contribution of the newer or older aid modalities to this dependency, it seems that there are a substantial number of countries – many of them in Sub-Saharan Africa – where external aid is running at between 40 and 50 per cent of the government's entire recurrent budget. It is hard to be sure of these figures as some aid money is allocated to the development budget even when it is recurrent. We can be fairly certain, however, that for instance in Zambia the overall contribution of donors to its recurrent budget is 45 per cent. And of the total budget of the Government of Zambia, 17 per cent is being allocated to education, of which about 60 per cent is provided by external actors.[19] Meanwhile, Uganda is said to be receiving over 50 per cent of its recurrent budget from outside sources, and Mozambique is receiving at least 40 per cent from external funding. In addition, many of the Francophone African countries are said to be highly aid dependent.[20]

Perhaps the much clearer focus of the world's development agenda on the IDTs and then MDGs has encouraged a greater readiness in certain agencies to use the new modalities to put more money directly into the national budget as opposed to in self-standing projects. But it is crucial to ask whether the target-focus of much aid may produce a situation where it is unclear what happens when the targets – for example, in health or education – are actually reached. What does it signify, in terms of sustainability, to reach UPE – or any of the other targets – by 2015, but to do so with 60 per cent dependency on external funding?

At a time when ownership, autonomy and self-reliance are on the lips of many agencies which help Africa, it is important to look at the scale of this help. Has the extent of aid dependency increased as a result of focusing more narrowly on particular targets and goals? As yet there is no clear answer but there are some hints that this may be the case, as a series of initiatives and 'flagship programmes' target different dimensions of the millennium goals in particular countries. For instance, in the first *EFA Global Monitoring Report* it is noted of the Fast Track Initiative (FTI) (which for a group of 18 core countries stipulates a set of key policy and financing norms against which their EFA plans may be evaluated and costed) that:

> ... there is an obvious risk that the higher levels of external support entailed by FTI will increase aid dependence, as the extent of

national ownership of plans and policies formulated via the PRSP instrument remains uncertain (UNESCO, 2002: 177).

It may also be the case that, compared to the separate financing of a whole series of individual aid projects, the sheer scale of what is needed to achieve EFA, and the availability of SWAPs and DBS as new modalities to move larger amounts of money may encourage both donors and recipients to do just that.

A very tentative conclusion about the conjunction of a global aid agenda with new ways to deliver aid is that, for all the rhetoric about country ownership and autonomy, aid dependency may actually have increased. Without detailed work at the national level it is difficult to understand precisely how the new aid architecture intersects with what remains of national planning processes in the economically weaker states. But it seems just possible that with the setting of a single set of targets for the whole developing world, individual countries may well decide to take on greater dependency or indebtedness in order to be seen to be 'on target'. As far as the specific education goals were concerned, the *EFA Global Monitoring Report* of 2002 offered, for all individual countries, 'an interim answer to the question as to whether the world was on track to achieve Education for All (EFA) in 2015' (UNESCO, 2002: 12). For the no less than 71 countries judged to be at risk of missing one or more of the quantitative goals, there could well be temptations to take on greater commitments than are economically sustainable. Countries that decide on such a route may turn out eventually to be in the very position that Ellerman so eloquently analyses:

> Conventional development assistance in Africa typically tries to transplant a 'best practice' backed up by conditionalities on policy-based lending or aid to motivate the country to implement the best-practice recipes. Yet, this policy reform process is designed to promote neither active learning nor lasting institutional change. The substantial external incentives may temporarily overpower the springs of action that are native to the institutional matrix of the country, but that will probably not induce any lasting institutional reforms (Ellerman, 2004: 10).

In this extended case study of the role of research in education in the construction of the global development agenda, it seems clear that it was agency-commissioned research that played the key initial and subsequent roles in the formulation, confirmation and monitoring of a part of the world agenda. There is little or no evidence of research from the South having played a part, though there are clearly voices from the South that are critical of the trends that have been described here (see Coraggio, 2001; Tilak, 2001; and Torres, 2001).

There may be a parallel to this lack of local influence and autonomy at the institutional level also – in the tertiary education systems of highly economically dependent countries. In higher education environments where the bulk of the development budget as well as almost all moneys for research are sourced externally, and predominantly from the development assistance community, there is a conspicuous absence of longer term basic research, and a predominance, instead, of research and consultancy associated with the agency policy concerns (Court, 1983; World Bank, 2002b; Olukoshi in UNRISD, 2004).

The era of the knowledge agency

Knowledge management and sharing within agencies

It was noted at the outset of this chapter that the era of the knowledge revolution within development agencies might not substantially alter the role of agency-commissioned research and agency knowledge in the construction of international policy. Indeed, as the new ideas about multilateral and bilateral bodies becoming knowledge agencies and learning organizations, and being involved with knowledge-based aid began to circulate from the late 1990s, it was plain that they were sourced very much from the corporate sector in North America and in Europe. There was, accordingly, a powerful tendency for the emphasis to be on the capture, synthesis and more cost-effective utilization of the agencies' enormous existing knowledge bases rather than on the generation of new knowledge. The private sector's interest in tapping the tacit knowledge of its employees was an obvious dimension of its concern with comparative international advantage. And the transfer of this preoccupation with leveraging staff knowledge across the many branches of multinational firms was one of the first influences on the shape of knowledge agencies. Paradoxically, it was an early report by the consultancy firm, Arthur Andersen, that fed into the World Bank's emerging knowledge management (KM) system (Arthur Andersen, 1996). Arthur Andersen used to claim that within 24 hours, by tapping its worldwide network of expertise, an answer to any staff member's question anywhere should be delivered. Its report for the Bank stressed the need for the new system to provide information and knowledge to managers on a just-in-time basis, and the information and knowledge had to be authoritative and definitive (Carayannis and Laporte, 2002). Similarly, DFID in the United Kingdom was clearly influenced in its early thinking about KM by British Petroleum (BP), and not least by the KM text, *Learning to Fly* (DFID, 2000b; Collison and Parcell, 2001).

From 1996 in the World Bank, and from 2000 in some other bilateral and multilateral agencies, the focus was on mechanisms for sharing and synthesizing the huge amounts of operational knowledge that was already held by staff members of agencies. A series of more or less formal knowledge sharing networks[21] was encouraged, as were advisory services and Web sites, to facilitate the spreading, first round the World Bank, and then other agencies, of just-in-time development knowledge. These exercises were hugely helped by new information and communication technologies. There are now some 80 of these Thematic Groups in the World Bank alone, down from over 120 in the late 1990s; and there are smaller numbers in some of the other agencies.

In terms of our current concern with the relation between research and policy, their focus has certainly been less on knowledge generation than on knowledge dissemination. Following the words of O'Dell et al. (1998) – 'If only we knew what we know', their emphasis has principally been on making World Bank, Canadian International Development Agency (CIDA), Japan International Cooperation Agency (JICA) or DFID's existing knowledge better known to like-minded groups within their respective organizations (King and McGrath, 2004). There have been one or two groups which have clearly had a link to policy – notably the Tertiary Education Group in the World Bank, that is said to have played a supportive role in the development of the Bank's recent policy text on *Constructing Knowledge Societies: New Challenges for Tertiary Education* (World Bank, 2002b). But, overall, it would seem, to judge from the World Bank's own evaluation of *Sharing Knowledge* in the institution, that there has been insufficient connection between the Thematic Groups and the Bank's research programme (World Bank, 2003b).

In general, it could be said of several agencies which took seriously the challenge of knowledge and learning that the focus of internal knowledge sharing has been relatively low-key and almost invisible to the outside world. It has involved better agency intranets, better connectivity between headquarters and country offices, and more staff development activities. But it could hardly be called a knowledge revolution, and it does not appear to have significantly affected traditional operational work.

One of the key issues is whether agencies have rethought their organizational and professional work in terms of the new aid modalities that were analysed above. It is difficult to judge merely from the names of the groups, but it does appear that though the majority of the World Bank groups continue to represent traditional professional fields such as Early Child Development or Tertiary Education, others such as Pro-Poor Growth and Inequality, or Empowerment and Social Capital, are much more cross-cutting. However, it is in some of the bilaterals that the new approaches to aid delivery seem to be more explicitly reflected in the agency. In the Swedish International Development Cooperation Agency (Sida), for instance, there is a separate unit charged with thinking about the new ways of delivering aid, and they have produced a series of analyses of Sida polices on *Capacity Development* (Sida, 2000a), on *Sector Programme Support* (Sida, 2000b), and on *Sida at Work* (Sida, 2003). What is striking, particularly about *Sida at Work*, is that it examines in some 80 pages the new roles for Sida staff, as 'analyst', 'dialogue partner', and 'financier', over and above their continuing roles as sector specialists. The sheer complexity of the new cooperation approaches has some resonance with what we said earlier about the demands of the new aid modalities. Sida argues that 'Gradually, a technical approach has given way to a more comprehensive approach involving socio-economic and legal structures' (Sida, 2003: 29).

Naturally, Sida points to the fact that their cooperation partners continue to have primary responsibility for analytical work at all levels, from comprehensive poverty reduction strategies to specific analyses of programmes/projects. But it is difficult not to reach a conclusion that the 70 pages of *Sector Programme Support* as well as *Sida at Work* merely confirm a likely new imbalance in policy dialogue between the donor and the recipient in the new modalities of aid. This notwithstanding, *Sida at Work* provides a uniquely thoughtful and unprecedented insight, amongst bilateral donors, into the complexity of the aid process in the early twenty-first century. Despite what has been said above, Sida's attitude towards knowledge in development remains firm: 'The process of learning needs to be based on the realisation that no party can claim superior knowledge that should be superimposed on other parties' (Sida, 2003: 38).

If Sida offers one insight into organizational learning to face new knowledge conditions, DFID offers a rather different one. Sharing a similar concern to move away from the traditional role of the sectoral specialist with sectoral knowledge, the whole of the large policy divi sion in DFID has been restructured, to break down the old sector silos, and to bring new teams together to collaborate on the basic cross-cutting themes of development knowledge. Groupings now have names such as: 'Reaching the very poorest', 'Service delivery', 'Drivers of change' and 'Growth hub' (DFID, 2003).[22] DFID's research, too, has been broken out of its original separate silos and integrated into a central research department, the better to meet the overarching millennium poverty reduction goals.

By contrast, JICA has been moving in the opposite direction. From its long tradition of using generalists – in JICA as in the rest of government – to deliver projects, it has for the first time in 2003, under the influence of the KM initiative, begun to introduce sectoral expertise and sectoral teams.

Our preliminary conclusions on what is termed internal KM in the agencies, therefore, is that for the first several years of aid agencies seeking to become knowledge agencies, or learning organizations, the predominant focus was on the development of the knowledge of their own staff rather than on knowledge development in the South.

Knowledge management and sharing with partners

Even though external knowledge sharing came later and was secondary, in some agencies, the privileging of knowledge development in and with the South had been there long before the new knowledge discourse arose in the late 1990s. Sida and its research wing, the Department for Research Cooperation (SAREC), had, like the International Development Research Centre (IDRC) and the Ford and Rockefeller Foundations, been in the business of supporting Southern knowledge and research development for years. What the arrival of the knowledge-for-development discourse did was to focus much more sharply on the centrality of knowledge in aid modalities. And again the vision was perhaps clearest and most partner-oriented in the case of Sida:

> The central issue of all development cooperation is to contribute to the development of knowledge – in the partner country, in Sweden and internationally (Sida, 1997: 28).

The danger for agencies that started with several years of sorting and synthesizing their own knowledge resources – in what has been termed internal knowledge sharing – is that when they finally turn their attention to their clients and partners in the South, the agencies might well have decided on what was their priority knowledge for development. There is more than a hint of this in DFID's development of its TSPs, discussed earlier. These derived directly from the IDTs, as we saw, but it has been estimated that only a minute proportion (less than 4 per cent) of the bibliographic research resources that sustained them were taken from the South. More than 84 per cent were themselves agency-commissioned work (King and McGrath, 2004: 119). Furthermore, as DFID rethinks its now centralized research strategy, there are powerful forces suggesting that DFID's entire research strategy could be made more coherent by being organized around the MDGs. This is of course more coherent; but the question must be whether the whole process of agreeing the IDT–MDG goals, followed by the elaboration of the TSPs, and then, finally, the setting of research priorities are really a completely Northern process.

The World Bank, by contrast, has stated explicitly that not only should their repository of development knowledge be shared with clients, but that Southern research and knowledge should themselves be prioritized. For an organization which had been on its back feet in defending some of their other global knowledge initiatives, such as the Development Gateway and the Global Development Network for privileging Bank knowledge, this was a major shift. It is worth quoting at some length:

> Changing the way we think about development to integrate knowledge as a central driver of growth, security and empowerment; update our view of the Bank's business and the way we measure and value our outputs and impact – from transferring knowledge and resources, to enabling learning and building capacity.... We need to move beyond the idea of the Bank as the repository of finance and knowledge that is transferred to clients, and towards the idea of the Bank as a facilitator and enabler of client learning – the crux of capacity building, and the best way to create sustainable policy shifts and development (World Bank, 2001b: 33–4).

This is a powerful vision, and it reminds us that capacity building – so widely used in the 1960s and 1970s by Ford, Rockefeller and IDRC – had come in from the cold in the early twenty-first century. And it might appear to be the key concept that has been missing from the construction of the global development agenda with which we have been concerned.[73] In a series of studies, led by the United Nations Development Programme (UNDP), but supported in their dissemination and promotion by other donors, notably JICA, the World Bank Institute, CIDA and Deutsche Gesellschaft für Technische Zusammenarbeit (GTZ), the crucial role of capacity development has been mapped out as central to the new aid relationship (UNDP, 2001, 2002, 2003b). Indeed, capacity development is presented as a crucial complement to the global architecture of the MDGs. Like *Shaping the 21st Century* (OECD/DAC, 1996), seven years earlier, the final report of the three UNDP volumes is replete with the language of 'Ownership', 'Leadership' and 'Policy Dialogue', and, naturally, capacity development is analysed in all its main guises – individual, institutional and societal.

But there is one dimension that is, surprisingly, virtually absent from UNDP's final volume, *Ownership, Leadership and Transformation: Can We Do Better for Capacity Development?* (UNDP, 2003b), namely, the core modality of capacity development via the formal education system, and especially higher education and the maintenance of national research capacity. Almost every other kind of capacity is illustrated in the 56 case studies of successful capacity development except this, which is arguably a precondition for many of the others. This is a particularly important oversight in a volume that situates capacity development so close to the MDGs, when the MDGs themselves have nothing to say about education above the basic level.

In reviewing the most recent preoccupation of agencies with both knowledge and capacity development, we would argue that the agencies have not started with the dramatic knowledge deficits of the South, nor with the key question of how KM could assist knowledge development in the South. A continuation along their present internal trajectories could be counter-productive; it could end up making agencies more certain of what they themselves have learnt, and more enthusiastic that others should share these insights, once they have been systematized. While on the external knowledge sharing side, there is still little evidence of dramatically increased support to knowledge development in the South.

Missing elements in the linking of knowledge and policy

The last 15 years have seen the creation of the MDGs which, in the opinion of the UNDP, do 'provide a strong, unequivocal political framework to orient international development aid' (UNDP, 2003b: xiii). Whether they may also come to be seen as a new set of aid conditionalities, following the era of structural adjustment, it is too early to say.[24] The history of their construction, examined through the single lens of education, would suggest that a very specific strain of agency research contributed to this process, and that the further elaboration of the Targets through the OECD/DAC and individual agencies such as DFID drew very little from Southern research or even consultation. Particular research on education executed within the World Bank, and principally by economists, translated into a key segment of the world's global agenda for education. Some of the other IDTs or MDGs may also have been shaped by World Bank research.[25] More widely, it could be argued that the salience of key concepts such as the informal sector in international policy agendas owe their position to agency-commissioned rather than academic research (King, 1991; Bøås and McNeill, 2004).[26]

The interplay between the global agenda, the new aid modalities, and the realities of development in the economically weakest countries has been little researched, but questions need to be asked about the centrality of time-bound MDG targeting by agencies and the massive, and possibly increasing aid dependency of a substantial number of countries.

The discovery of KM and knowledge sharing by agencies, and the rediscovery of capacity development, have done little in most agencies to alter the aid relationship. It is particularly striking that the celebration of knowledge for development in agencies happens to have coincided with a period of continued deterioration of the higher education and research environments in many parts of the developing world, and especially in sub-Saharan Africa (World Bank, 2002b; UNRISD, 2004). The World Bank's identification of knowledge accumulation and application as the major drivers of economic development in the twenty-first century has served merely to underline the continuing knowledge deficits in many countries. For these states, the weak and externally dependent condition of higher education and research is doubtless a contributory factor to the erosion of the policy terrain which we described earlier, both in government and in civil society. Equally, the absence of sufficient and sustained critical work on the new development architecture in sites in the South leaves much of the agency consensus unchallenged. It is vital that national researchers, think-tanks and knowledge networks in the South engage with the structures and modalities that have emerged, and explore in detail, at both the macro and institutional levels, their implications for the ownership of knowledge and of the development project more generally.[27]

6
The Quest for Gender Equality[1]

Gita Sen

Introduction

The field of gender and development is often viewed as a sterling example of researchers and activists working together to bring about policy change. A cursory glance at the kinds of policy changes that have occurred in the latter twentieth century suggests strong confirmation for this view. Across a sweeping range of issues, from macroeconomics to human rights and political participation, feminist researchers and activists from women's movements[2] appear to have succeeded in bringing about significant changes both in discourse and in actual policy.

Furthermore, this happened in a relatively short 30-year time span during which the field of gender and development was itself evolving and taking definition. Perhaps this openness and fluidity in the analytical underpinnings of the field brought a salutary humility to the ways in which researchers were willing to listen to and learn from ground-level activists! Be that as it may, during this time policy was made, changed and shaped by the agglomeration of researchers and activists that call themselves part of the women's movement. And policy makers who rarely have time or patience to deal with the intellectual vagaries of a newly evolving field appear to have paid attention.

What lessons are there to be learned by those who attempt to create knowledge to support social policy? Is the experience of the women's movement unique or special? Was it the result of the serendipitous presence of the right people in the right places at the right times? Were there critical elements of conscious planning? And central to the concerns of this chapter, is social activism the key to effective translation of research-based knowledge into policy? On the other hand, can activism by itself effect policy change? When and to what extent is research necessary? Are different combinations of research and activism required in different circumstances? The experience of gender and development provides a rich basis for addressing some of these questions. Looking more closely at this experience offers insights into how the relationship between research and policy is mediated by politics, discourse, subjectivity and learning.

The discussion of the chapter draws from three illustrative examples of policy change: engendering macroeconomics; sexual and reproductive health and rights; and human rights, especially violence against women. In discussing these, we show that the relationship of activism to research has been far from smooth, and continues to be fraught with challenges. Nonetheless, it offers a number of lessons for how a better understanding of the politics of policy, and the politics of discourse may actually help to close the gaps between research and policy.

Illustrations of policy change

The three illustrations below raise a number of common issues that are addressed in later sections.

Illustration 1: engendering[3] macroeconomics

The field of gender and development took shape in the 1970s following the pioneering work of Ester Boserup (1970). Its evolution was informed by the critical research of feminist anthropologists and historians, many of whom drew from and counterposed their work to that of socialist historians and analysts. Particularly influential were the two volumes of anthropological writing edited by Rosaldo and Lamphere (1974) and Reiter (1975), the latter including Rubin's (1975) important essay on 'the traffic in women'; the work of historians such as Scott and Tilly (1987) who brought a gender lens to earlier gender-blind depictions of the industrial revolution; the analytical integration of production and reproduction in the research of the British 'subordination of women' group (Edholm *et al.*, 1977); and the critique of Boserup's argument that the problem for women was lack of 'integration' into development (Beneria and Sen, 1981). This research was analytically rigorous, grounded in history and ethnography, and critical. It helped the field overall to assimilate these characteristics from its early beginnings.

These analytical underpinnings also helped feminists to interpret the difficulties faced by early policy attempts to integrate women in development (Tinker, 1976; Buvinic, 1984), as well as to develop new ways of understanding the experience of organizations working with women on the ground. The 1970s were not a period of major oppositional activism on gender and development. It was rather a period of developing analytical tools, gathering experience and sharpening understanding.[4] There was not, at this time, a sharp distinction between researchers and activists; this blurring of roles may also have been due to the importance of universities in the social uprisings of the 1960s. Researchers wore the badge of activism with honour, and activists turned overnight into respected analysts and researchers.

The period of the 1970s saw the beginnings of the feminist critique of growth processes that are inimical to equity and sustainability, even as they ignore the requirements of human survival and reproduction where women hold central responsibility. Feminists were not as yet thinking or writing in terms of macroeconomics, but their work was focused on understanding the place of gender in socioeconomic systems. As such it sharpened feminist ability to use system-focused approaches that are central to macroeconomics.

This preparation came to quick fruition in the conservative policy climate of the 1980s – the Reagan–Thatcher revolution in the North and the Washington Consensus-based structural adjustment programmes promoted by the Bretton Woods institutions (BWIs) in the South. Feminists were among the early critics of structural adjustment programmes, following closely and in parallel to the critique contained in the United Nations Children's Fund's volumes on the importance of putting a human face on adjustment (Cornia *et al.*, 1987). The Women's Tent in the Nairobi conference of 1985 that was the culmination of the United Nations Decade for Women (1975–85) saw activists and researchers coming together with a powerful critique of the growth-focused development paradigm. The Development Alternatives with Women for a New Era (DAWN) network's platform *Development, Crises, and Alternative Visions: Third World Women's Perspectives* (Sen and Grown, 1987) articulated an understanding gained through research and field-based experiences.[5] It was the product of what was at the time a new and unusual process of bringing women from different geographical areas, backgrounds, and experiences together to develop a common understanding and analysis. The circles of interaction that DAWN used not only brought researchers and activists together, but also makers and shapers of policy. As a consequence, its critique spread quickly through the wider gender and development networks.

At the same time, feminist economists began addressing the problem of engendering macroeconomics directly even as their understanding of the phenomenon of globalization and its implications for the gender division of labour grew (Beneria and Roldan, 1987; DAWN, 1995). The growing work on engendering budgets and budget processes was a spin-off of this attention (Budlender, 1996).

On the ground women working in organizations were experiencing the feminization of poverty, and deepening their understanding of the impact of macropolicies beyond the traditional social sectors, health and education. The links between macroeconomic policies, poverty and inequality, environmental sustainability, and the newly emerging concern of trade policies (and later, the World Trade Organization – WTO) were articulated by an overwhelming number of the groups that took part in the 35,000 strong non-governmental organization (NGO) forum held in Beijing in 1995.[6] They also began drawing the connections to the growing crisis of violence against women and to the rise of a conservative backlash against women's autonomy and agency in the public domain. Research and activism came together powerfully and drew a promise from the new president of the World Bank that he would respond and address some of the concerns raised.[7] The period since Beijing has seen further strengthening of feminist analysis of trade,[8] and integration, albeit slowly, of women's concerns in the movement for global economic justice as represented in the World Social Forum (WSF).

Sexual and reproductive health and rights

Women's struggle for control over their bodies is currently in its second phase. The first phase occurred during the birth-control movement of the late nineteenth and early twentieth centuries. This movement was interwoven with the suffragist struggle for the recognition of women as citizens in Europe and North America, and to some extent the anti-colonial movements of that time,[9] although the relationship was by no means straightforward. The period between the first phase and the second phase that goes back to the last 30 years or so saw the population policy field and the discipline of demography grow substantially.

Population policy as it evolved in the period after the Second World War was largely Malthusian. The concern of the policy establishment in the North with protecting the North from the growing brown, yellow and black peoples of the world was barely concealed in document after document of the 1960s and 1970s. Population growth was portrayed as the single most serious threat to economic development and population control was the policy answer (Ehrlich, 1971). Despite the South versus North skirmishes over the relative importance of 'development' versus family planning in controlling population growth,[10] there was very little real challenge to this consensus about population policy.

Most demographers have had little to do with or say about the evolution of population policy. Demography developed as a largely technical discipline concerned with the calculus of birth, death and migration, with relatively little interest in social and behavioural issues.[11] Perhaps for this reason, not only have few demographers focused on policy questions, but the field as a whole was able to close itself off from attention to the causes and consequences of sexual and reproductive behaviour, and the social institutions, practices and norms within which that behaviour is embedded in different cultures and societies. It was not until the rise of the modern women's movement in the 1960s and 1970s that real change became possible in the field.

The international women's movement had coined and been using the term 'reproductive rights' for about 20 years before the paradigm shift that transformed the population field at the International Conference on Population and Development (ICPD) in Cairo in 1994. Much of this work was motivated by activist concern to challenge coercion, human rights abuses, and unethical practices in population policies and programmes.[12] A strong focus of this work was to challenge the ways in which new contraceptive technologies were introduced in family planning programmes. This activism was not matched by significant feminist research effort until the 1990s. During the 1980s feminist demographers remained concerned with the question of whether and through what pathways women's education or autonomy impact on fertility and related behaviour (Mason, 1988).

The upcoming United Nations (UN) conferences of the 1990s galvanized both research and activism. The fact that the United Nations Conference on Environment and Development (UNCED) was coming up in Rio in 1992 acted as a major challenge to the women's movement, since many major North-based environmental groups viewed population growth as a major threat. Feminist activists began a process of consolidation of a counter-position that was articulated in the *Planeta Femea* (the women's tent in the NGO Forum of UNCED) in the presence of a large number of women from environmental organizations. In the next two years, women's organizations worked together to develop a consensus position on population policy that would bridge the considerable differences and mistrust that existed among groups from different regions and backgrounds. While some of these differences were the product of mistrust of Northern by Southern groups, there were also tensions among groups within each global pole.[13] A major and conscious effort at bridging gaps and building agreement was critical in allowing the women's move-ment to turn its attention to two tasks: the first was to negotiate an alliance with the family planning lobbies, and the second was to develop the political capacity to challenge the growing bloc of religious conserva-tives that was being created by the Vatican. The success of the women's movement in accomplishing these two tasks is the history of ICPD.

Again, the role of research and activism combined was critical. Although somewhat slow to get off the ground, feminist research opened up the field in ways that brought new issues and concepts to the table. A new framework for population-related policy was created that affirmed women's right to control their fertility and meet their needs for safe, affordable and accessible contraceptives, while recognizing the social determinants, and health and rights consequences of sexual and repro-ductive behaviour (Dixon-Mueller, 1993; Correa and Reichman, 1994; Sen *et al.*, 1994). New and radical concepts such as reproductive and sexual health and rights had to be clarified in a field that had been an 'odd mixture of technocratic modelling and doomsday scenarios until then' (Antrobus and Sen, forthcoming). A significant part of this research reflected the combined and collective effort of feminist researchers, activists and a growing number of people from the policy establishment. This again was done consciously to win a place for activists at the policy table, and to build support for the paradigm shift within the policy establishment.[14]

Human rights and violence against women

Women's organizing in preparation for the 1993 International Conference on Human Rights in Vienna set the stage for the broadening of the human rights framework. Until then there had been two major contro-versies in the field of human rights. The first was the priority given by Northern governments and organizations to political rights and abuses over economic, social and cultural rights; the struggles to gain recognition for the 'right to development' during the conferences of the 1990s provided continuing evidence of this imbalance. The second controversy was over the political use of human rights by powerful countries as a stick to selectively beat countries into submission on various unrelated issues. Women's activism brought a third issue – women's human rights – squarely to the centre of the human rights debate (Bunch and Reilly, 1994). With this came the question of the universality of human rights versus practices that violate women's human rights but are upheld by some as cultural norms, for example, female genital mutilation or honour killings.

Violence against women became the lever that moved the opposition argument that there was no need for specific recognition of women's human rights. The presence of women in Vienna testifying to their experiences of violence – systematic rape and war crimes, genital cutting, domestic violence, dowry deaths, honour killings, sexual violence to name only a few – created a climate that made it possible for violence against women to be placed for the first time on the agenda of a major human rights conference. Until then, the UN and governments had tended to treat violence against women as a private, familial or cultural matter; in many instances the official approach was to treat it as a matter of abuse of male private property[15] rather than an abuse of the woman's human rights. The recognition of women's rights as human rights in Vienna in 1993 also made possible the significant advances made in Cairo in 1994 and Beijing in 1995.

This struggle brought together a powerful combination of activists who could identify and document experiences, and feminist lawyers who could translate those experiences into the legal terminology and concepts needed for negotiation. This experience of working together also gave the women's movement analytical and negotiating skills and very impor- tantly the language skills needed to become effective players in official negotiations. Women in these conferences were present not only as NGO delegates but also on official delegations; effective lobbying required rapid development of a very specific set of strategic and tactical negotiating skills that major networks developed through sheer learning by doing. Mistakes were undoubtedly made, but the ability to put tensions aside to work together and to learn from mistakes was a major reason for the effec- tiveness of the women's movement in these negotiations.

The politics of policy advocacy

The three examples above appear to indicate a relatively smooth rela- tionship between researchers and activists in the process of policy advocacy. This was not really so. It is true that the achievements of the women's movement in these situations were due in no small measure to the ability to work through internal differences and develop common positions. However, the differences were sometimes quite significant and often very difficult to transcend; sometimes the differences would be set aside in the face of a common 'enemy' only to resurface when the situation became easier.

Three sets of issues were the source of recurring tensions between researchers and activists: issues of substance, issues of power and issues of sociology. These issues were not in water-tight compartments more-over and would often be mixed up in practice.

Substantive differences often arose around the relative importance of immediate ground-level perceptions and understanding versus analytical discussion and extrapolation or abstraction. Whose 'reality' has greater validity when there are differences? While such tensions are inevitable, given the varying grounds of research and activism, they have become sharper in the era of globalization. Activists continue to function by and large where they have been,[16] but researchers have the possibility and are more often required to compare and analyse across larger geographic spans. Their generalizations have necessarily to deal with the wider variations in ground level reality this entails.

For instance, the history of population policy has varied considerably across major continental and subcontinental lines. While the traditional concerns of activists in South Asia have been about coercive practices in family planning programmes, the problem in Africa has been one of availability of services particularly in the context of HIV/AIDS. Latin America's major problem has been one of getting services through the public sector in a political context where conservative Catholicism, including the Opus Dei, is influential.[17] The unwillingness of some activists in South Asia to recognize that the issue of coercion is not all there is to the demarcation of reproductive rights created major tensions before and to a lesser extent during ICPD.[18] It required greater flexibility and a willingness to cross boundaries, something researchers tend to do more naturally and that some activists at least found difficult. Another example of tension, on the economic front this time, was the major 'crisis' that erupted in Latin America post-Beijing about the legitimacy of engaging with national or global institutions. Accusations of co-optation were in the air and issues of accountability within the movement became the hot subject of a somewhat rancorous debate.

On the surface it may appear that these were not primarily debates between researchers and activists, but between two tendencies within the women's movement. I believe nonetheless that the basis of the argument was fundamental differences in the substantive ground of experience – more local or national and specific, as associated with activism, or more global as associated with research.[19]

These differences often translate into differences of *power*. Challenges to the links between knowledge and power have a long tradition in the women's movement. Power may appear to be embodied in researchers who have access to resources and connections that activists do not. In the early days of the field of gender and development, this often took the form of a South versus North divide as Northern researchers with research grants appeared in the South to write about Southern experiences.

This has changed considerably as direct links between activist organizations in the South and funding agencies have grown. Ironically, the result has been greater 'research' demands (framing proposals, monitoring, analysis and report-writing) being imposed on organizations that have little capacity for research.[20] Activist organizations now perforce have to search for more qualified professional staff who can fulfil these requirements, and this has its own dynamic for the internal hierarchies within an organization. What has tended to happen as a result is that what used to be a struggle for power between an activist organization and external researchers has been displaced to two other levels: the level of an internal struggle within organizations, and a new form of struggle between funding agencies and organizations. The more 'technisized'[21] form of the latter struggle makes it appear more natural and more difficult to see the shift in power relations it entails.

A more symbiotic relationship between researcher and activist is now evolving as a result. In all of the illustrations given above, this symbiosis was very much in evidence. But this does not mean that the relationships are now free of tension. As organizations attempt to develop new internal relationships between research and activism, major power struggles often develop.[22] All of the 'chips' in these games of power are not on the side of research however. In the women's movement in particular, many organizations profess a strong ethos of collective action, of breaking power hierarchies and of empowering the activist. Laudable as these objectives may be, they have sometimes been naïve in their application, attributing achievement and capacity to inappropriate levels.[23] This can result in a paralytic inability to address the issue squarely. It can also lead to disillusion on the part of professional staff who are asked to go along with the practice of attributing the work they feel *they* have done to the collective, while the work done by field staff is not. Unless the place of different kinds of knowledge and their relationship to power is addressed squarely, it can leave organizations incapable of moving forward to strengthen their work. Tensions can simmer and keep resurfacing even though everyone may be willing to pull together during key moments. It can also put funding agencies or research convenors in the awkward position of having to play the arbiter, or of wielding more power as a result of the internal tension than they ought.

A closer look at the *sociology* of research and activism may provide another perspective on these issues. Tension between researchers and activists is by no means the same or evenly distributed in different countries and regions. In some locales there is very little disagreement while in others conflict appears to lurk constantly beneath a thin veneer of solidarity. Even in the same country, some relationships are smooth while others are fraught with potential for conflict. The explanation may lie in the background and history of who researchers and activists are.

My thesis is that the potential for tension is greater when researchers and activists come from similar social and economic backgrounds, but have made different life choices early on which then affect their life trajectories and life chances. Competition may sometimes appear in the guise of disagreements over the basis of knowledge or the extent of commitment to a cause. Such competition may be more or less severe depending on whether life choices once made are difficult to alter, or whether people can move more fluidly from being a researcher to being an activist and vice versa, that is, it depends on how irrevocable the choice is.[24] It is not accidental, I believe, that tensions of this sort are less severe in Europe or North America (at least until recently) where the educated segment of the labour force can move with relative ease from activist organizations to research or policy analysis. The research-activism nexus is not congruent with the researcher-activist relationship. The tensions are probably most severe in Asia[25] where the market for educated labour is demand-constrained. Tension over the control of knowledge and who gets credit for it can be quite severe in such circumstances.

This would explain why the attempt to combine research with activism is greeted with suspicion and wariness. If the researcher begins to combine in herself field-level knowledge obtained from the ground, or if the activist develops the capacity for more rigorous analysis, it can make her a far more formidable competitor in the struggle for funds and recognition. This is particularly ironic because almost everyone in the movement would argue that it is important for researchers to have activist experience and for activists to have greater analytical capacity. This may also explain why the relationship of researchers to larger, mass- or community-based organizations (CBOs) can be easier than their relationship to smaller NGOs. The social and economic background of the large majority of activists in CBOs (although not perhaps of their leadership) is often vastly different from that of most researchers, thus reducing the perception of competing interests.

Displacement of such tensions on to the loftier ground of greater or lesser sacrifice of personal interest or commitment can only serve to conceal and confuse the real dynamic of relationships. I do not hold that all the differences that surface between research and activism are only manifestations of such displacement. But the issue is present enough and important enough that it has to be addressed in a more straightforward manner. People who work within or in support of social movements are not very different from others in their susceptibility to competitive or other pressures, although the fact that they make commitments and difficult personal choices also plays an important role in shaping who they are, and setting the ideals and norms of the organizations with which they work.[26]

The politics of discourse

In the International Feminist Dialogue, a two-day meeting that preceded the WSF 2004 in Mumbai, there was an argument made that the language of human rights and reproductive rights has been so co-opted by powerful institutions that women's organizations should no longer use these concepts or the related frameworks. This is neither the first nor will it be the last time that such an argument is heard. Its source is frustration at the slow pace of change and mistrust of the organizations entrusted with change, or who may be the self-anointed agents of change.

All of the three illustrations provided above are based on very significant transformations in the language and content of discourse. One of them, ICPD, represented a full-scale paradigm shift, while the others witnessed major conceptual changes. How did this come about, and what is its significance for policy change? And why do some people believe that the change is temporary?

To understand the politics of discourse is to understand a key element of how research gets translated into policy, and the role that activism can play, both positive and negative. The typical trajectory whenever significant changes in discourse occur is that critical research supported by activism first wages a major struggle to change old concepts and frameworks and introduce new ones. In the field of gender and development, many such struggles have been waged to gain acceptance and use for concepts such as 'gender', 'empowerment', 'women's human rights', 'reproductive and sexual health', and 'sexual and reproductive rights'. But such a struggle is not a once-and-for-all event. As the new frameworks and concepts begin to be used, they are also interpreted and reinterpreted to suit the predilections of the user. In the process their meanings may become more fuzzy and multivalent with different people and institutions using the same terminology in very different ways. As Humpty Dumpty said to Alice, a word can come to mean whatever the user wants it to mean!

This is the point at which two different routes can be taken. One is that chosen by the speakers in the International Feminist Dialogue who argued that it is time to drop the use of terms that have been co-opted and, by implication, corrupted and rendered bereft of transforming power. The other route is one that I believe has more potential for moving debate forward. It is to recognize that the fact that the new terms and frameworks are being taken up by the opposition is an important sign not of failure, but of success in the first level of the struggle for change. If knowledge is power, then changing the terrain of discourse is the first but very important step. It makes it possible to fight the opposition on the ground of one's choosing.[27]

By way of example, in the pre-ICPD days, all discussion about gender or women's autonomy had to be cast in terms of its efficacy for population control. The paradigm shift of ICPD made it possible to begin to ask entirely new questions that were not focused on population control but on the guaranteeing of rights and the meeting of needs. The terms of discourse determine both what can be asked and what cannot be asked, and how it can be asked. It is very difficult within a Malthusian discursive framework to seriously entertain questions about quality of health care or the meeting of individual health needs.

Powerful institutions understand the importance of controlling discourse only too well. It is not accidental that the rise to dominance of the Washington Consensus during the 1980s and 1990s was mirrored by a very real decline in the ability of the United Nations Development Programme (UNDP) or other institutions outside the Bretton Woods system to find the resources for research or knowledge building.[28]

But winning the struggle over discourse (as happened at Vienna or Cairo) is only the first step. The greater the victory the more the likelihood that others will attempt to take over the discourse and subvert its meaning. The battle is not over; it has just begun. The real struggle to transform the new discourse into effective policy change has to move on to the level of changes in institutions, laws, practices and norms. In this struggle, terms and language will be interpreted and reinterpreted. This fact does not automatically mean co-optation. It simply means the struggle has moved on to another phase. Giving up one's concepts and frameworks at this stage is a sure guarantee of losing both the battle and the war!

Are activists or researchers more likely to follow one or the other trajectory? I do not believe that the research-activism distinction is a particularly strong predictor of behaviour in this regard. However, those who were more involved in making the change in discourse happen in the first place are more likely to want to hold on to it, and this is but natural. Those more distant from the making of discursive change and who are more interested in knowing whether it has made impact on the ground are less likely to be patient. For the field of gender and development, much of the recent discursive change that has occurred was struggled over in the terrain of UN conferences, a locale far removed, not only physically but also in terms of cultural and sociological distance, from many in the women's movement. Those who were present when the negotiations were going on in conferences tended to be from global networks whose links to activists on the ground may be ambivalent, but whose connections to researchers may be stronger.

It may be useful to reflect here on the changes of the last few decades in the way in which social policy change occurs. I do not possess a clear understanding of the time phasing of discursive pressure versus activist mobilization on the ground in earlier historical periods. But more than the time-phasing question, the fact that changes in discourse and changes in ground-level mobilization have happened in the recent past in different geographic and political locales may be crucial. Ground-level mobilization (except perhaps for the WSF and anti-WTO rallies) still happens, by and large, at *local and national* and, possibly, at regional levels. This is especially true for the women's movement. But the struggles over language and discourse have happened in the first instance at the *global* level, particularly for many in the South. The gap between the two is literally oceanic! Great efforts have to be made to communicate the content, meanings and implications of the conceptual changes that have occurred. And this *has* to happen if activists in local and national locales are to play the role of interlocutors of governments to ensure implementation – the changes in laws, institutions, practices and mind-sets – that are necessary in the next phase.

The transformation of discourse into policy change – implementation in a word – is bound to be a time of great turmoil and clashes of interests as those who were favoured by the status quo ante are challenged. Backlashes and foot-dragging are par for this course. This is also therefore the time that requires clarity, ingenuity, flexibility and, above all, stamina on the part of those who are attempting to change social policy. Ambiguity and confusion within social movements may weaken the potential for real change. Especially, this is not the time to be backtracking on hard-won concepts and frameworks on the grounds that they have been co-opted. The need of the hour is to push hard so that actual changes can occur.

Implications for the making of social policy change

How effective has the combined research and activism of the women's movement been in making an impact on social policy? The changes in discourse have been almost monumental in some instances. Changes on the ground within countries have been more mixed as might be expected, and have depended on the nature of the barriers faced and the capacity of the movement to chart a clear course for itself as the discussion in the previous section suggests.

Three sets of issues are particularly important in this regard: the nature of the 'opposition'; the positions of allies; and the internal capacity and self-reflexivity of the protagonists.

In the case of gender and development, explicit opposition has come from social and religious conservatives opposed to gender equality at global, regional, national and local levels; this opposition continues until today, and is able at different times to mobilize support from powerful governments. Although the overt issue is often abortion or 'family values', this is a veneer for real and implacable opposition to the very idea of gender equality. For the gender and development field therefore, there is no compromise possible with this strand of opposition; the world-views are diametrically opposed.

The action of the BWIs has been more indirect and complex. As stated earlier, the women's movement was one of the early opponents of the Washington Consensus. Globalization, insecurity of livelihoods and inequality have proceeded in pace with the entry of women into labour markets and the breaking of traditional barriers. The BWIs are not on the same side as the social conservatives on the issue of gender equality (World Bank, 2000b) but they would like to believe that their policies are favourable to women. The evidence does not however point in this direction.

The presence and articulation of these two sets of actors have shaped both research and activism on gender and development. The relationship to allies has been even more complex. On issues of reproduction, sexuality and women's human rights, the traditional family planning lobbies have in the course of the hammering out of the Vienna, Cairo and Beijing agreements become the partners of the women's movement. But not everyone among them is happy. Some family planning organizations and demographers continue to believe that ICPD was a mistake, and that a narrower focus on family planning is more likely to lead to greater funding and more effective policies. While these are a minority, some of them hold positions of power and influence.

The relationship between the women's movement and another important ally, the movement for global economic justice is quite complex (Sen and Correa, 2000; Petchesky, 2003; Antrobus and Sen, forthcoming). Some organizations and individual members of the latter believe that the women's movement represents a narrow identity politics without transformative potential. Many are reluctant to internalize the implications of the 'personal as political' in their own lives. Worse, some are allied to the most implacable opponents of gender equality – the religious conservatives – in the name of a common platform on poverty eradication, debt removal or cultural conservation. Expanding its space within the global justice movement and transforming these positions has been extremely difficult for women activists, and is an ongoing struggle.[29]

Engaging in these relationships with allies and opponents has been essential for the field of gender and development to really be able to transform policy. But the women's movement's own capacity to engage has had many sociological limitations. Challenging the BWIs, for instance, requires familiarity with the concepts and language of mainstream economics, but very few women are actually trained as economists. Women also have relatively little experience with making policy since they have, by and large and with few exceptions, been outside the mainstream of policy institutions and structures, and even marginalized from the institutions of representative democracy. They have little experience, as a result, of the politics or mechanics of policy making and implementation. Women also have little background in negotiating power within large organizational structures such as bureaucracies or other institutions of the state, which men have dominated from time immemorial. This may result in their falling back to personalized, 'familial' modes of dealing with power, with which they may feel more comfortable but which may be inappropriate and ineffective.

These weaknesses have often meant that feminist activists are more comfortable with oppositional politics that requires them to be on the streets rather than in the offices and corridors where negotiations occur and power is brokered. This is not a problem for feminists alone but for all social policy whose protagonists (dalits, racial or ethnic minorities, indigenous peoples) have been historically marginalized from political power.

Conclusion

The introduction to this chapter contained a set of questions about the lessons that the experience of gender and development provides for the making of social policy. Some answers have been developed although they are uneven and in some cases fragmentary. Nonetheless, there is an important set of lessons to be learned. While the experience of the women's movement certainly contains unique and special elements deriving from the nature of gender power in society, it has much to offer for a reflection on the relationship of social research to social activism.

When dominant social paradigms have to be changed, one is inevitably in the terrain of power where a combination of research, analysis and activism is essential for the protagonists of change. But the relationship between researchers and activists is by no means simple, and requires careful negotiation and great patience if it is to fulfil its potential. In such situations, neither research by itself nor activism by itself can bring about change in policy discourse or policy implementation. Different combinations may be necessary in different circumstances, but the two must come together nonetheless. The terrain of power in which social change movements have to operate is a complex one where opponents can be obdurate or wily, where alliances can shift like quicksand. Self-reflexivity, patience and stamina are essential ingredients for forward movement.

7
Global Social Policy Reform
Bob Deacon

Introduction

This chapter addresses the challenge of global social policy reform and the relationship between ideas and politics in processes of policy change. To write by oneself 'What is to be done?' is a foolhardy exercise when the task at hand requires an effective movement for shifting us from a world framed by the idea of global neoliberalism to one framed by the idea of global social reformism or global social justice. This has to be a collective endeavour emerging out of an emancipatory counter-hegemonic project rooted in the emerging transnational civil society. However, following Gramsci, I do believe that ideas matter and, backed by institutional power, make a difference. In this sense, there is a role for 'organic intellectuals' in attempting to bridge the disparate struggles of particular interests (which are generated by the globalization process) into a vision that might facilitate a more inclusive and solidaristic globalization. As Cox (1999: 26) argued, 'the challenge is to bridge the differences among the variety of groups disadvantaged by globalisation so as to bring about a common understanding of the nature and consequences of globalisation, and to devise a common strategy towards subordinating the world economy to a regime of social equity'.

In a globalized world this struggle has to take place at several levels simultaneously including the local, national and international. Within this context this chapter will attempt to address aspects of the recent and ongoing struggle of ideas between a neoliberal approach to social policy at a national, regional and global level and the (re)emergence of more equitable approaches at all levels. It also makes some suggestions for how this more progressive approach to globalization might be

144

furthered by intellectuals and research activities within and around United Nations (UN) agencies and other international organizations, and considers some possible objections to these proposals.

The focus of the chapter is social policy or, more particularly, global social policy. Social policy within one (capitalist or market-based) country may be understood as those mechanisms, policies and procedures used by governments, working with other actors, to alter the *ab-initio* distributive and social outcomes of economic activity. These mechanisms and policies may be conceptualized as being constituted of three strands. Redistribution mechanisms alter, usually in a way as to make more equal the distributive outcomes of economic activity. Regulatory activity frames and limits the activities of business and other private actors normally so that they take more account of the social consequences of their activities. The articulation and legislation of rights leads to some more or less effective mechanisms to ensure citizens might access their rights. Social Policy within one country is made up then of Social Redistribution, Social Regulation and the promulgation of Social Rights. Social policy within the world's most advanced regional cooperation (the European Union/EU) also consists of supranational mechanisms of redistribution across borders, regulation across borders and a statement of rights that operates across borders.

Global social policy is, by extension, the mechanisms, policies and procedures used by intergovernmental and international organizations, working with other actors to do *two* things: first influence and guide *national* social policy and second provide for a supranational or *global* social policy. Within this second sense Global Social Policy is about global social redistribution, global social regulation and global social rights. Global social policy in this sense embraces the emerging mechanisms of global social transfer (for example, the Global Fund to Fight AIDS, Tuberculosis and Malaria [hereafter referred to as the Global Fund]; differential drug pricing; and the projected Global Social Trust Network), global social regulation (the UN global compact, core labour standards, international food quality regulation) and global social rights (the advancement up the UN agenda of social rights and their monitoring and enforcement through soft law). One of the questions in this chapter is whether this concept of 'global social policy' (Deacon *et al.*, 1997) has taken root among scholars and international organizations as a way of thinking about the international policy that is necessary to re-embed free floating global capital in a set of international institutions which might ensure that the global economy has a social or public purpose.

The chapter is structured as follows.

- First, the analytical framework for understanding the role of ideas in policy making is briefly set out.
- Secondly, it examines the long decline and recent reassertion of the idea of equity and universalism as an organizing principle for national social policy within the social policy discourse within and between international organizations.
- Thirdly, it considers the idea of global social policy as international redistribution, regulation and rights, and asks whether this concept has taken root. The section will show that not only is there a substantial amount of scholarly work articulating a global social reformist project within which global social redistribution, global social regulation and global social rights plays an important part but also that this approach is now entering the global policy making agenda.
- Finally, the chapter turns to the institutional framework of global social governance and addresses the problem of the stalemated and stalled institutional and policy reform debates surrounding them and finally asks how progress towards a more socially just global social policy might be made despite this situation. Here we consider the recent emergence of reformist inclined global social policy making through international networks, task forces and projects. And we ask how these might be steered towards a more coherent global social reformist political project in alliance with other global social actors from below, and whether a global counter hegemonic project is re-emerging.

The struggle over ideas matters

In my view, ideas about what constitutes desirable national and international social policy in a globalizing context as articulated and influenced by epistemic communities within and around international organizations are every bit as important in influencing national and international social policy as the ('perceived') constraints of a deregulated global economy. Bøås and McNeill (2004) have discussed the relationship between institutional power and the power of ideas in social development and argue that 'powerful states (notably the USA), powerful organisations (such as the IMF [International Monetary Fund]) and even, perhaps, powerful disciplines (economics) exercise their power by "framing" (the terms of the policy debate), which serves to limit the power of potentially radical ideas to achieve change'.

Within a matrix of state and global institutional power ideas do have a part to play in both sustaining those relations of power and in challenging them even if radical or socially progressive ideas have had a hard time of it in the last decades (Weiss *et al.*, 2005).

In terms of theoretical reference points, we need then to include the work of Haas (1992 and so on) on epistemic communities. Focusing on national states, he concluded that 'epistemic communities (networks of knowledge based experts) play a part in . . . helping states identify their interests, forming the issues for debate, proposing specific policies, identifying points for negotiation' (Haas, 1992). The same can be said about international epistemic communities, their associated think-tanks and invisible colleges and the shaping of an international social policy agenda (Stone, 1996, 2000). But equally important is the work on transnational social classes and the associated international class struggle that is identified within this framework by Sklair (2001) and others. If national welfare state formation was in part the outcome of class (and gender and ethnic struggle [Williams, 1987]) and the resultant formation of cross class (and gender and ethnic) alliances so will be any transnational social policy. To this we must add the concept of hegemonic struggle from Gramsci as used by Gill (1993, 2003), Cox (1995) and others. As early as 1993, Gill and Law were suggesting that a counter-hegemonic bloc (to global neoliberalism) existed in embryo in the shape of Amnesty International, Greenpeace, Oxfam and the World Council of Churches. This was before The World Social Forum and the alliance of Brazil and China with India creating the G20. Arrighi (1993) even suggested at that point that 'the next hegemony would have to be world social democracy'. Within the same debate it is interesting to note, however, that post-modernism was influencing Cox (1993: 286) to depart from the search for a new progressive hegemony and suggested a search for 'a new form of world order; post-hegemonic in its recognition of co-existing universalistic civilisations, post-Westphalian in its restructuring of political authority into a multi-level system and post-globalisation in its acceptance of the legitimacy of different paths towards the satisfaction of human needs'. Whatever view we take about the desirability of a *global* social democratic hegemony (within which a major role would be played by global social policy mechanisms of redistribution, regulation and rights) compared to a decentred globalization with strong *regional* social policies the concept of hegemonic struggle is I believe a useful reference point for scholarly work on the global struggle for a post-neoliberal global economic and social policy. This chapter is written within the context of this kind of understanding of how global social policy is being made and changed. The question of whether to privilege a global or regional strategy is returned to at the end.

The fall and rise of universalism in international discourse about national social policy

Before turning to the question of the emerging global social policy, this section of the chapter stays at the level of national social policy and national social development and reviews the role of ideas within and between international organizations in influencing the debate about desirable national social policy. The focus is the retreat within international social policy discourse during the 1980s and 1990s from the idea of universal entitlement to social provision and welfare and its replacement by the idea of targeted and selective allocations to the poor with private provision for the better-off. This tendency is now in retreat, as I show below.

In the context of work on the making of post-communist national social policy, I argued and demonstrated that:

> the opportunity created by the collapse of communism for global actors to shape the future of (national) social policy has been grasped enthusiastically by the dominant social liberal tendency in the World Bank. In alliance with social development NGOs [non-governmental organizations] who are being given a part to play especially in zones of instability, a social safety net future is being constructed. This ... is challenging powerfully those defenders of universalist and social security based welfare states to be found in the European Union and ILO [International Labour Organization] (Deacon *et al.*, 1997: 197).

The struggle between 'Europe' and 'America' to fashion the social policy of post-communist states continues with many countries still balancing between these two forces/approaches (Deacon, 2000b). The Bank itself has recently reflected upon this story in terms of the attempt to move countries towards more privatized and individualized funded pension schemes.

> When examining the circumstances that enabled pension privatisation ... it turned out that the driving forces of pension privatisation proved to be the neo-liberally minded ministries of finance and economics, backed by the International Financial Institutions' policy advice and financial support (Holzmann *et al.*, 2003: 68).

More generally Orenstein (2003: 188) goes on in the same volume to suggest that, while path dependency may be a factor limiting radical reform and that historical–institutional theories and path dependency may explain a lot about why countries adapt innovations in particular ways to suit their conditions, 'countries reform in response to global and regional models, under the influence of norms and ideas spread by the leading international organisations and epistemic communities of the day'.

He continues to argue for analysts of policy change to take account of what he calls the 'Global Politics of Attention'.

> Why has the World Bank focused so much attention on promoting pension policy diffusion in Central and Eastern Europe ... are [these] states seen as targets of opportunity because of ongoing economic transformation and the impending European Union accession process ... are [these] countries seen by others as global pension reform leaders and thus potential models? ... whatever the reason it would seem important to investigate further the link between the internal processes of global policy advocates and global patterns of policy diffusion (Orenstein, 2003: 189).

In a later paper for the United Nations Research Institute for Social Development (UNRISD) (Deacon, 2000a), I subsequently argued that certain tendencies in the globalization process and certain policy positions adopted by international organizations give cause for concern with regard to social policy *in more southern and more underdeveloped economies*. My concern with this emerging consensus was that the coexistence of four tendencies would undermine an equitable and universalist approach to social policy in a social development context. These tendencies were:

- The World Bank's continuing belief that governments should only provide minimal or basic levels of social provision and social protection.
- The Organisation for Economic Co-operation and Development's (OECD's) Development Assistant Committee's concern (subscribed to in Geneva 2000 by the UN as well as the Bank and IMF under the banner of the Millennium Development Goals/MDGs) to focus on only basic education and health care with its new international development targets.
- International NGOs' (INGOs') continuing self-interest in winning donor contracts to substitute for government social services.

- The moves being made within the World Trade Organization (WTO) to speed the global market in private health, social care, education and insurance services.

My concern was that where state provides only minimal and basic level health and social protection services the middle classes of developing and transition economies would be enticed into the purchase of private social security schemes, private secondary and tertiary education and private hospital level medical care that are increasingly being offered on a cross border or foreign investment presence basis. The result would be predictable. We know that services for the poor are poor services. We know that those developed countries that do not have universal public health provision at all levels and public education provision at all levels are not only more unequal but also more unsafe and crime ridden. Unless the middle class is also catered for by state provision good quality social provision cannot be sustained. This was the prospect for many countries that might buy into this new development paradigm.

In other words, while in practice most West European universalistic welfare states are proving to be largely sustainable in the face of neoliberal globalization,[1] the global hegemonic approach to social policy making in the context of development was still a safety net or residual approach. This concern was echoed by both Townsend (2002) and Tendler (2002) within the context of an UNRISD-sponsored research project mentioned below.

How did the idea of social policy geared to securing greater equity through processes of redistribution and universal social provision get so lost in the context of the global discourse about desirable social policy? Four reasons might be offered. Globalization in terms of the form it took in the 1980s and 1990s was primarily a neoliberal political project born at the height of the transatlantic Thatcher–Reagan alliance. This flavoured the anti-public provision discourse about social policy within countries and contributed to a challenge to the idea of the EU's social policy agenda. The collapse of the communist project, coinciding as it did with the height of neoliberalism, gave a further push to the rise of the myth of the marketplace. Most importantly, the perceived negative social consequences of globalization generated a new concern for the poor. In the name of meeting the needs of the poorest of the poor, the 'premature' or 'partial' welfare states of Latin America, South Asia and Africa were challenged as serving only the interests of a small privileged work force and elite state employees. A new alliance was to be struck between the Bank and the poor (see Graham, 1994; Deacon *et al.*, 1997).

The analysis of the privileged and exclusionary nature of these provisions made by the Bank was accurate. However by destroying the public state services for this middle class in the name of the poor, the politics of solidarity, which requires the middle class to have a self-interest in public provision which they fund, was made more difficult. The beneficiary index measures of the Bank showing how tertiary education spending, for example, benefited the elite contributed in no small measure to this development. The Bank's technical expertise was ill-informed about the political economy of welfare state building which requires cross-class alliances in defence of public expenditure. Once again American exceptionalism (in this case in terms of its residual welfare state) was sold as the desirable norm. Finally in the late 1980s and 1990s the self-confidence of defenders of the social democratic and other equitable approaches to social policy was temporarily lost. The critics of neoliberal globalization came to believe their worst-case prognosis.

Are there signs of a shift in the global discourse leading to a reassertion of the politics of social solidarity and universalism? There are a number of global initiatives that have the aim of re-establishing the case for, and finding ways of implementing, universal public provisioning as part of an equitable social policy in Southern countries. Among them are:

1. The UNRISD research programme on Social Policy in a Development Context has the stated objective to 'move (thinking) away from social policy as a safety net ... towards a conception of active social policy as a powerful instrument for development working in tandem with economic policy'.
2. The rethinking presently being undertaken within the ILO concerning the sustainability of its traditional labourist approach to social protection. Particularly notable is the Socio-Economic Security In Focus work programme which is searching for new forms of universalistic social protection such as categorical (by age) cash benefits to complement the very limited coverage in the South of work-based social security schemes. Good practices being revealed within this programme could inform southern social policy making.
3. The report of the UN Secretary-General (E/CN.5/2001/2) (see ECOSOC, 2000) on 'Enhancing social protection and reducing vulnerability in a globalizing world', prepared for the February 2001 Commission for Social Development, almost became an important mile-stone in articulating a UN social policy. Among the positive features of the report were: (a) the fact that it was the first comprehensive UN

statement on social protection; (b) the thrust of its argument was that social protection measures serve both an equity-enhancing and an investment function and such measures need to be a high priority of governments and regions; and (c) it argued that social protection 'should not (serve only) as a residual function of assuring the welfare of the poorest but as a foundation for promoting social justice and social cohesion'. It has to be said, however, that discussion on even this paper became bogged down at the Commission and was never approved. It remains a non-paper. While the EU were supportive, the G77 wished again to link it to issues of global financing and governance arrangements (Langmore, 2001). The North–South impasse on global social standards stemming from the labour standards and global social policy principles stand-offs bedevilled the Commission's work. This demonstrates the importance of linking global social polices of redistribution to global social policies that attempt to set norms for improved Southern country social policies.

4. The 2004 meeting of the Commission on Social Development (47th Session on 4–13 February 2004) seems to have managed to avoid this pitfall in terms of its discussion of the issue of Improving Public Sector Effectiveness. However the Report of the Secretary General on this topic (E/CN.5/2004/5) (see ECOSOC, 2003) did contain among its recommendations the sentiment that international cooperation should 'include the elaboration of norms and guidelines . . . on the respective roles and responsibilities of the public and private sector' (para 59a) but such an idea did not find expression in the (advanced unedited version) of the agreed conclusions now published on the United Nations Department of Economic and Social Affairs (UNDESA) web pages. These agreed conclusions rather stress 'that each government has primary responsibility for its own economic and social development, and the role of national policies and development strategies cannot be overemphasised' (para 7). On the more central question of the issue of universalism versus targeting and the balance of public and private provision, the agreed conclusions are very much in favour of universalism and equity. 'The Commission emphasise the crucial role of the public sector in, *inter alia*, the provision of equitable, adequate and accessible social services for all so as to meet the needs of the entire population' (para 1) and again in the context of assessing the choice between public and private provision the Commission notes that while services can be provided by private entities it also 'reaffirms that any reform of public service delivery

should aim at promoting and attaining the goals of universal and equitable access to those services by all' (para 12).

5. Perhaps it is within attempts to steer developing countries towards the meeting of the MDGs that are, after all, focused on *basic* education and *basic* health and *basic* sanitation and water services that we should look to see if my earlier concern that these would lead to targeted residualism was soundly based or not. Certainly the United Nations Development Programme's (UNDP's) *Human Development Report* (2003), which focuses on these goals, balances in an interesting way a focus on basic services for the poor with a concern for equity. In general terms it firstly reasserts some of the lessons of high human development achieving countries. In high achievers such as Botswana, Kerala in India and Cuba, 'public finance was adequate and equitable. In high-achieving countries political commitment is reflected not just in allocations of public spending to health and education but also in their equity' (UNDP, 2003a: 87).

Recognizing the concern of the Bank and others that none-the-less public spending on health and education can be 'captured' by the better off, it strikes a balance between the need to maintain public expenditure for all social groups while also giving priority to the poor. In education it asserts the need to increase expenditure on primary education (to benefit the poor), but at the same time argues: 'Still, additional resources are needed for higher education as well if countries are to build capacity to compete in the global economy – but not at the cost of primary education. Entire education budgets need to increase' (UNDP, 2003a: 94). Within health policy the balancing of the concern with equity with a pro poor focus is handled by arguing for rationing and regulatory measures that ensure some health service workers are directed to work for the benefit of the poor. Thus for example countries could 'use service contracts to require medical personnel to spend a certain number of years in public service' (UNDP, 2003a: 101). The report notes that in some regions, for example Latin America, there has been a massive push to private health provision because of pressures to liberalize combined with low public sector health budgets. Here it is concerned that 'because managed care organisations attract healthier patients, sicker patients are being shifted to the public sector. This two-tier system undercuts the pooling of risks and undermines cross-subsidies between healthier and more vulnerable groups' (UNDP, 2003a: 113). Apart from addressing these concerns about within-country equity the report's main thrust is to argue for a global contract between richer and poorer countries to ensure a greater degree of global equity. We return to this in the next section.

It will be important to track this issue of reaching the poor while maintaining equity through the work of the Millennium Project through which the UN hopes to meet the Development Goals.

While attempts to restore the case for an equitable approach to social policy may not be unsurprising coming from UN agencies, a more important indicator as to whether the global ideological tide is shifting would be what the World Bank is saying. A Nordic evaluation of the 2000/2001 World Bank Development Report on Poverty (Braathen, 2000) concluded that although the Bank at least at the discursive level had shifted from its 1990 focus of social paternalism to a 2000 focus on social liberalism and even social corporatism within which the poor are to be given a voice, it still did not embrace in any significant way the social radicalism approach which would involve redistributive policies, except perhaps in the sphere of land reform.

The *World Development Report 2004* (World Bank, 2003a), which focused on making services work for poor people, suggests that there might be some movement. There is a tension within the text (and probably among the authors) between the position that much public spending by developing countries benefits the rich and is therefore to be refocused on the poor (for example, figure 2, page 4) and the argument that 'cross class alliances' between the poor and non poor are needed to pressure governments to 'strengthen public sector foundations for service delivery' (figure 10.1, page 180). Most striking is the assertion that 'In most instances making services work for poor people means making services work for everybody while ensuring poor people have access to those services. Required is a coalition that includes poor people and significant elements of the non-poor. There is unlikely to be progress without substantial "middle class buy-in" to proposed reforms' (World Bank, 2003a: 60). This section of the report goes on to quote the words of Wilbur Cohen, US Secretary of Health, Education and Welfare under President Lyndon Johnson in the 1960s: 'Programmes for Poor People are Poor Programmes'. The report itself is extraordinarily complicated in its recommendations and prescriptions and concludes with a rejection of the one-size-fits-all approach, which the Bank used to be accused of when it tried to sell Chile to the world. Instead it adopts an eight-sizes-fits-all model. Which model is to be applied depends on such aspects as the capacity of government, its openness to influence by the poor and the degree of homogeneity of the country. At least two of the models involve a strong emphasis on government being the major provider at either national or local level.

It is interesting to note that a Finnish economist was influential in leading some of the thinking of this report. This pattern whereby Nordic countries have sought to engage with Bank neoliberal economists to shift the terms of the discourse is reflected also in the work of the large Trust Fund for Environmentally and Socially Sustainable Development (TFESSD) funded by Norway and Finland. A seminar in June 2003 on progress of this fund drew the same conclusion about the significance of an emerging paradigm shift inside the Bank on these issues. My conclusion is that the intellectual tide has turned against the feared neoliberal social policy prescriptions arguing everywhere at a *national* level for privatization and targeted benefits only for the poor. The restoration of the case for good quality public services universally available with additional measures to ensure they are accessed by the poor is once again being made. We now turn to whether we can see signs of the case being made for transnational or *global* social policies of redistribution and equity.

Global social policy: has its time come?

Is the case for a *global* social policy of redistribution, regulation and rights being put by scholars and listened to by policy advocates within and around international organizations? In 1997 my colleagues and I asserted: 'There is now a global social policy, constituted of global redistributive mechanisms, global regulatory mechanism, elements of global provision and empowerment' (Deacon *et al.*, 1997). Given this, we went to on to argue our preference for

> a global social reformist project which would call for more rather than less redistribution of resources between states, for more rather than less global social and labour regulation as framework for the operation of corporations, for more rather than less authority to be given to supranational bodies to intervene in the affairs of states where those states fail their citizens.

The argument continues by insisting on the linkages between the elements.

> There should be no free trade without global social regulation. There should be no global social regulation without global redistribution.

To ensure citizens (and not their governments) benefit there should be no global social redistribution without the empowerment of citizens before a global court of social rights. Trade, regulation, redistribution and empowerment go hand in hand.

In many ways all that has happened since has been the unfolding of global politics of this project and its stumbling on four counts:

(i) the unilateralism of the United States;
(ii) the social protectionism of the EU;
(iii) the opposition of many Southern governments and voices to a Northern driven agenda especially when the resources to fund one key element of the matrix – redistribution – is missing; and
(iv) a concern that this modernist project does not respect immense cultural differences. As Yeates (2001: 169) put it: 'It must be acknowledged that historical, cultural, ideological, religious and institutional differences render the pursuit of "universal" public goods, or an agreed global cosmopolitan form of progress particularly difficult'.

Nonetheless others within academia continued to develop the idea of a global social policy. Townsend and Gordon (2002: 421) acknowledge that 'what remains is perhaps the most difficult: to bring about extensive redistribution of resources between and within countries to eradicate poverty and establish decent human rights'. But they argue that this objective 'is more plausible to world opinion than it was even five years ago'. George and Wilding (2002) devote a whole chapter to 'The Future of Global Social Policy'. They argue for seven major roles for social policy at a global level.

- The promotion and establishment of basic human rights at an international level.
- To supplement and complement national social policy (because of cross-border social issues: drugs, AIDS, crime, migration).
- To create an international level playing field.
- To raise standards internationally by action at the global level.
- To reduce poverty and inequalities and to provide a safety net for global capitalism.
- To provide the services which global capitalism needs to survive and prosper (environmental law, employment law, migration regulation).

- To promote a sense of one inextricably linked global world (bringing into being the emergent ideas of global citizenship and global responsibility).

To achieve all of this, they argue: 'global social policy will be multi dimensional – a mix of regulation, redistribution, provision of services and guaranteeing of basic rights' (George and Wilding, 2002: 192). They conclude that the bringing into being of such a comprehensive global social policy will require 'creative thinking about...a radically new approach to global governance' (George and Wilding, 2002: 210). This is something we return to in the next section.

The case for a social democratic approach to the management of globalization has been made by scholars working in disciplines other than social policy. Political scientists (Patomäki, 1999; Patomäki and Teivainen, 2004; Held, 2004; Lent, 2004) are among such contributors. The political desirability and viability of this wider global social demo-cratic project will be returned to in the closing section of the chapter. The next section of this chapter, keeping its focus on social policy, examines in some detail proposals and ideas arising across the three dimensions of *global redistribution, global social regulation and global social rights* with a main focus on the polices, practicalities and politics of redistribution.

Global social redistribution, regulation and rights

In the context of widening global inequity there is a case for *global redistribution* and for establishing a global levy through international taxation and other means. How might this new money be spent? How might international social transfers take place? What mechanisms for global resource allocation might be developed? Who would decide and on what criteria would allocations be made? Are there steps being taken upon which this project could be built? Some initial answers to these questions are suggested below. How far these are developed further in practice will be the outcome of a period of international and suprana-tional debate and consensus building.

It is likely that steps towards a formal system of global redistribution that might eventually involve a Global Tax Authority and a Global Social Affairs Ministry will build upon firstly existing ad hoc mecha nisms and, secondly, proposals for such mechanisms that are already within the global policy debate. Among existing mechanisms for inter-national redistribution are the ones used by the Global Fund (Global

Fund, 2003). It uses a combination of criteria and mechanisms to allocate resources where they are needed most in the world. Using the World Banks' categorization of countries into low and middle income, the Global Fund firstly distinguishes between low-income countries which are fully eligible for monies and lower-middle-income countries which must match international funds with national funds and focus activities on the poor and vulnerable and aim to be self-sufficient over time. A few upper-middle-income countries are also eligible in much the same way as lower-middle-income countries if they have exceptional need based on disease burden indicators.

In this case the procedure used for allocating funds within the constraints above is based on a competition between bids from Country Co-ordinating Mechanisms (CCMs) within each eligible country. A partnership is aimed at between the Global Fund and national political effort that also embraces, through the CCMs, national partners drawn from the private sector, the professions and users groups. Where governments are non-functioning, the applications can be made for NGOs. A board of internationally appointed technical experts adjudicate between competing applications using the following list of criteria: epidemiological and socioeconomic criteria, political commitment (of recipient governments), complementarity (to national effort), absorptive capacity (of governance mechanisms), soundness of project approach, feasibility, potential for sustainability, and evaluations and analysis mechanism in place. There are arguments for and against this responsive mode of resource allocation. Such an approach might miss the most needy who are unable to bid but it does involve a partnership between national and global effort. At the same time there is room for debate about the implicit conditionality built into the allocation mechanism. Good national governance is likely to be rewarded (except where it is recognized that no effective government exists). On the other hand a global fund that simply poured money into the coffers of a corrupt national government is likely to be criticized. All of the above criteria in various combinations are eminently suitable for decision making about the allocation of monies arising from a proposed Global Levy. They might be used either in response to bids or in the context of a top-down planning/allocation system. Details could vary depending on whether the monies were to be used for health or education or social protection purposes.

Critics (Ollila, 2003) have, however, pointed to a worrying aspect of the Global Fund and other initiatives, such as the Global Alliance for Vaccination and Immunization (GAVI) based upon research undertaken within the context of the Globalism and Social Policy Programme.[2] The concern is that such funds lack democratic accountability and detract from more systematic processes of global health funding which could be developed under the auspices of the World Health Organization (WHO) (Ollila, 2003: 53). These criticisms stem from a wider concern that partnerships between multilateral agencies and corporate interests, such as those involved in some of the ad hoc health funds, may erode the existing government-based multilateral system rather than lead to its strengthening and democratization (Martens, 2003). My point would be that some of the technical allocation mechanisms used by the Global Fund might be built upon by a democratized and strengthened global social governance system within the context of the sustainable resources available from a Global Levy based on global taxation.

An idea on the drawing board and ready to be experimented with is that of the Global Social Trust Network (Cichon *et al.*, 2003). It builds on the idea and practice of social partnerships that fund social protection in many richer countries, seeking to extend this to international social partnerships between people in richer countries and those needing social protection in poorer countries. It will involve resources voluntarily committed (at the suggested level of 5 Euro a month or 0.2 per cent of monthly income) by individuals in OECD countries via the agency of social partner organizations such as Trade Unions or National Social Security funds. National Social Trust Organizations would then be established in both donor countries and recipient countries and transfers would be organized through a Global Board with technical assistance provided, in this case by the ILO. Monies would then be spent by the National Social Trust Organizations with poorer countries in partnership with embryonic social protection mechanisms at the local level. One suggestion is that the Global Social Trust Network would finance universal pensions at the level of one dollar a day. Pensions are recognized as being a very good cash benefit that actually meets the needs of whole families within extended family networks in poorer countries. The Director of the Social Protection Network of the World Bank has commented favourably upon the ideas so long as the payments are linked to its Poverty Reduction Strategy Papers (PRSPs) process (Cichon *et al.*, 2002). These ensure that Countries do not receive cheap loans from the Bank or have debt written off unless there is a public and transparent policy process in place within the recipient country to reduce poverty. There is room for discussion as to whether the priority for international social protection expenditure should be old-age pensions or, as favoured by Townsend (2002: 368), universal child benefits. Any Global Levy could usefully provide additional resources to put into this Global Social Trust and thereby build upon the eloquent idea of the international social partnership embodied in it. The Global Levy proposed here could also supplement incomes being argued for, or already being collected for, other global funds such as those for cheap drugs or those for the World Water Contract (Petrella, 2001).

This proposed Global Levy, in addition to building on the practice of, and complementing, the emerging global funds discussed above, which seek to supplement national resources, will also make a major contribution to the realization of the provision of global public goods and the prevention of global public bads. Sustained intellectual work being undertaken under the umbrella of the UNDP by Inge Kaul and her colleagues (Kaul *et al.*, 1999, 2003) is now shaping a conception of global public goods that goes beyond the mere formal economist's criteria of goods which are technically non-excludable and non-rival in their consumption (for example, world peace) to embrace goods such as basic education and health care which are (or should be) 'socially determined public goods', that is, goods which might be considered rival and excludable but which by political decision could be regarded as non-exclusive (Kaul *et al.*, 2003: 83). Political decisions about this could reflect the list of global social rights embodied within the 1967 United Nations Covenant on Economic, Cultural and Social Rights. Another approach would be to regard as socially determined global public goods those goods listed within the internationally agreed MDGs being progressed through the UN Millennium Project Task Force. In other words, those things that we all benefit from but that no individual entrepreneur has an interest in providing, such as education and health in poor countries, should be considered as global public goods which international effort should ensure is provided either by public service or privately in ways and with access criteria that enable all to benefit. A Global Levy could be used for such purposes.

Kaul and her colleagues make a useful distinction between development assistance, whereby richer countries donate monies to enable poorer countries to catch up in the development stakes, and global public goods (Kaul *et al.*, 2003: 358). Development assistance might continue in the context of progressive globalization and could be provided with additional funds from a Global Levy. Additionally mechanisms need to be set up to manage the provision of genuinely global public goods and diminish the existence of global public bads. Kaul and her colleagues envisage the establishment over time by each country of

Global Issue Ambassadors located within international development departments. These ambassadors would work for policy coherence towards global issues across ministries such as trade and aid. There would be ambassadors for climate stability, food safety, international drug running and so on. National ambassadors would liaise with, and develop, international policy under the guidance of a Global Chief Executive (CEO) (for example, food safety). Such a CEO would be advised by a global board drawn from relevant international organizations and be responsive to global civil society and global business interests (Kaul *et al.*, 2003: 395). This approach effectively adopts a networking and partnership form of global policy development and practice-shifting, which involves the collaboration between stakeholders in the international organizations, the global corporate sector, INGOs and civil society organizations (CSOs). These problematic governance questions are returned to in the next section.

To what extent is the idea of a *redistributive, regulatory and rights*-based global social policy finding its way into the lexicon used by international organizations? Has the concept of global social policy taken root? Will it fly? Are the initiatives to be supported? It is possible to argue that many of the new international initiatives particularly, but not exclusively those arising from within the UN Secretary General's Office, embody in practice such concepts without using the terminology. The MDGs and associated work touch on *global redistribution* as does the Global Fund, as we have just seen. Differential North–South drug pricing embodies the idea of global redistribution.

In terms of *global social regulation* the UN Global Compact encourages the voluntary adoption of international soft regulations for international corporations. The discussion of the MDGs in the UNDP *Human Development Report* (2003a) has a strong emphasis on an international compact. The aforementioned work within the UNDP on Global Public Goods is an important component of these trends. Each of these initiatives is subject to some of the same criticisms that we saw were levelled at the global funds discussed earlier. The Global Compact in particular has been condemned as a vehicle for the promotion of corporatist interests and image building without embodying any mechanisms for policing bad corporate practice (Richter, 2003). It is poor substitute for compulsory global business regulation and indeed its existence is seen as a block on such developments. On 23 June 2004, a Global Compact Counter Summit, sponsored by the Global Policy Forum in New York and involving several INGO and social movements which share these concerns, took place.

There is no space within this chapter to discuss at any length the vast literature on the emergence and effectiveness of the UN system of *global social rights*. An excellent review of the state of the global debate and the case for an obligation upon the international 'community' towards upholding rights, including social rights with poor countries, has been made by the Geneva-based International Council on Human Rights (ICHRP, 2003). It concludes that a major factor in the promulgation and realization of international rights to secure global social justice is not so much the absence of agreement on the foundation of such internationally recognized rights, rather it is 'political and administrative capacity'.

> We may be fully aware that economic and social rights are being violated...(but) the point at which transnational obligation breaks down is...the incapacity of decision-making and administrative systems to cope with the additional complexity of working outside the traditional national frameworks of governance and decision-making that manage most societies and which underpin the international frameworks of governance that have evolved (ICHRP, 2003: 75–6).

These international, or rather global, social governance questions are returned to later.

The World Commission on the Social Dimension of Globalization (WCSDG)

Where does the attempt by the WCSDG to reach a global consensus between North and South, business and labour and other voices fit in terms of this discussion? Does the WCSDG (ILO, 2004) adopt the language and concepts of global social policy in its attempt to chart a path towards 'A Fair Globalization'? In the words of the press release:[3] 'The Commission argues that a broader Globalization Policy Forum is required, to bring together international organisations and other key actors and participants in global debates on globalisation and its impact, and the design of *global economic and social policies*'.

In terms of *global social redistribution*, the report however continues to mince words about global taxation but argues that: 'A greater effort of resource mobilization at the international level is a basic requirement. The commitment to the target of 0.7 per cent of GDP [gross domestic product] for ODA [official development assistance] must at long last be respected. (453–458)' 'A wide range of options for additional sources of funding should also be actively considered... (463–470)' 'The potential of voluntary private contributions and philanthropic endeavours for global solidarity should be more fully tapped. (471–472)' Interestingly it argues that: 'International action is likewise needed to support national social protection systems, in order to ensure that there is a minimum level of social protection in the global economy. (488–491)'

In terms of *global social regulation* the report argues: 'The rules of the global economy should be aimed at improving the rights, livelihoods, security and opportunities of people, families and communities around the world. That includes fair rules for trade, finance and investment, measures to strengthen respect for core labour standards, and a coherent framework for the cross-border movement of people...(361–367)' It continues treading delicately around the ILO/WTO social clause/labour standards issue by saying that: 'The capacity of the ILO to promote respect for core labour standards should be reinforced. All relevant international organizations should assume their responsibility to promote these standards and ensure that their policies and programmes do not impede their realization. (426)' Perhaps its most radical ideas are to be found in the sections dealing with migration. 'Steps should be taken to build a multilateral framework that provides fair and trans-parent rules for the cross-border movement of people. We recommend a systematic approach which (a) extends and revitalizes existing multilateral commitments on issues such as the rights and protection of migrant workers and trafficking, especially of women; (b) develops common approaches to major policy issues through dialogue between countries of origin and destination and (c) seeks to build a global framework for an orderly and managed process in the common interest. (433–444)'

In terms of *global social rights* some of the above points also apply. In addition it is to be noted that the report links the issue of social rights to the resources needed for their realization in practice: 'Education, health, human rights, the environment and gender equality should all be addressed through an integrated approach to economic and social goals. (511–514)'

The report seems to back two horses with regard to the reformed *global governance* arrangements that might be needed to bring these changes about. It argues both that: 'There should be serious considera-tion of existing proposals to create an economic and social security council, and a global council on global governance (530–531)' and that 'ECOSOC's [United Nations Economic and Social Council's] capacity to coordinate global polices in the economic and social fields should be strengthened by upgrading its level of representation, including an executive committee at ministerial level and inter-ministerial interaction on key global policy issues, and the adoption of new forms of functioning. (533–534)' It also calls for interparliamentary oversight of the UN system and greater national public scrutiny of national actions in international bodies. Its most important proposal that paves the way from here to there is the idea that: 'International organizations should launch Policy Coherence Initiatives in which they work together on the design of more balanced and complementary policies for achieving a fair and inclusive globalization... (608–611)' And that 'A Globalization Policy Forum should be established by interested international organizations. The Forum will be a platform for regular dialogue between different points of view on the social impact of developments and policies in the global economy. Participating institutions could produce a regular "State of Globalization Report". (618–622)'

With the publication of the WCSDG, the time for the articulation of an effective Global Social Policy has arrived. In the next section we turn to some of the implications for action within and around the existing inadequate instruments of global social governance and ask questions about the kinds of international alliances, networks and social pressure which might combine to further this shift from a world run within a neoliberal hegemonic framework of ideas to one run within an ethic of global social solidarity and responsibility.

Network, projects, task forces and policy coherence initiatives: elements of the counter-hegemonic project?

How then do intellectuals in and around international organizations act in relation to the existing global governance institutions and in some kind of alliance with global social movement from below who are also concerned (or some of them are) to fashion a socially just globalization to make progress in this direction? The problems of trying to fashion a common interest out of the myriad intergroup conflicts thrown up by globalization has been usefully rehearsed by Cox (1999) and Gill (2003). Industrial workers in developed and polluting economies clash with environmentalists, workers in developed economies share little common interest with those taking their jobs in emerging economies, indigenous peoples clash over land and resources with those who claim these raw materials for production. This is still to say little about reconciling the diverse paths to social progress that different cultures have thrown up.

The focus here is not so much building such alliances between civil society movements from below. The analysis of steps being made through the World Social Forum in that direction still needs to be undertaken.

I do not believe, as Callinicos (2003) seems to, that they represent a fifth international ready to overthrow the capitalist world order in favour of some unspecified 'socialist' one. I am more inclined to see this movement as contributing to the reform, and not the overthrow of, capitalist globalization. The focus here, however, is rather the struggle within and between international organizations and policy advocates at the international level, but this is of course based upon the broader global social struggle. The specific questions we now turn to are those concerned with (a) the reform of existing institutions of global social governance; and (b) the prospects of the adoption by them of a socially redistributive, regulatory and rights-based globalization agenda.

What passes for a system of global governance in the social sphere is a complex of overlapping and competing agencies all seeking to influence policy. At the global level there are a number of competing and overlapping institutions and groupings of countries all of which have some stake in shaping global social policy towards global social problems. This struggle for the right to shape policy and for the content of that policy is what passes for an effective system of international social governance. The fragmentation and competition may be analysed as being made up of five groupings of contestations. First the World Bank, IMF and WTO are in competition for influence with the rest of the UN system. The Bank's health, social protection and education policy for countries and for the world is, for example, not the same as that of the WHO, ILO, or the United Nations Educational, Scientific and Cultural Organization (UNESCO), respectively. While the world may be said to have one emerging Ministry of Finance (with lots of shortcomings), it has two Ministries of Health, two Ministries of Social Security and two Ministries of Education.

Then again the UN social agencies (WHO, ILO, the United Nations Children's Fund/UNICEF) are not always espousing the same policy as UNDESA and, furthermore, the Secretary-General's initiatives, such as the Global Compact or the Millennium Project, may by-pass and sideline the social development policies of ECOSOC.

Quite apart from conflict between the UN and the Bank as well as within the UN system, there is also the G7/8, the Canadian-led G20 meetings of finance ministers, the G77, the new G20 initiative promoted by Brazil, China and India at Cancun and other groupings of countries. While the rich G7/8 continue to assume the right to make global policy, the Canadian-led G20 is struggling to forge a broader global consensus, and the G77 remains more a party of opposition to the Northern agendas, although the emergence of the alliance of China, Brazil, India,

South Africa and the G20 at Cancun suggests the ground may finally be shifting. Regional groupings of countries also have to be brought into the picture.

Interaction between all of these actors has led to international social policy making in recent years becoming stalemated with the EU, G77 and United States adopting entrenched positions. Significant global institutional reform seems checkmated and major global social policy change is difficult to achieve. This is the case notwithstanding the new proposals on institutions and policies by the WCSDG.

Because there are now so many loci of action and initiatives on global social issues, we may be witnessing a shift in the *locus* and *content* of global policy debate and activity from those more formally located within the official UN policy-making arenas (whether of ECOSOC in New York or in the councils of the ILO and WHO in Geneva) and focused on UN/Bretton Woods institutional reform, such as the establishment of an Economic Security Council to a set of practices around Networks, Partnerships and Projects, which in some ways by-pass these institutions and debates and *present new possibilities for actually making global change in particular social policy arenas*.

Ngaire Woods in a chapter in Held and McGrew's (2002) *Governing Globalization* argues:

> The global governance debate is focused heavily on the reform and creation of international institutions...yet global governance is increasingly being undertaken by a variety of networks, coalitions and informal arrangements which lie a little further beyond the public gaze and the direct control of governments. It is these forms of governance that need sustained and focussed attention to bring to light whose interests they further and to whom they are accountable.

Among examples of these networks, partnerships and projects are the UN Secretary General's Millennium Project involving ten task forces to manage the implementation of the MDGs and the problematic Global Compact. The essence of this emerging networking and partnership form of policy development and practice-shifting through a focus on specific projects is the collaboration between stakeholders in the international organizations, the global corporate sector, INGOs and CSOs. Such a shift in the locus and substance of global policy making and practice has received support recently from commentators coming from very different intellectual positions. Rischard (2002), the World Bank's Vice President for Europe in *High Noon: 20 Global Problems, 20 Years to*

Solve Them, argues that global multilateral institutions are not able to handle global issues on their own, that treaties and conventions are too slow for burning issues, that intergovernmental conferences do not have adequate follow-up mechanisms and that the G7/8 type groupings are too exclusive. Instead what is needed are Global Issues Networks (GINs), involving governments, civil society and business facilitated by a lead multilateral organization, which create a rough consensus about the problem to be solved and the task to be achieved, establish norms and practice recommendations and then report on failing governments and encourage good practice through knowledge exchange and a global observatory which feeds a name and shame approach. Charlotte Streck (2002) in *Global Environmental Governance: Options and Opportunities* argues for Global Public Policy Networks (GPPNs) that bring together governments, the private sector and CSOs. She insists that recent trends in international governance indicate that the focus has shifted from intergovernmental activity to multi-sectoral initiatives, and from a largely formal legalistic approach to a less formal participatory and integrated approach. Such GPPNs can agenda-set, standard-set, generate and disseminate knowledge and bolster institutional effectiveness. Streck is building here on the work of Witte *et al.* (2000) who argued that international organizations had a particular role they could play in GPPNs as convenor, platform, net-worker and sometimes partial financier.[4] To these ideas have to be added the proposals of the WCSDG for Policy Coherence Initiatives, multi-stakeholder Policy Development Dialogues and a Globalization Policy Forum.

There is clearly something in these accounts of the way policy making has become projectized and task-centred. Indeed this trend has led to some sustained criticism that these initiatives are undermining the more formal multilateral system (Martens, 2003). My view is that, while the global institutional and global policy impasse continues, we have to work with such initiatives while at the same time continuing to put the case for a more effective system of global social governance (Deacon *et al.*, 2003; Deacon, forthcoming). A key question becomes how intervention in these tasks, projects and dialogues might become subject to some principles of justice and equity. There is a case therefore for not only the networks and partnerships focused on short-term projects and tasks but also for longer term *global political alliances* that might fashion sets of principles of the kind espoused by the WCSDG and steer members of the task forces. If intervention to mend neoliberal globalization is project-and task- and initiative-based, then the actors in those projects and tasks need a solid ethical reference point and set of policy principles against which they can assess their proposals for action. We are back to global social policy, but not a policy to be debated and won in the chambers of the UN or won in intellectual dialogue with Bank experts (though these activities need to continue), but a policy implemented in practice by those who find themselves on such projects. A global reformist political alliance would act as a reference point for actors in practice.

Perhaps this is happening *soce voce*. Perhaps the choice of experts to sit on the Commission, perhaps the choice of people to serve on the Millennium Task Force, perhaps the work of the Helsinki Process[5] which has launched three tracks within which international dialogue between Northern and Southern voices will take place, leading to a major conference in 2005, is evidence of such an implicit anti-neoliberal global political alliance within and between international actors. Perhaps the conference convened by Gordon Brown on 16 February 2004, at which the new President of Brazil and many INGOs spoke about the need to get other countries signed up to his International Finance Initiative to double overseas aid, is a sign of the emergence of a global social democratic alliance. Perhaps this is a kind of war of position, albeit at a fairly reified level, whereby the dying global hegemony of neoliberalism is being contested and outmanoeuvred. Perhaps if countries follow the Swedish initiative and legislate to ensure that *all* government policy is subordinated to a responsible approach to globalization, progress will be made. Perhaps if countries follow the proposals of Kaul to appoint issues ambassadors for global public goods issues, such as education, health and water, these ambassadors will in effect be participants in this war of positions. Perhaps the US Treasury does not have total grip anymore? Perhaps as Bøås and McNeill's book (2004) concludes, powerful states (notably the United States) contend with other powerful states (notably Europe, China and Brazil), powerful organizations (such as the IMF) contend with other powerful organizations (such as the ILO) and powerful disciplines (notably economics) contend with other disciplines (notably social and political science) to wage a war of positions as to how the terms of debate about globalization should be framed. To the extent that this is the case, the role of intellectuals and their ideas struggling in and against the international organizations will have been important but not decisive. The shift in influence of contending ideas will reflect a shift in the balance of power whereby social movements from below will have had an impact upon national governments and international actors.

Regionalization or globalization?

There is an important caveat or corrective to enter at this point that unfortunately this chapter does not have space to develop in any depth. It is conceivable that because of the continued opposition by the world superpower to any kind of strengthening of the UN system and any talk of global taxation and redistribution, an alternative route to a more systematic global governance might need to be looked for in the concept of a strengthened Regionalism with a Social Dimension (Deacon, 2001; Room, 2004; Yeates, 2004). Within this scenario the EU that anyway 'offers novel ways of thinking about governance beyond the state' (Held and McGrew, 2002) would be joined by the Association of Southeast Asian Nations (ASEAN), the Southern African Development Community (SADC), the Mercado Común del Sur (MERCOSUR), the South Asian Association for Regional Cooperation (SAARC) and new regions in a global federation of regions linked to, say, the Canadian-led G20 international governance mechanism. In this case an international redistribution would be handled on an interregional basis and funds allocated on socioeconomic criteria of need to some regions, which would then decide to allocate it to activities and projects within the region using mechanisms already established by the EU or by new mechanisms, such as those being experimented with by the Global Fund, discussed above. Such a regional approach to a global social policy might also chime with the sentiments of many Southern voices which react against a Northern-driven global social democracy as strongly as they react against a Northern-driven global neoliberalism (Bello, 2004). It might also embody at a global level the post-hegemonic, relativist, and multicultural global order that we saw Cox had argued for in 1993. One of the problems is of course that many regions are not so coherent and in some cases the more protectionist inclined regions listed above compete under US influence with more open free-trade mega-regions like the Asian Free Trade Area (AFTA) and the Asia-Pacific Economic Cooperation (APEC). The social dimensions of most regions are also still fairly weak by comparison with the EU.

Researching global social policy

The challenge of developing a global social policy or a pattern of regional social policies has implications for the type of research and policy advocacy carried out by UN social agencies and their research networks. Currently there is an overemphasis on researching and advocating policies for *national* governments. UN researchers see

themselves as working for inter-*national* agencies and in some sense
they are bound to offer advice to the countries that fund the agency. By
the same token it does not come naturally to researchers within (and
paid by) international organizations to research the organizations
themselves and the shortcomings they collectively exhibit in terms of
any desirable system of global social governance. If the analysis in this
chapter is correct, the spotlight does, however, need to be turned on the
emerging system of global social governance and the emerging practices
of global redistribution, regulation and rights.

The moment is ripe, given the recommendation of the WCSDG
report that 'Research programmes and data collection on the social
dimension of globalisation should be strengthened (623–629)', to work
towards the establishment of a Global (and Regional) Social Policy
Research Centre or Programme serving a Global (and Regional) Social
Policy Observatory and acting as a Global (and Regional) Social Policy
Advocacy Think-Tank whose purpose would be to track, monitor, and
analyse for effectiveness all the elements of the emerging global and
regional policies of social redistribution, regulation and rights. It would
be an institute or programme which shadowed and contributed to both
the Globalization Policy Forum that the WCSDG report said should be
established by interested international organizations and the Policy
Coherence Initiatives within which international organizations would
work together on the design of more balanced and complementary
policies for achieving a fair and inclusive globalization as well as
shadowing and commenting on all the other parallel global policy
dialogues which are emerging at the moment. If an initiative like this
were taken then, in the words of the conference title for which this
paper was originally prepared, research would not only, as it has done,
make a difference to national policy making but would also make a
difference to *international* policy making.

Back to the politics of global social policy

The case for a centralized global research and policy evaluation and
advocacy project might be objected to in a diverse world. Equally the
case for a unified and global social reformist project might have objectors.
The argument for attempts to create a socially just 'capitalist' globalization might need to be defended against the 'de-globalizers' and others
who favour its demise.

Indeed the comments on an earlier draft of this chapter suggest some
of the possible criticisms (Hopenhayn, 2004). While welcoming the call

for such research and sharing the same political project of a socially just globalization, there were concerns about the mismatch between, on the one hand, a meta narrative and an all encompassing agenda that was to be set and monitored at a global level, and, on the other hand, the disparate movements and diverse critiques of globalization emerging in localities.

In the context of the foregoing considerations, Bob Deacon's paper is enlightening. The basic premise is that we are at a turning point where the neo-liberal hegemonic model must be countered with a counter-hegemonic project rooted in the emerging global civil society. Counter-hegemony, however, is not a univocal concept. On the one hand, it may be understood as global thinking which encompasses the United Nations system, a profuse range of non-governmental organizations and academics around the world, connected through cross border networks and in which the production of knowledge advocates the three 'musts' that Deacon has advocated: greater social justice, greater regulation and a global order based on rights. In addition, counter-hegemony is rooted in a set of local actors who may or may not be part of trans-national networks and who construct practices and discourses from the margins and interstices of economics, politics and global culture. These actors undertake actions and send out messages that imply solidaristic and horizontal forms of sociability, denounce the violation of civil, social and cultural rights in different places and nations of the globe, champion the cause of cultural minorities, and vulnerable and ethnic groups who are discriminated against, advocate environment preservation, and struggle for fair and egalitarian treatment in terms of gender, community management, local democracy and others (Hopenhayn, 2004).

The task for UN research, policy analysis and policy dialogue, Hopenhayn argued, must 'adapt to this emerging idea of bottom-up globalization where all voices can be heard'. He continued:

given this decentring in the production of knowledge and its feedback through networks, it is not easy to adhere to the proposal of a 'Global Social Policy Research Centre serving a Global Policy Observatory and acting as a Global Social Policy Advocacy Think Tank whose purpose would be to track, monitor, and analyse for effectiveness all the elements of the emerging global and regional policies of social redistribution, regulation and rights'. In my view, such an aspiration embodies a development paradigm according to which a central agent would embody the lights of reason, both in terms of interpreting the destiny of history and of guiding it. I am not sure that nowadays the global civil society can withstand this type of rationality (Hopenhayn, 2004).

Reflecting Yeates' (2004) concern that 'historical, cultural, ideological, religious, and institutional differences render the pursuit of... an agreed global cosmopolitan form of progress particularly difficult', are the objections of Hopenhayn to a proposed research centre embodying the light of reason.

Elsewhere I have defended the global social reformist project against five types of criticisms (Deacon *et al.*, 1997: 213). They included those of socialist or Marxist fundamentalists who saw it as a project to legitimate global capitalism, and those of post-modernists or relativists who saw it as an unacceptable imposition of Western democratic and constitutional ideas. With regard to the anticapitalists, the issue for the foreseeable future *is* one of the *reform* of (global) capitalism not its overthrow. Furthermore, this project has to be a global one in so far as much of capital has escaped the regulatory and embedded frameworks of national regulatory authority. This does not preclude, however, the option for countries to try to regain control of capital flows and manage foreign direct investment (FDI) and engage in protectionist measures.

This is not to dismiss the possibility of the re-emergence of a genuinely revolutionary post-global capitalist project. Callinicos (2003) might see the emergence of a fifth international in the World Social Forum. I am not convinced. Hardt and Negri (2000) are, I think, correct to see globalization as the final 'progressive' arrival of Empire within whose terrain the class struggle will finally be fought.

> Class struggle, pushing the nation state towards its abolition and thus going beyond the barriers posed by it, proposes the constitution of Empire as the site of analysis and conflict. Without that barrier, then, the situation of struggle is completely open. Capital and labour are opposed in directly antagonistic form. This is the fundamental condition of every political theory of communism (Hardt and Negri, 2000: 237).

They write (Hardt and Negri, 2000: 411) of the 'organisation of the multitude as a political subject, as posse, thus begins to appear on the world scene' but note that 'the only event we are still awaiting is the construction or rather the insurgence of a powerful organisation.... We do not have any models to offer for this event... only the multitude through its practical experimentation will offer the models and determine when and how the possible becomes real' (Hardt and Negri, 2000: 411).

While 'waiting' we should seek to reform global capitalism. Indeed, in doing so, we may not be asking for anything very different from that which Hardt and Negri's 'powerful organisation' might want. After all, the first two of the three political demands of the multitude are, according to Hardt and Negri (2000: 400–3):

(a) 'The general right to control its own movement (across borders) is the multitude's ultimate demand for global citizenship' and
(b) 'A social wage and a guaranteed income for all... once citizenship is extended to all we could call this guaranteed income a citizenship income, due to each member of society'.

It seems to me that a global social policy observatory and think-tank could well model such ideas as part of a global reformist project, which might indeed turn out to have revolutionary implications.

With regard to relativists, I concluded then, and repeat now, that:

> the respect for cultural diversity, and respect for the right to seek different paths towards meeting human needs, does not mean endorsing inhumanity, accepting injustice, or denying people's rights to a creative and full life. To uphold these things in a globalised world calls precisely for a global ethic, a global regulatory authority, a global process of ironing out injustice and the right of legitimate global authority to intervene when cultural differences becomes an excuse for the blocking of individual access to the emerging rights of global citizens. The global social reformist project stands or falls by these values (Deacon *et al.*, 1997: 213).

This is not to dismiss the question that progress towards this end needs not only to be articulated at a global level but also engage with, and reflect, the disparate voices of opposition in localities. The suggestion in this chapter of a decentred globalization involving strong regions each with their own social dimension is one possible response to this problem.

There is of course the wider issue of the global North–South impasse or stand-off in the politics of globalization reform which lies behind some of these comments. For some years now, Northern-driven progressive global policies have been rejected as readily by some Southern activists and governments as by Northern neoliberals (Deacon, 1999, 2000c). The history of colonialism, followed by structural adjustment combined with the hypocrisy of Northern governments with regard to trade and rights and their refusal to pay for the implementation of global standards, led understandably to the Southern rejection of the Social Clause, the Social Policy Principles and more latterly the process conditionality of the PRSPs. The progressive ideas of Northern-based intellectuals got so caught up in the impasse that this author argued some years ago that the batten needed to be passed to the South on the issue of global reform (Deacon, 2000c). Progress beyond this realization is difficult. It is not made easier by the appearance of more recent Northern publications arguing the case for a global social democratic project that singularly fails to address explicitly the question of why the South should buy in to the ideas (Jacobs *et al.*, 2003; Held, 2004). At the same time, many Southern intellectuals are concerned about the erosion of scholarly capacity in the South resulting from a combination of underfunded universities and co-option of the best scholars into a Northern-driven, often World Bank-driven, intellectual agenda via consultancies (see Girvan and Sen in this volume, and UNRISD, 2004). Within this context a Southern response to globalization is to want to rescue national intellectual and development policy, and not so much to reform globalization but to retreat from it, defend against it, rebuild and engage again later on more equal terms.

Nonetheless, as argued above, the political task that faces us (within which the global and regional social policy research agenda will play one part) is, indeed, requoting Cox (1999: 26):

> to bridge the differences among the variety of groups disadvantaged by globalisation so as to bring about a *common* understanding of the nature and consequences of globalisation, and to devise a *common* strategy towards subordinating the world economy to a regime of social equity.

What is needed is more dialogue based on humility and mutual respect between progressive social policy and social development intellectuals North and South, in the context of listening to the voices of social movements. This might facilitate the marriage of diversity in culture and experience with a common set of values concerning social justice and rights, as well as their conversion into a shared international political project to secure a socially just world. This would require some combination of restored and equitable national social policies, strengthened regional social policies, a measure of global social redistribution, effective regulation, and the articulation and realization of rights.

8
Generating Knowledge in the United Nations

Louis Emmerij, Richard Jolly and Thomas G. Weiss

> You can record the 20th century as a story of astonishing technical progress. You can tell it as a rise and fall of powers, or as a painful recovery from modern society's relapses into barbarism. But if you leave out ideas, you leave out what people were ready to live and die for (*The Economist*, 17 January 2004: 72).

Introduction

It may come as a surprise that there is no comprehensive history of the United Nations (UN), neither institutional nor intellectual. Several specialized agencies have written or are in the process of writing their institutional histories, which is indeed what all organizations need to do. In this respect, the Bretton Woods institutions (BWIs) are far ahead. The World Bank has published two massive histories on the occasions of its twenty-fifth and fiftieth anniversaries. The International Monetary Fund (IMF) has an in-house historian who ensures the capture of its place in history with regular publications (Mason and Asher, 1973; Kapur *et al.*, 1997; Boughton, 2001). The UN story deserves to be better documented.

The United Nations Intellectual History Project (UNIHP) is tackling one aspect of this neglected task, a history of ideas launched or nurtured by the world organization.[1] Begun in 1999, the UNIHP is producing a host of products that shed light on the role of the UN system in creating social knowledge and in influencing international policy making. Drawing on the work of this project, this chapter reflects upon the contribution to development debates and policy of research and knowledge associated with UN agencies. We begin by identifying a number of methodological and conceptual issues related to the study of ideas and the challenges they pose for the UNIHP. We then go on to examine what constitutes ideas and social knowledge in the UN system, their impact on international policy making, the linkages between research outside and inside the UN, and the question of whether UN research is sufficiently independent and critical. A concluding section considers some of the lessons learned from studying the intellectual history of the UN as well as a number of policy implications.

Towards an intellectual history of the United Nations

Ideas are a driving force in human progress. They may be the most important legacy of the UN for human rights, economic and social development, as well as for peace and security. Because of this, the lack of attention to the UN's role in generating ideas is perplexing. But this neglect is part of a more general blindness. As Ngaire Woods has noted, 'ideas, whether economic or not, have been left out of analyses of international relations' (Woods, 1995: 164).

The study of ideas, although relatively new in analyses of international politics and organizations, has long been common bill of fare for historians, philosophers, economists, and students of literature. Peter Watson in a recent book on intellectual trends puts the point dramatically: 'Once we get away from the terrible calamities that have afflicted our century, once we lift our eyes from the horrors of the past decades, the dominant intellectual trend, the most interesting enduring and profound development, is very clear. Our century has been dominated intellectually by a coming to terms with science.' Watson's intellectual focus is on science. We would emphasise the contribution of a wider range of ideas in the international arena. But we share the conviction that ideas are so often central (Watson, 2001: 4).

What, then, is an intellectual history, and how does one go about writing one? Although the term can have a variety of meanings, 'intellectual history' in our case seeks to explain the origins of particular ideas; trace their trajectories within institutions, scholarship, or discourse; and in some cases, certainly in ours, evaluate the impact of ideas on policy and action. We focus upon and seek to analyse the role of the UN as an intellectual actor.

Four questions often arise about existing approaches to the study of ideas. The first question is: Which comes first, an idea or a policy challenge? Most approaches to international relations do not explain the sources of ideas, just their effects. They rarely explain how ideas emerge or change. By ignoring where ideas come from and how they change, we cannot ascertain cause and effect. Do ideas shape policy? Or does a policy challenge call existing ideas forward and perhaps generate new ideas that may emerge in response to that policy or action? As the reader will discover, the UNIHP is finding many variations and is coming closer to answers, but a synthesis of the research findings still has to be undertaken.

A second question is whether ideas arise and exist in particular situations, or whether they have a life of their own. We are trying to trace the trajectory of ideas within the UN and examine how individual leadership, coalitions, and national and bureaucratic rivalries within it have generated, distorted, and implemented particular ideas. At the same time, we also hope to discern how ideas, in and of themselves, have helped to shape policy outcomes at the UN. There is a related, long-standing debate among intellectual historians whether an idea should be analysed in the light of the historical and social context within which it emerged, or whether it can be understood on its own, without reference to context. We favour the former school and thus assume that economic and social ideas at the UN cannot be properly understood if divorced from their historical and social context. The birth and survival of ideas in the UN – or their death and suppression – invariably reflect events and are contingent upon politics and the world economy.

A third question is when to begin tracing the trajectory of a particular idea. Ideas are rarely totally new. At what point in its life or in which of its many possible incarnations should one begin to study an idea? We explore antecedents wherever possible, and often go back before the beginning of the UN in 1945. A related issue is ownership. The difficulty of identifying a single individual or institution responsible for the creation of an idea is one illustration of this problem. We decided not to undertake the type of historical analysis pioneered by Arthur Lovejoy, who sought to trace an idea 'through all the provinces of history in which it appears' (Lovejoy, 1960). Rather, we pick up an idea at the time it intersects with the UN, and then trace its most important antecedents.

A fourth and final question relates to the influence of ideas versus the individuals who put them forward (Yee, 1996). There is little consensus here. It can be argued that the more influential the purveyors, and the more powerful the countries or interests supporting them the greater the odds that their ideas will be adopted. Ideas presuppose human agents, which is why we are documenting through oral history the role of individuals in the evolution of international economic and social development. Did ideas emanate from within UN secretariats, or from outside the world organization through governments, non-governmental organizations (NGOs), experts, or consultants? What happened to these ideas? Were they discarded without discussion or after deliberation? Were they discussed, adapted, distorted, and then implemented? What happened afterwards?

UNIHP involves 12 thematic studies, 2 synthesis volumes and some 75 oral histories. This article draws upon the first five published volumes in the UNIHP book series, as well as on the oral histories.[2] We have focused on concrete illustrations as the best way to stimulate debate as well as foreshadow what is forthcoming.[3]

The second main activity of the Project has been conducting oral history interviews with key participants in the work of the UN, especially in the evolution of UN thinking and ideas. A method of research for preserving and creating knowledge of historical events as recounted by participants in those events, oral history also allows us to identify ideas that never made it beyond closed-room discussions, and to explore the debates about and circumstances of their demise. The UNIHP archive includes some 75 personal testimonies and recorded life narratives of individuals who have served the world organization in key positions as staff members, consultants, researchers, diplomats, or members of commissions.[4] They include the four living Secretaries-General.

There are shortcomings in concentrating the oral histories on an 'elite'. But we had to begin somewhere, and one of the justifications for the effort is to rectify a woeful lack of attention to such learning. The importance of the collection of taped memories cannot be overemphasized, as there is precious little institutional memory at the UN and even fewer resources to capture the historical record.[5]

Ideas and social knowledge in the UN system

Throughout the project we have tried to maintain the distinction between the 'two UN's': the arena where states make decisions, on the one hand, and the leadership and staff of international secretariats, on the other hand (Weiss *et al.*, 2004). The 'first UN' focuses on states and their decisions and actions. The 'second UN' focuses on the secretariat, institutions and staff members of the UN, and for our project on their contributions to research and thinking.[6]

Here we essentially embroider the final two sentences of *Ahead of the Curve?*: 'Ideas matter. People matter.' (Emmerij *et al.*, 2001: 214). What are the economic and social ideas coming out of the UN, and which key ones should be analysed? The answer to this is, in many ways, necessary background for addressing the other issues analysed in this chapter. For us 'ideas' are defined as normative or causal beliefs held by individuals or adopted by institutions that influence their attitudes and actions.[7] Ideas are analysed in our studies when they intersect with the UN – that is when they appear as major thoughts or concepts in UN documents, speeches, or conferences or as analyses, policy decisions or guidelines for action. Normative ideas are broad, general beliefs about what the world should look like; causal ideas are more operational motives about what strategy will have a desired result or what tactics will achieve a particular strategy. At the UN, causal ideas have often taken an operational form, such as the target of 0.7 per cent of gross national product (GNP) to be contributed as official development assistance (ODA). An example of a normative idea would be the call for eliminating all forms of discrimination against women or ensuring the rights of the child, and more generally that the international community bears a moral responsibility to promote social progress and better standards of living in all countries.

Historical context, of course, is important, though by no means always a determining influence. The International Labour Organization (ILO) many times discussed employment during the 1920s and 1930s, to little practical effect – except that some of its interesting ideas helped lay the foundations for post-war UN contributions. Another example, the inclusion of human rights in the Charter and the adoption of the Universal Declaration in 1948 appear, in historical perspective, mind-boggling in their boldness. In the words of Stéphane Hessel, an early UN recruit who sat at Eleanor Roosevelt's side in 1948 and later became *Ambassadeur de France*, human rights are 'what makes the second half of the 20th century such an important moment of world history'.[8]

Ideas that have mattered over the world organization's six decades cover the waterfront. At least those that emerge from the first five books in the UNIHP's publication series suggest a host of ideas that have mattered from the narrowly specific to the more sweeping. Here are some examples.

Though often neglected, the UN's contribution to the political arithmetic of statistics has been a major influence. This is an engrossing story told by Michael Ward (2004) in *Quantifying the World: UN Ideas and Statistics*. An engagingly written tale of pioneering work in the early years in national accounting and of the subsequent move into social and environmental accounting, the study also represents an account of the UN's statistical leadership in such fields as population, employment, and gender. The battles over what to count, how to count it, and what to ignore suggest the extent to which UN-generated ideas and conventions have been taken seriously by the member states whose economies are being measured and compared. We are reminded that the crucial importance of statistics was captured by Dudley Seers some two decades ago:

> We cannot, with our own eyes and ears, perceive more than a minute sample of human affairs, even in our own country – and a very unrandom sample at that. So we rely on statistics in order to build and maintain our own model of the world. The data that are available mould our perceptions.... It is for this reason that a statistical policy – (i.e. the policy of statistics offices) – exerts a subtle but pervasive and lasting influence on political, social and economic development. This is why the apparently dull and minor subject of statistical priorities is of crucial importance (Seers, 1983: 130).

UN Contributions to Development Thinking and Practice by Richard Jolly, Louis Emmerij, Dharam Ghai and Frédéric Lapeyre (2004) represents an ambitious attempt to identify whether the UN has contributed anything new to development discourse that was not already said by the classicists. The volume begins with an inventory of ideas on development from Adam Smith to John Maynard Keynes via Malthus, Ricardo, Friedrich List, John Stewart Mill, Marx, Schumpeter and others. Standing on the shoulders of those thinkers, the book traces the contributions to development thinking since 1945 by the UN, often assisted by many outside consultants who later turned out to be intellectual giants in their own right. The book analyses the early UN work on economic development and global income distribution. It also follows the development of new perspectives on employment, the informal sector and basic needs in the ILO as well as the influence of the work of the Dag Hammarskjöld Foundation; the United Nations Research Institute for Social Development's (UNRISD's) unified approach; and the Bariloche Foundation during the 1970s. The four development decades provide snap-shots for tracking the evolution of other thinking and ideas in the UN from the 1960s onwards.

One often overlooked practical contribution of the UN is target-setting, another story told in some detail by Jolly *et al.* The recent focus on the Millennium Development Goals (MDGs), for instance, brought forth many skeptical catcalls. Careful analysis shows that the UN over the last 40 years has set some 50 development goals, with a record of performance that is more encouraging than often realized. A few targets have been fully, or almost fully, achieved – for instance, the eradication of small pox, major reductions of infant mortality, and the near elimination of polio and guinea worm. Many other goals have been largely achieved in a considerable number of countries. It is in fact, only a small minority of global goals for which hardly any progress has been made – the reduction of maternal mortality being a prime example and, revealing and more serious, the 0.7 goal for development assistance in general and the goals for assistance to least developed countries in particular.

The terms of trade debate in many ways started the North-South battle, and this intellectual history is told in brilliant detail by John and Richard Toye (2004) in their volume on *The UN and Global Political Economy*, which recounts the story of the terms of trade controversy initiated by Hans Singer and Raúl Prebisch around 1950 (Prebisch, 1950; Singer, 1950: 473–85),[9] the failure to establish the International Trade Organization (ITO) anticipated as the third leg of the BWIs, the creation of the United Nations Conference on Trade and Development (UNCTAD), and much more. It also contains a forward-looking chapter regarding possible adaptations in the international financial institutions (IFIs) as well as in the World Trade Organization (WTO). The book has used extensively available archival evidence in New York, Geneva, Santiago de Chile, London and Washington, DC, as well as interviews with personalities from the region.

The book also tells the story of the struggle between the Group of 77 (G77) and the bulk of the Western countries members of the Organisation for Economic Co-operation and Development (OECD) and how UNCTAD was squeezed. The antecedent of this struggle was already visible during the campaign for the Special United Nations Fund for Economic Development (SUNFED) in the 1950s. The developing countries aimed not only to set up a soft loan agency; they also wanted to create it as a new financial executing agency under UN control. They succeeded in the first but failed in the second aim. This gave further substance to the struggle between the UN and the BWIs that is also reflected in the idea to replace the Economic and Social Council (ECOSOC) with a new Economic Security Council with a voting system half-way between the UN's one-country-one-vote and the BWIs' weighted model of voting.

The volume traces the decline of the UN as a vibrant centre of thinking on issues of trade, finance, and development as well as of the rise – particularly after 1980 – of a neoliberal consensus on these issues, orchestrated by the World Bank. It advances the thesis that in international organizations the degree of creative thinking – as opposed to the synthesizing and recycling of existing ideas – is inversely related to the ability of their top management to exercise strong editorial control over the research process, for the purpose of preaching a doctrine that they think promotes the aims of the organization.

Regional variations are, of course, to be expected and welcomed; and the volume *Unity and Diversity in Development Ideas*, edited by Yves Berthelot (2004), substantiates this generalization. It depicts the UN regional commissions, with all their differences and idiosyncrasies, and fills a gap in the existing literature. For instance, Berthelot and Paul Rayment analyse in great detail the problems of transition in the economies in Central and Eastern Europe and the former Soviet Union after 1989. These constitute a special but not unique case where the United Nations Economic Commission for Europe (ECE) was clearly in the lead. It advocated a gradual approach emphasizing institutional reform that with hindsight was much better policy advice than the 'big bang' policies emanating from the World Bank and IMF (ECE, 1990: 5–26; 1991). In part this related to the fact that the ECE had long been the only place during the Cold War where East and West met *and* worked together on a range of very specific economic issues, including such bread-and-butter problems as road transport and electricity grids. In spite of this experience, the 'big bang' advocated by the BWIs and also by several very visible international consultants won the day. The economic and human costs of this missed opportunity have been, and still are, extremely large (see Emmerij *et al.*, 2001: 146–65; Berthelot, 2004: 111–20). We come back to this issue later.

Along with the Europe story, the collection traces the ideas on economic and social development launched by the UN regional commissions.[10] Each has operated quite differently, depending on leadership and objective circumstances with respect to the political and economic situation in their region. The United Nations Economic Commission for Latin America and the Caribbean (ECLAC) has been the most active in developing policy ideas that it considered crucial for the region, such as the centre–periphery framework, import substitution policies and dependency analysis. The United Nations Economic Commission for Africa (ECA) also provides examples such as its important work and many battles to adapt the orthodoxies of structural adjustment policies to African circumstances, although its independent dynamism has diminished during the last few years. In Asia and the Pacific there is such diversity at the country level (great successes, steady progress, and erratic performances side by side) that the Economic and Social Commission for Asia and the Pacific (ESCAP) has been more pragmatic in its approach to development ideas. As West Asia is the most politically troubled region, there has been little room for original economic thought. The United Nations Economic and Social Commission for Western Asia (ESCWA) has been a follower rather than an innovator of ideas. However, it has done important work on water security, gender, and population.

One of the reasons why the ECE and the United Nations Economic Commission for Latin America (ECLA) were so creative, particularly in their early years, was the creativity and independence of their first executive-secretaries (Gunnar Myrdal and Raúl Prebisch). Dissenting voices were allowed. This was the case, for instance, with dependency theory within ECLA.[11]

The impact of ideas on international policy making

The impact of ideas on the 'first UN', where member states make decisions, is one important dynamic in determining how ideas matter. The influence of ideas on international actions, transnational corporations, social movements, advocates, and the like is noticeable. But the UN is an inter-*governmental* organization. And in a world in which states remain the primary actors, we concentrate on how UN ideas change their thinking and actions. Ideas are important determinants of change. We take inspiration from John Maynard Keynes, who wrote of 'academic scribblers' that 'The ideas of economists and political philosophers, both when they are right and when they are wrong, are more powerful than is commonly understood. Indeed, the world is ruled by little else' (Keynes, 1936: 383).

The questions that we have attempted to keep in mind are: What impact, if any, did particular ideas have? Once adopted in original or distorted form, did ideas make a difference outside of the UN? If so, how? Even partial answers to these difficult questions could constitute an essential research finding. For even if ideas are one of the main legacies of the UN, harsh critics may well ask, 'So what?' The reply that is emerging from the UNIHP involves an examination of four ways to measure the impact of intellectual debates on the framing of development issues.

The first is that UN ideas can change the nature of international public policy discourse and debate, and, as a result, often help states to define and redefine their interests to be more inclusive of common concerns. The litany of changes in vocabulary is one of the most obvious ways to demonstrate that UN ideas have at least altered the way that we talk and think about international development. They have at times transformed the intellectual environment or at least changed the nature of international public policy discourse.

The very focus of the UN on economic development from its early years is one of the key examples. Economic development as presented by the UN was the idea of *purposeful* policy and action to accelerate the process of development, an approach initially denounced by some critics as primarily 'an intellectual or artistic exercise' at variance with 'existing realities in underdeveloped countries' (Frankel, 1953: 275; Emmerij *et al.*, 2001: 42). Purposeful development meant not only changes in national policy and the need for national planning but the recognition that development in other countries, especially in other poorer countries, was a matter of more general international concern. The UN, in the early 1950s, advocated an *international* development strategy to back up national efforts of developing countries. What happened was the Marshall plan for Europe (implemented outside the ECE) while the developing countries were left in the cold. But the idea of a necessary international development framework was there to stay.

Another area where international discourse has been totally altered by the UN has followed from its leadership in the area of universal human rights. Over the last half century, the UN has fundamentally transformed the way in which the rights of people all over the world are perceived. In parallel with this has been growing attention to the obligations of governments and other parties, including over the last two or three decades, transnational corporations, to demonstrate commitment and practical action in response to such rights.

These are examples of major changes in perceptions and attitudes in which the UN has had a major and probably *the* major role in leading the way. There are many others – for instance, in promoting attention to education for all or health for all, in changing attitudes to population policy, to the rights of women and the gender dimensions of development, to concern for children as a central focus in development policy and strategy and, more recently, to the promotion of human development, as a norm and approach which should underlie all development policy, national and international.

The UN has also had a major impact on thinking and ideas of a more technical sort. For example, the Prebisch–Singer thesis about deteriorating trends in the terms of trade of developing countries changed the discourse about fairness and the reasons to support or reject liberalization of markets, a debate that continues. Ideas about 'centre–periphery' and 'dependency' that were developed by Latin American economists within ECLA in the 1950s and 1960s altered the discourse on modernization theory, at least for a while.

Less successful were ideas about the need for a New International Economic Order (NIEO), developed by the UN in the 1970s, though largely killed off by the end of that decade. Over a much longer period, the UN analysed and emphasized the links between disarmament and development. Interestingly, some of the early leads for this came in the 1950s and 1960s from governments – France, the Soviet Union, and Brazil – but the UN undertook sporadic work over several decades. This continued until the 1980s, when the United Nations Institute for Disarmament Research (UNIDIR) was established, and the UN issued the pioneering Thorsson Report on the relationship between Disarmament and Development, for which Wassily Leontief, the Nobel prize-winning economist, prepared one of the background papers. All this is in sharp contrast to the World Bank and the IMF. The World Bank's historians comment that 'arms reduction is sensitive as well as political and was typically avoided by the Bank until – in the aftermath of the cold war – the presidents of the Bank, first Conable, then Preston, joined Managing Director Camdessus of the Fund, in making borrower's allocations to defense a matter of greater Bank-Fund concern' (Kapur *et al.*, 1997: 533).

The second type of influence is when ideas provide a tactical guide to policy and action especially when norms conflict, or when sequencing and priorities are disputed, and thus when states need to define their interests. The necessity to balance belt-tightening with the requirements of a 'human face' in structural adjustment was one such dispute in the 1980s where the United Nations Children's Fund's (UNICEF's) ideas provided a roadmap to navigate between apparently conflicting priorities and needs (Cornia *et al.*, 1987), a theme strongly promoted by ECA as well. The UN, and UNCTAD in particular, also took the lead in calling for more rapid and more fundamental international action to tackle the debt crisis and to take more seriously the problems of the least developed countries as a group. Indeed, for most of the issues where the UN has raised awareness of problems and new challenges, it has also generally helped define an agenda for policy and action. This is true in a wide range of development areas from accelerating economic growth, to trade and finance, agriculture and industry, population, education and health, to changing the economic structure of developing countries and international support.

The third kind of impact is when ideas alter the prospects for forming new combinations of political and institutional forces, thereby altering prospects for forming bargaining coalitions. For example, early calls to take seriously the Prebisch-Singer thesis about declining terms of trade for developing countries stimulated UNCTAD'S work in the 1960s and the demand in the 1970s for a NIEO became the veritable glue of G77 solidarity – though like many glues, not always as strong or long lasting as originally expected. Indeed, perhaps the most spectacular illustration of this phenomenon is the coming together of various groupings of developing countries over time in order to pursue jointly the calls for changing the rules of the international economic game. Although the solidarity has weakened over time, other coalitions (of least developed countries, of like-minded countries, of donor governments, of NGOs) clearly represent other manifestations of this third impact. One concrete illustration is the Doha Round of WTO negotiations where the possibility existed to establish trade of developing countries on a more equitable basis than at present. When that possibility was not transformed in reality at Cancún in 2003, a new coalition of developing countries decided to break off negotiations rather than continuing to play the game with industrial countries that do not practise what they preach.

The fourth kind of impact is when ideas become embedded in institutions, sometimes in the form of new units or programmes, sometimes in the form of new institutions. UN-bashers in Washington and elsewhere are uncomfortable with such institutions or programmes because they imply a commitment of financial and personnel resources. But what could be a more concrete demonstration of why ideas matter? The establishment of new agencies – for instance, the United Nations Environment Programme (UNEP), the International Fund for Agricultural Development (IFAD), and the United Nations Development Fund for Women (UNIFEM) – is the most visible manifestation of ideas taking root. But no less striking or important is the 'mainstreaming' of issues (for example, human rights into the formerly 'rights-free' areas of agriculture, trade and environment) and the creation of new units within established bureaucracies (for example, of a gender unit in the Department of Peace-keeping Operations or the ECA setting up a whole string of sub-regional organizations). All of the volumes have explicit examples of such creations, at every level. Perhaps the most spectacular is the creation of UNCTAD, masterfully told in the volume by John and Richard Toye (2004).

A major task is to explore whether the UN has demonstrated unique attributes or a comparative advantage in creating, nurturing, and diffusing ideas, and if it has anticipated global and regional challenges by responding earlier than other institutions. This was of course implied in the title of UNIHP's first publication, *Ahead of the Curve?*, albeit qualified with a question mark. As our research has proceeded, we are inclined to drop the question mark! We have found more and more examples of how the UN has been in the international lead, most notably and most frequently being ahead of the BWIs in such areas as setting up international economic development frameworks, global income distribution, the environment, gender, population, employment, human development, children and human rights.

When analysing how ideas relate to policy making, it is crucial to consider the issue of organizational learning. The kind of learning that accompanies UN research and ideas is quite different to that associated with business research and analyses. This is a variation on the theme of 'you can lead a horse to water, but you can't make it drink'. In business literature, learning is comprised of diagnosing a problem, devising a solution, and taking concrete actions to address the problem by implementing some of the prescriptions. At the global level, UN ideas – whether solid or inept – typically are restricted to the first two steps because the final, and some would say most essential, step of implementation is not in the hands of the idea-mongers, but of states. Hence, the criticism that too many UN ideas remain on coffee tables or in file drawers has some truth but is often beside the point. Those who create normative or causal ideas are usually not those who are responsible for their implementation. The host of 'lessons learned' might better be organized under the rubric of 'lessons spurned' in that the governments of member states who may have initiated policy documents and negotiated policy conclusions, frequently have failed to make decisions about implementation. Again Doha and Cancun are an illustration of this in the international trade field.

It might be helpful to elaborate a little upon another example of the disconnect between knowledge creation and implementation. We are struck by the absence of meaningful international reaction when an idea that is oversold then becomes counterproductive. For instance during the 1980s, the neo-classical development paradigm took hold again with a vengeance. Initially, this neo-classical resurgence in development did not get a strong response from within the UN. We had to wait till the mid-1980s for a reaction to occur – and that came from an unexpected place within the UN, namely UNICEF, and less surprisingly from the ECA, but not from the UN in New York.

Why so late and why so timid? Why did the UN proper not confront the BWIs head on? Why did the world have to wait until well into the 1990s for a more systematic reaction to occur, including by then from within the World Bank itself, and then only after many countries of

Latin America and sub-Saharan Africa had been deep into a tail-spin for a decade or more? Was it solely the might of the industrial countries and their commitment to the neo-classical model that made it so difficult to resist? Or was it the lack of quality and imagination by UN economists and the accompanying timidity by the UN's organizational leaders? Clearer answers than we have at present would be of the utmost importance for the future of the UN.

In 1996 one of us organized a conference on development policies into the twenty-first century at which Ajit Singh forcefully asked the question how long it would take Latin American policy makers to admit that the Washington Consensus had been a failure. 'Five more years', was the reply by people like John Williamson and Andres Bianchi (Singh, 1997: 257–9). Five years later, in 2001, Argentina was in a deep financial crisis, Fujimori was in Japan, Hugo Chavez in Caracas, Carlos Salinas de Gortari in Cuba, Ecuador dollarized – hardly a successful picture! Over the last 20 years, the UN has frequently missed the chance to emphasize the failures of such overconfident predictions.

The linkages between research outside and inside the UN

Most observers think primarily about the political and security institutions and individuals when mention is made of the UN, including the latest High-level Panel on Threats, Challenges, and Change. Nobel Peace Prizes awarded to the UN come to mind, including to Ralph Bunche, Dag Hammarskjöld, the Office of the United Nations High Commissioner for Refugees (UNHCR), UN peacekeepers, and recently Kofi Annan and the UN itself. In fact, the impact of the UN economic and social institutions may have been more quiet but often more effective. Indeed, two development agencies – the ILO and UNICEF – have also been recognized with a Nobel Peace Prize. More importantly, from the point of view of this intellectual history, ten Nobel laureates in economics (Jan Tinbergen, Ragnar Frisch, Gunnar Myrdal, Wassily Leontief, James E. Meade, W. Arthur Lewis, Richard Stone, Lawrence Klein, Theodore W. Schultz and Amartya Sen) have spent a substantial part of their professional lives working as UN staff members and/or consultants contributing to the UN ideas and activities.

Notwithstanding such intellectual 'giants', it cannot be implied that most UN ideas and research under discussion emanate from the UN system itself or are commissioned by it. The UNIHP approach has cast its net more widely in trying to determine how knowledge and ideas about social development are generated and find themselves on or off the agendas of various UN organizations. We find that identifying 'who conducts UN research' (one of the main background questions in the Oral History component of our Project) is profoundly ambiguous. Margaret Joan Anstee argued for a different approach to this issue during a session of our International Advisory Council. This alliterative approach suffuses UNIHP research: The UN sometimes has been a 'fount' (or original source) for ideas, but more frequently a 'funnel' for outside ideas, a 'forum' where controversial ideas are debated and subsequently modified or a 'font' for their blessing. In addition, the UN has at times provided a 'fanfare' to announce them and at times the 'funeral' for their burial. For us, all parts are valid components of an intellectual history of the world organization because all are parts of a puzzle that can lead to explaining the impacts noted above.

We locate some sources of ideas within international secretariats: individual leadership, UN researchers, reports of eminent commissions, global conferences, and inter- and intra-agency co-operation and tensions. If a particular idea was developed largely within the UN, it is important to determine whether key individuals brought it with them and subsequently fought successfully for its organizational adoption, or whether it emerged from ongoing group negotiations. There has been both a two-way street as well as international secretariats acting as more independent purveyors of ideas.

We also examine which ideas originated outside the UN system, perhaps from expert groups, NGOs, and national decision-makers as well as outside the UN family. Were they in response to a particular event or crisis? Some ideas originated within an elite, whereas others, such as the Universal Declaration of Human Rights, were more the consequence of a 'mass base' and rather widespread popular support, notwithstanding the enormous contributions of people like Eleanor Roosevelt, René Cassin, and John Humphrey.

The oral history interviews and the books attempt to tease out the importance of various linkages between 'external' and 'internal' ideas. Here we emphasize four in particular that emerge from the oral history transcripts.[12]

Academics, consultants, and expert groups are seen by many of our interlocutors as useful channels for injecting outside expertise and formulating new ideas and concepts. Others are more cynical, believing that UN agencies more typically call upon 'known quantities' whose views coincide with in-house ones and who thus will parrot what the commissioning agency wants, said Robert Cox, who chose to leave the ILO and pursue an academic career at Columbia University and the

University of Toronto was perhaps the most cynical: 'I learned that you don't invite a consultant in when you want good advice about management. You invite them in when you want to do something, and they're going to help you to make the recommendations that will result in a structure coming out which is the one you wanted to begin with.'

UN agencies frequently organize expert groups to examine specific issues. In examining the output and impact of such analysts over the years, Mahfuzur Rahman has written: 'The quality and composition of these expert groups varied greatly over time, but they generally had considerable influence on policy decisions of intergovernmental bodies. In fact, expert-group studies in general had more prestige attached to them than authors of secretariat studies could normally aspire to' (Rahman, 2002: xiii).

In *Ahead of the Curve?*, we examined the early use of high-level expert committees in three major UN publications that helped define the future international development agenda: *National and International Measures for Full Employment*, 1949; *Measures for the Economic Development of Under-Developed Countries*, 1951a; and *Measures for International Economic Stability*, 1951b (United Nations, 1949, 1951a, 1951b; Emmerij *et al.*, 2001: 26–42). These pioneering reports contributed much new thinking about the situation and needs of developing countries. The process of drafting these reports also pioneered a pattern. Each was prepared by a small team of prominent economists from different parts of the world, notably including subsequent Nobel laureates W. Arthur Lewis and Theodore W. Schultz, with support from the UN secretariat. There was a strong ethical commitment – acceptance that the purpose was to contribute to a world of greater economic and social justice with less poverty, and that work for the UN was a service to the larger community of states and peoples in addition to being professional work.

Many of our interlocutors appreciated the role of universities and think-tanks in generating ideas, but they were split about the relative importance of internal and external sources of UN ideas. Gerry Helleiner, now a retired professor of economics from the University of Toronto, and who has frequently been consulted by the UN and other international institutions, remarked that 'these expert groups are devices for demonstrating that ideas can be shared among people of quite different interests and origin when they gather as independent people, not representing their constituencies ... Now that you mention it, I prefer expert groups to jamborees. If I had my druthers, I think that is a much better use of money. Now I show utterly my biases. I show support for research. I guess that goes without saying or I wouldn't be in academia.'

Sartaj Aziz, who has assumed a university presidency in Pakistan after a long career in government and the UN, quipped: 'Obviously there is a lot of cross-fertilization of ideas. All the UN agencies which have people who are either from an academic background, or interact with the academic community, do manage to pick up a number of ideas. And the academics, if they come up with major breakthroughs in ideas, like Arthur Lewis' book, *The Theory of Economic Growth*, or Schumpeter's *The Theory of Economic Development*, or Gunnar Myrdal's *Asian Drama*, all had a major impact on development thinking. So then everybody else built on them.... But below that, even less important ideas in institutions which have close interaction with the academic community can become significant. More agencies invite members of the academic community to lead missions, for example, to different countries. They get enriched because they go to the countries. And at the same time, the people learn from them.'

NGOs and other associations of what increasingly is called 'global civil society' – defined as 'the sphere of ideas, values, institutions, organisations, networks and individuals located between the family, the state, and the market and operating beyond the confines of national societies, polities, and economies' (Anheier *et al.*, 2001) – are inserting themselves into a wide range of inter-governmental deliberations. How significant is this flurry of activities in terms of generating new ideas, norms, and principles?

'NGOs are an increasingly important piece', according to one observer, 'of the larger problem of global governance. Although the state system that has governed the world for centuries is neither divinely ordained nor easily swept away, in many ways that system is not well suited to addressing the world's grown agenda of border-crossing problems' (Florini, 2000: 3). The presence of alternative voices has become an integral part of the UN system's processes of deliberations and of world politics more generally. One could even make the case for considering a 'third UN,' although the analytical boundaries would be extremely difficult to define. The creation of the 'global compact' as a result of the Millennium Summit would imply that both non-profit NGOs as well as increasingly for-profit corporations would need to be included in this 'third UN' (see Ruggie, 2001).

NGOs are seen by virtually everyone among our interviewees as an essential component of ideational change, either themselves pushing forward their own ideas or badgering governments to consider ones already on the table. In terms of specific ideas, most interviewees attributed the recognition of gender and human rights concerns to the advocacy work of civil society groups. Leticia Shahani noted that the UN's influence 'moves like an iceberg. But eventually, again because of the pressure of people and NGOs, the women's issue emerged'. And Brian Urquhart, in his usual self-depreciating manner, remarked that, 'the NGOs, god bless them, have made life unsafe for established international bureaucracies'.

In specific terms, Jacques Polak remarked that even the IMF has been influenced by NGO pressures. He attributed the incorporation of social policies into the financial mainstream not only to Managing Director Michel Camdessus, the Americans, and the British, but also to pressure from NGOs: 'The influence of the NGOs on the Fund', he said, 'is really more indirect through the U.S. Congress, and through the British Government too, I think. On those two governments, they have an important influence and they guide, to a certain extent, the positions taken by the Executive Directors, how they push the organization.'

At the same time, others were uncomfortable with either the non-representative character or the clear political agendas of NGOs. The late Bernard Chidzero drew upon his experience in Zimbabwe: 'There may be a tendency on the part of some NGOs to operate as agents of multi-nationals or transnationals. . . . If they can remain in the areas of serving mankind without taking sides with political groups, they will serve a very useful purpose. But, if they become associated with eroding or opposing parties, they become part of a political system. They become political agents. And, I think, this would destroy or minimize their roles . . . [and] bypass certain market forces and civil government bureaucracy. That is a virtue but it is also a danger, because the NGOs . . . may be promoting projects which are not those of government, or which are even anti-government.' In a similar vein, after leaving the secretariat and returning to his home country, James Jonah did not wish to have uniform categories of 'saints' or 'sinners': 'Not all of them are solid. Some of them are outright 'crooks,' sorry to say, engaged in smuggling commodities and diamonds. In Africa in particular, some of these NGOs have links with rebel movements. I think that raises questions. Governments are raising questions – and I know we did in Sierra Leone – about the accountability of NGOs in terms of how they run their show. Because they are politically powerful in many countries like the United States, and in Europe, these governments channel their assistance through NGOs.'

A particular type of international expertise – which combines knowledge and political visibility and has been influential in nourishing economic and social ideas – has emanated from reports of independent commissions of eminent persons. This technique was launched in 1969 with *Partners in Development*, the report of a commission chaired by Canadian Prime Minister Lester B. Pearson (Commission on International Development, 1969). The Pearson Commission was followed by a host of others, including: two commissions on development issues headed by German Chancellor Willy Brandt (Independent Commission on International Development Issues, 1980, 1983); on common security by Swedish Prime Minister Olav Palme (Independent Commission on Disarmament and Security Issues, 1982); on environment and development by Norwegian Prime Minister Gro Harlem Brundtland (World Commission on Environment and Development, 1987); on humanitarian problems by Iranian and Jordanian Princes Sadruddin Aga Khan and Hassan bin Talal (Independent Commission on International Humanitarian Issues, 1988); on South-South cooperation by Tanzanian President Julius Nyerere (South Commission, 1990); on global governance by Swedish Prime Minister Ingvar Carlsson and Guyana's Shridath Ramphal (Commission on Global Governance, 1995). The two most recent ones have been on humanitarian intervention and state sovereignty by Australian Foreign Minister Gareth Evans and Algeria's Mohamed Sahnoun, issued in 2001 (ICISS, 2001) and on human security by Sadako Ogata and Amartya Sen, issued in 2003 (Commission on Human Security, 2003). There are also such commissions that are recalled more by the names of their sponsors rather than of the chairs – for example, the Club of Rome report on the limits to growth (Meadows *et al.*, 1972, 1992) and the Carnegie Commission on preventing deadly conflict (Carnegie Commission on Preventing Deadly Conflict, 1997).

These commissions get mixed reviews, from our interviewees, with many judging them to have produced creative new ways to deal with emerging or problematic issues – 'sustainable development' emanating from the Brundtland Commission is cited as such by virtually everyone even though the concept was first developed in UNEP several years earlier. Mostafa Tolba, Executive Director of UNEP from 1973 to 1992, explained to us that the concept of sustainable development took eight years to evolve. Maurice Strong came up with 'eco-development' in 1974. In 1975 it became 'development without destruction', and by 1981 'sustainable development' had been crafted. But it was the Brundtland report that brought the term into common international parlance in 1987.

Coming back to commissions in general, judgments about the quality of the analyses as well as the ultimate political impact of such commissions vary substantially across our oral history interviews. But the three functions that emerged from interviews are awareness and consciousness-raising; advocacy for particular ideas; and lending legitimacy to programmes and ideas. Some interviewees qualified their success, and thought that they could only be successful when their initiatives are backed by major powers, and when the subject matter is narrowly focused. Gerry Helleiner thought that 'if you put the right kind of group together, a mixed kind of group, it does have an impact on people. It is like social scientific research. The impact may not occur for 25 years.' Bernard Chidzero, who was more positive, said: 'I think these commissions were not just academic exercises. They were intended to produce results which would be applicable to real situations and which would necessitate governments' policies and institutional arrangements. . . . [They] have generated an awareness of the real problems which we face, not just of academic ideas. They have underpinned the necessity for governments to take action.' Sadako Ogata was less enthusiastic about the efforts of the 1990s than of the 1970s: 'The utility of the big commissions has receded in the 1990s. That's my impression. So in terms of agenda-setting, I don't know how far commissions can provide impetus. Is it because the world is saturated with too much information? Globalization? Maybe, but I think it is difficult to see who is really setting the agenda now.' Ironically, Mrs. Ogata agreed to co-chair the Human Security Commission.

Global, ad hoc conferences are seen as important occasions to push ideas – on the environment, women, human rights, population, children. At the same time, many interlocutors wondered about their cost-effectiveness, especially now that follow-up had been routinized in the form of +5 and +10 conferences. Viewed from the vantage point of the beginning of the twenty-first century, it may be difficult to believe that as late as the 1960s environmental degradation, population growth, urbanization, and women's rights were being discussed in specialized circles but were largely invisible on the radar screen of international development. This changed during the 1970s, and one reason was that the UN system launched a series of global conferences on emerging global challenges.

The UN institutionalized the conference system as a relation to common, global concerns (Fomerand, 1996; United Nations, 1997; Schechter, 2001). The major goals of these conferences were to raise awareness of common problems, to promote a change in the dominant attitudes toward them, to define solutions, to generate commitment and to stimulate the establishment of programmes of action to confront the challenges.

The 1972 Stockholm Conference was the first of the series and, from this perspective and in virtually everyone's opinion, a resounding success. Its worldwide publicity largely contributed to the inclusion of environmental concerns in national and international policy discussions and in the recognition that environmental challenges had to be tackled as part of development in poorer countries not instead of it. Environmental problems have played a crucial role in the growing awareness of interdependence and problems that countries could not solve alone (see Commoner, 1971). The Stockholm Conference illustrated also the importance of naming a strong personality like Maurice Strong to head the effort and of choosing a sympathetic host like Sweden. It also demonstrated the importance of intellectual preparations by experts at Founex before the actual conference, as interviews indicated with Ignacy Sachs and Michael Zammit-Cutajar who were there.

During the 1990s, the UN system went back to this method and built upon the series begun in the 1970s, but this time as summits and media events for heads of state and government rather than for 'mere' ministers. In a new era after the Cold War, a series of world summits promoted agendas for the 1990s and beyond. The objective was to mobilize governments and international civil society and to build a consensus around alternative approaches to development, centred on human beings and the protection of the environment.

Our interviewees are not of one voice about the value of global, ad hoc conferences. Most were supportive. They agree that public opinion was mobilized and long-run dynamics altered, but some are dubious about the precise impact and especially cost-effectiveness of such gatherings. Gert Rosenthal thought back to his experience as a national and international civil servant. 'I happen to think that one of the things the UN does best', he stated, 'is to impact on public awareness through either global conferences or reports or just the repetition of certain topics. Sooner or later, people start repeating certain basic propositions. Usually they are born in the UN secretariat, or the UN secretariat buys in when they are developed somewhere else and popularizes them. The UN does that very well. It takes time. No single document, no single conference is a watershed event. Oftentimes a report's ideas find sudden wide repetition in public circles up to five years after a report's release.' James Jonah also pointed to their potential for institution-building: 'Well, the general view was that they are good in terms of raising consciousness. That is one major goal which I would accept. But frankly, realistically, and honestly, it was also as a bureaucratic device by the secretariat to create institutions. If you look, many of these things came out of the conferences. Someone in the secretariat would be planning,

'How many posts am I going to get?'...Most of it is conceived by people who want to advance their careers.'

One crucial difficulty in unpacking the exact influence of the UN vis-à-vis other means of promoting ideas is that people often wear many hats – at the same time, or certainly over the course of careers. The previous discussion and much of what has been written, attempts to keep the above categories distinct for analytical purposes. Reality is usually more blurred.

An excellent example of this phenomenon and of the problems in determining the precise role of the UN in the production of key ideas can be found in an example from the 1970s (see Emmerij *et al.*, 2001: 60–79). The ILO developed and launched the so-called basic needs approach to economic and social development. But where did this idea come from? Did it come from within the secretariat of the ILO World Employment Programme or did it originate outside? The origin of the idea is difficult to unravel. Already the psychologist Abraham Maslow, in a 1942 article, talked about basic needs as the lowest rung on a five-rung ladder that culminated in spiritual and cultural needs (Maslow, 1942). India promoted a strategy of meeting 'minimum needs' in the early 1950s, heavily influenced by the economist Pitambar Pant. Ideas never develop in a vacuum. During the 1970s there were at least three places where the idea of basic needs was developed. One was at the Dag Hammarskjöld Foundation that culminated in 1975 in 'What Now? Another Development' (*Development Dialogue* 1975). A second place was in Argentina in 1976 where the Bariloche Foundation publication *Catastrophe o Nueva Sociedad: Modelo Mundial Latinoamericano* (Herrera, 1976) dealt with an analogous approach. The third place was in Geneva where the ILO prepared its 1976 World Employment Conference and produced a draft report in 1975 and a final one in 1976 where the concept of basic needs took central place (ILO, 1976).

How can one disentangle the exact origin of this idea, when several individuals were involved in all three projects? And that is the norm and not the exception. An idea 'suddenly' appears in different places at the same time. It is 'in the air'. However, at UNIHP the important thing is that in 1975–76 it arose and had international policy traction, especially because of the UN setting.

An important question is the extent to which researchers in and from developing countries are engaged in the process of knowledge production. Our impression is that especially since the 1960s, prominent individuals from the Global South are more and more present in research as in other positions within international secretariats. Our own interview pool contains a number of them – for example, Samir Amin, Lourdes Arizpe, Fernando Henrique Cardoso, Celso Furtado, Dharam Ghai, Noeleen Heyzer, Enrique Iglesias, Devaki Jain and Amartya Sen. The institutional connections are perhaps more problematic. James O.C. Jonah commented provocatively in an interview that commissioning outside papers 'is not an answer' because it comes from 'mostly Western institutions, which is why most of the things the Secretary-General does are not embraced by Third World countries'. This seems overly simple since, as we just mentioned, there is an increasing participation of institutions and individuals from developing countries.

Independent and critical thinking

Is independent and critical thinking within the UN system alive and well, or is it being weakened or compromised? We have learned from our research and interviews, for example, that research was de-emphasized during Boutros Boutros-Ghali's tenure, but that Kofi Annan has been more supportive of scholars, including placing several senior academics on the thirty-eighth floor to maintain liaison with the academy. In interviews as well as published memoirs, UN secretaries-general basically confirm that political and security crises expand to fill all available time, and that economic and social issues assume a lower priority. The present Secretary-General, Kofi Annan, nonetheless has taken the lead on the Millennium Summit and on pressing for action to reduce poverty and to implement the MDGs. In contrast, Javier Pérez de Cuéllar wrote about his sense of irony: 'Coming from the Third World, I was especially unhappy during my ten years as Secretary-General with the failure of the United Nations to work as a system more effectively for economic and social development.... It can be persuasively argued that, over the years, there has been inadequate leadership on the part of the Secretary-General and the UN Secretariat in placing the United Nations in the forefront of economic thinking.... Moreover, the political and administrative demands on the Secretary-General have always come first' (Pérez de Cuéllar, 1990: 4–5).

In trying to determine the UN's comparative advantage in the production or commissioning of research, it is clear that a direct comparison with a social science faculty of a major research university is not appropriate. The world organization's emphasis is on applied research and workable policy recommendations and not on the generation of basic knowledge. The UN system's emphasis is as much or more upon the politics of mobilizing political support for new undertakings as probing basic scientific facts. Doing something about global warming through a Kyoto or Montreal Protocol is the UN's comparative advantage, not measuring ozone levels.

What happened to particular ideas within the UN? In tracing the sources and distortions of ideas, we explore the importance of leadership within the UN and specialized agencies as well as the contributions by international civil servants. We also look at the importance of institutional rivalries or coalitions, particularly tensions within the UN system, and between the world organizations and the BWIs, which for our purposes are *de facto* independent even if *de jure* they are part of the system. The impact of rivalries or even of outright hostilities, within and among diplomatic coalitions is another important and underdocumented variable. We also seek to determine how the 'culture' of the world organization – for example, its institutional style and hiring practices – determined the decibel levels surrounding ideas, and thus influenced what ideas could be heard and eventually implemented.

Analysing failures is as important as analysing successes as a means to understand the UN role in facilitating consensus, and in perpetuating or exploding myths and reigning orthodoxies. The effort to document less as well as more 'successful' UN ideas is one means to foster more fruitful international discussions, negotiations and common approaches.

An example of the vagaries of measuring 'success' comes from the UN's approach after the physical collapse of the Berlin Wall and the ideological collapse of socialism in Central and Eastern Europe and the Soviet Union. As explained earlier, there were two schools of thought about the way ahead. There was the 'impatient' school emanating from the World Bank, the IMF, and European Bank for Reconstruction and Development (EBRD) as well as from several high-profile Western consultants. These were in favour of a big-bang, a one-leap, or a shock-therapy approach, undertaken as fast as possible whatever the point of departure and the absence or presence of certain institutions like financial and banking facilities. The second school – promoted by the UN, and more particularly by the ECE, argued in favour of a more cautious, gradual approach. A 'crawl', was needed because modernization was not a quick fix but demanded setting up appropriate institutions, careful trade liberalization policies, substantial inward transfer of resources, free access to major markets on which export-oriented growth could be based, and a sensitive treatment of the complicated heritage of 'social welfare'. This more deliberate school stressed the need for a wide social backing for the reform programme in order to maintain a social consensus in favour of a shift to the market. It also underlined the inevitable painful effects of the transition on the population.

The ECE framework for transition focused on comprehensiveness (how much to change), speed (how to introduce change), and sequencing (what to change first). It presented a set of institutional reforms to be implemented at the outset: property rights, micro reforms at the enterprise level, the establishment of a commercial banking infrastructure, social safety net and labour market changes – as well as macroeconomic stabilization and price liberalization in the short run. Afterwards would come reforms with a lower priority, including current account convertibility, easier foreign investments, and the like. Finally, the ECE proposed changes that simply could not be addressed in the short term, such as large-scale privatization, the creation of an adequate regulatory environment and of capital markets, and reform of the pension system.

Should the ECE's ideas be counted as a failure because they were not implemented? There are several reasons why the ECE approach did not prevail. Most importantly, it had no resources to put on the table, whereas the IFIs backed their ideas with billions of dollars of investments and grants, albeit not as many billions as they first argued would be necessary. The UN obviously had the experience (it had been the only organization where Eastern and Western Europe had co-operated on the ground) and the better strategy – as subsequent experience as well as the experience of China have shown. But superior ideas do not necessarily win out in the face of superior resources.

One of the more important and potentially disconcerting considerations is the extent to which UN research – conducted in-house or commissioned – is obliged to be 'politically correct'. And in determining correctness, whose definitions carry the most weight? Major donors? Countries most affected by a topic? Leadership in a particular secretariat? All of the above?

While the jury is still out, the five published volumes and oral histories show how much vision and creative thinking emerged from the first generation of UN leaders and how great was the input of their colleagues and academic consultants. In later decades, and particularly since the 1980s, the vision was less bold, the ideas more blurred, and the UN, at least in the development arena, often sidelined. This was less a question of political correctness than a failure to speak out with analytical boldness. In the 1990s, with a new emphasis on human rights and human development there was a revival of UN vision and intellectual creativity, and a new visibility often linked to the global conferences and summits.

Economic backing and resources, however, remained concentrated on the BWIs.

In keeping with this, the role of neo-classical orthodoxy and Western influence remains internationally dominant, even though collaboration across the different agencies of the UN and between the UN and the BWIs is increasingly encouraged. In particular, the Millennium Summit in September 2000 outlined a new development agenda for the UN and opened possibilities for a new and more balanced partnership with the BWIs and the WTO. Not that this is the first time the World Bank and IMF accepted outcome goals – as opposed to the process goals of structural adjustment in the 1980s.

It is difficult to assess whether or not these new possibilities are likely to be carried forward into action as terrorism and war have now moved to centre stage, at the UN and elsewhere. But development remains a central priority for the new millennium, and the UN with its universal membership and truly worldwide concerns is in a unique position to contribute to new thinking. Indeed, without it, the eradication of poverty, economic and ecological sustainability, and a world of greater justice will not only not be achieved; but the situation will actually worsen.

Conclusions

In keeping with the aim of the UNIHP to provide a *forward-looking* history, each volume attempts to draw lessons for the future. While it is too soon to draw all the threads together some conclusions for action seem clear.

First, the UN has had a more positive and pioneering record in the economic and social arena than is generally realized. This performance compares favourably with that of the BWIs, yet funding for development has increasingly flowed to the latter and away from the world organization. The UN's record in economic and social ideas and action deserves to be better known and the imbalance in funding corrected.

Second, more emphasis in the last few years has been laid by all countries on closer collaboration between the BWIs and the UN as well as on 'ownership' of development projects and initiatives by developing countries themselves, but the driving force for economic policy still rests with the IMF and the World Bank following the 'Washington consensus' orthodoxy. This is true both of the Poverty Reduction Strategy Papers (PRSPs) and of actions in pursuit of MDGs. The historical record of performance suggests that this is still too narrow an approach and at variance with what is required to achieve the MDGs. The multi-disciplinary approaches of the UN need to be given more attention in analysis and action – both by the UN itself as well as by other bodies – especially at country level, backed up with more staff and more resources.

Third, the UN's most important contributions in ideas and thinking have come from a diversity of places and people. Leadership in ideas has shifted over the years, waxing and waning in different agencies and institutions, though usually linked to some common factors: boldness of vision and leadership; high quality of professional analysis that is both multidisciplinary and pragmatic; close attention to country-level specifics and realities; freedom from tight government or bureaucratic control; and strong commitment to justice. These are the characteristics that need to be protected and carried forward in the organization and practice of the UN's future research and analysis.

Fourth, quasi-university public research institutes like the World Institute for Development Economics Research (WIDER) and UNRISD have a special place, since they hold out a credible hope for re-igniting the creative intellectual spark in UN economic and social work. Their mission is to pioneer applied research, to undertake policy advocacy and to strengthen capacity in the area of sustainable growth. They have a research staff and a worldwide network of collaborators, thereby avoiding problems of motivation that bedevil organizations that rely too much on permanent staff. Governments contribute funding to projects that they wish to support, thereby introducing multiple accountabilities that reduce the scope of a single country to exercise an overbearing financial leverage on the intellectual direction of the organization in question. For these reasons, 'it is still possible to believe that international organizations can be creative intellectual actors, and that there will be more intellectual history of the United Nations to be written in the future' (Toye and Toye, 2004).

Notes

Introduction

1. The author would like to thank Yusuf Bangura, Deborah Eade, Terence Gomez, Thandika Mkandawire, Shahra Razavi, Dennis Rodgers, and an anonymous reviewer for their comments on earlier drafts, and Kate Ives, Jenifer Freedman and Anita Tombez for research and editorial assistance.
2. Strictly speaking, Marx and Engels used these words in 'The Communist Manifesto' to refer to earlier historical epochs.
3. The 50 Years is Enough campaign was organized in various countries to protest against the policies and governance structures of the World Bank and the IMF on the occasion of their 50th anniversary in 1994. The campaigns were institutionalized with the formation of the United States Network for Economic Justice and initiatives and organizations in several other countries.
4. The World Summit for Social Development, held in Copenhagen in 1995, brought together many world leaders and civil society activists to explore ways of mitigating the social effects of economic liberalization and structural adjustment, and of eradicating poverty and promoting full employment and social integration.
5. The HDR is commissioned annually by the United Nations Development Programme (UNDP). It was first launched in 1990 'with the single goal of putting people back at the center of the development process in terms of economic debate, policy and advocacy'. From 1995 to 2000, the HDR was fairly outspoken in its critique of dominant patterns of globalization (HDR, 1999), consumption (1998), economic growth (1996), and focused on such issues as human rights (2000), poverty eradication (1997) and gender equality (1995) (see http://hdr.undp.org/aboutus/).
6. The World Bank refers to itself as a 'knowledge bank'.
7. 'Voices of the Poor' is the umbrella title for three reports published by the World Bank in 2000 (see Narayan *et al.*, 2000a, b; Narayan and Petesch, 2000).
8. 'Social capital' generally refers to the developmental benefits that can derive from relations of trust, reciprocity, associational activity and organizational density.
9. See World Bank, 2005.
10. PRSPs aim to identify the macroeconomic, structural and social policies and programmes, as well as the financial needs of low-income countries, that will promote growth and poverty reduction. Prepared by governments, they involve multistakeholder consultations with selected domestic and external actors and organizations.
11. In this framing process, other institutions also play a key role, notably the media (Carragee and Roefs, 2004).

12. I am grateful to Dennis Rodgers for his views on this issue.
13. For a summary of the conference discussions see UNRISD Conference News, *Social Knowledge and International Policy Making: Exploring the Linkages* (Report of the UNRISD Conference, 20–21 April 2004), which was prepared by Deborah Eade and this author. Support for this conference and preparation of this volume was provided by UNRISD's core donors, which include the governments of Denmark, Finland, Mexico, Norway, Sweden, Switzerland and the United Kingdom.
14. Such pretensions refer to the assumption that a particular world view or school of thought has universal applicability. This should not be confused with the notion of universal human rights.
15. The phrase refers to the critique of structural adjustment programmes emanating from research sponsored by the United Nations Children's Fund (UNICEF) in the mid-1980s. See Cornia *et al.*, 1987.
16. Regarding the principles and policy recommendations of the Commission, see ILO, 2004.
17. Such a position contrasts with the more antagonistic relations between certain parts of the UN system and TNCs in the 1970s, when attention focused on a New International Economic Order and a code of conduct for TNCs.
18. 'Post-Washington Consensus' refers to an enlarged package of policy prescriptions that succeeded a set of structural adjustment and economic stabilization policies, which was known as the Washington Consensus because it was promoted most explicitly by the World Bank, the IMF and the United States Treasury, all located in Washington, DC.
19. This agenda had expanded considerably as a result of a series of UN summits held in the 1990s on issues such as sustainable development, women, social development, population and urban development, as well as growing attention to human rights and 'rights-based development'.
20. The term has been used by French regulation theorists and others to refer to the compromise between capital and labour that was a feature of the so-called Fordist model of development (Lipietz, 1992).
21. This 'mission creep' is reflected in the topics addressed by the World Bank in its annual flagship report, which since the late 1990s has focused on knowledge (World Bank, 1999), 'attacking poverty' (World Bank, 2000a), institutions for markets (World Bank, 2001a), sustainable development (World Bank, 2002a), services for the poor (World Bank, 2003a) and equity (World Bank, 2005).
22. Such concerns figured prominently in discussions at the UNRISD conference on 'Social Knowledge and International Policy Making'. See, for example, the summaries of interventions by Rehman Sobhan, Adebayo Olukoshi and Marcia Rivera (UNRISD, 2004, pp. 10–11).
23. See, for example, Mark Weisbrot, 'The IMF has lost its influence', *International Herald Tribune*, 23 September 2005, p. 7.
24. See, in particular, *Economic Security for a Better World* (ILO Socio-Economic Security Programme, 2004), the *Human Development Report* (UNDP, 2005), *Report on the World Social Situation* (United Nations, 2005), *Economic Development in Africa: Rethinking the Role of Foreign Direct Investment* (UNCTAD, 2005), and *Gender Equality: Striving for Justice in an Unequal World* (UNRISD, 2005).
25. Such resistance was particularly evident in the case of the ILO and UNCTAD publications noted in the previous footnote.
26. See Oxfam International, 2005, and G8 Gleneagles, 2005.

2 The New Buzzwords

1. We are indebted to Jo Doezema and Keith Bezanson for leading us to the work of Georges Sorel, via that of Ernesto Laclau and Albert Hirschmann respectively, which proved so fruitful for our analysis. Thanks go to Katja Jassey, Rosalind Eyben, Mick Moore and Ian Scoones for their insightful comments on earlier versions. We would also like to thank Jenny Edwards, Georgina Blanco-Mancilla and Aaron de Grassi for locating some of the materials we refer to here. It goes without saying that all errors of interpretation are, of course, entirely ours.

2. See, for example, Crewe and Harrison (1999) and Mosse (2004b).

3. In doing so, we take our cues from the fascinating and important work that has been done in recent years on discourses of development, such as Gasper and Apthorpe (1996), Gardner and Lewis (1996), and Grillo and Stirrat (1997).

4. See, for example, Bebbington *et al.* (2004) on 'social capital' in the World Bank, and Cornwall and Pratt (2004) on 'participation' in Sida.

5. See Brock *et al.* (2001) and Cornwall (2000) for longer overviews of the uses of 'poverty reduction' and 'participation', respectively.

6. Threads of 1970s participation discourses, both radical and pragmatic, can be traced further back in the domestication of dissent through colonial community development (Presley, 1988) and 'decentralized governance' a.k.a. indirect rule (Ribot, 1996). Traces of these experiences patterned participation in struggles over political space in the global South; they were also, of course, patterned by shifting configurations of power in the political contexts that shaped the policies of development agencies, whether the waves of popular participation in America and Europe over the course of the 1960s, or the politics of the Cold War.

7. See Manor (1999) and Crook and Sverrisson (2001) for further, empirical, exploration of the limitations of 'participation' in decentralization narrative and practice, and for a critical view of the relationship between decentralization and 'poverty reduction'.

8. In 1996 the Development Assistance Committee (DAC) of the Organisation for Economic Co-operation and Development (OECD) published *Shaping the 21st Century: The Contribution of Development Co-operation*, which contained seven IDTs that aimed to halve the proportion of people living in extreme poverty by 2015.

9. Reflecting on the implementation of the Bolivian PRSP from the perspective of a bilateral donor.

10. For Craig and Porter (2003), these are: promoting opportunity (as broad-based growth); facilitating empowerment (by promoting good governance, especially anti-corruption); enhancing security (by investing in health and education), which often includes a fourth, social protection (to protect the marginal).

11. Indeed the MDD declares, 'we are committed to making the right to development a reality for everyone and to freeing the entire human race from want' (United Nations, 2000: 55/2, para. 11). For one Northern donor, the Department for International Development (DFID), this has led to some edgy positioning that places the emphasis firmly on the national government as duty-holder, carefully avoiding any implications for supranational actors or other foreign governments who are part of development activities in any given country (Piron, 2003).

12. See Gilbert Rist's (1997) brilliant and disconcerting analysis of the emergence of 'development', and the role of myth in its creation and continuity.
13. It needs to be borne in mind that these struggles are only ever partially over meaning: they are also over turf, and may be driven as much by bureaucratic convenience and organizational imperative, or by rivalry, ambition and a desire for personal power, as by moral and intellectual conviction.
14. Comment made in discussions of this paper at the UNRISD conference on Social Knowledge and International Policy Making: Exploring the Linkages, UNRISD, Geneva, 20–21 April 2004.
15. The full citation reads: 'Now we often hear sudden declarations of fashionable support for participatory approaches from politicians, planners, economists and technocrats. Social scientists should not confuse these statements with actual participatory planning because, under the cloud of cosmetic rhetoric, technocratic planning continues to rule' (Cernea, 1995[1985]:25).

3   The Search for Policy Autonomy in the Global South

1. I wish to thank participants at the United Nations Research Institute for Social Development (UNRISD) Conference on Social Knowledge and International Policy Making: Exploring the Linkages, held in Geneva, 20–21 April 2004, and especially Charles Gore of the United Nations Conference on Trade and Development (UNCTAD) for the many useful comments made on an earlier draft of this paper. The usual disclaimers apply.
2. The Bandung Conference, held in Indonesia in 1955, established the vision and principles that guided the Non-Aligned Movement, which was officially launched in 1961.
3. Blomstrom and Hettne (1984), Toye (1987) and Hettne (1995) provide useful reviews of the contributions of Southern thinkers and the evolution of the development debate in this period.
4. On this point, see especially Eichner (1983: 231–6), cited by Dr Glenn Sankatsing in a private communication.
5. This point is discussed with great insight by Wolf (1982: 9), Goonatilake (1984), and also cited by Dr Sankatsing (1998).
6. A recent example of this, in relation to the Argentine case, is to be found in Krueger (2004). The International Monetary Fund (IMF) has since admitted its errors in Argentina (see IMF, 2004).
7. The practice is reminiscent of those medieval doctors who firmly believed that the cure for certain illnesses was to draw blood from the patient. As the patient further deteriorated, additional bloodletting was prescribed, with predictable results.
8. This reflection was stimulated by a comment by Charles Gore on an earlier version of this chapter.
9. Critics of the PRSP process have noted the narrowly prescribed parameters in which it takes place with respect to participation of democratically elected actors, the absence of analysis of the structural causes of poverty and the distribution of power in the society, the lack of variety in the policies

proposed which correspond closely to the framework advocated in World Development Reports, and the fact that the process conditionality of the PRSPs has not replaced or reduced the use of policy-based conditionality. See Cornwall and Brock (2004), and Toye (2004).

10. Further elaboration of this idea with some illustrative examples can be found in Girvan (1995).
11. This may be because the most significant regional groups are either Northern-based (European Union/EU, North American Free Trade Agreement/NAFTA) or, in the case of the South, have until recently tended to engage in multilateral trade negotiations on terms set by the North.
12. The notion of 'epistemic communities' is taken from Byron (2003: 66).
13. At the UNRISD conference on Social Knowledge and International Policy Making, where an earlier version of this paper was presented, it was reported that in Eastern Europe, the United Nations Economic Commission for Europe (ECE) had advocated a more gradual and nuanced transition to market economy than that adopted under the aegis of the Washington-based institutions, with apparent vindication from subsequent events.
14. It should be noted that the Dominican Republic and Cuba also participate in the CRNM in certain areas.

4 The World Bank as a Knowledge Agency

1. Weber believed that the specific nature of bureaucracy 'develops the more perfectly the more bureaucracy is 'dehumanised', the more completely it succeeds in eliminating from official business love, hatred, and all purely personal, irrational, and emotional elements that escape calculation' (Gerth and Mills, 1946: 215).
2. In defining the criteria of the 'good researcher', we do not suggest that bad researchers, who fail to meet these criteria, cannot be found in academia as well as elsewhere. Our point is that good researchers face an additional hazard in the bureaucratic context.
3. For a detailed case study of such vetting at the World Bank, see Wade (1996).
4. In its early years, the Bank's most distinguished economist was Paul Rosenstein-Rodan, who had contributed one of the seminal works of the new sub-discipline of development economics in 1943 (see Rosenstein-Rodan, 1943). His sojourn at the Bank between 1947 and 1954 was a contentious and unhappy one, and after many conflicts with the management, he left for academic life at the Massachusetts Institute of Technology (MIT).
5. See Tinbergen (1958). His account of the publication delay, and the reasons for it, is given in Magnus and Morgan (1987).
6. Interview of Gerald K. Helleiner by Tom Weiss for the UN Intellectual History Project, Toronto, 4–5 December 2000, internal UNIHP document, p. 45.
7. See Chang (2001). Stiglitz's own account of his experience in the Bank is given in Stiglitz (2002).
8. Further US pressure, this time to change the draft of the *World Development Report 2001*, led to the resignation of the report's independent editor-in-chief,

Ravi Kanbur, in the following year. These two episodes are chronicled in Wade (2001).

9. It was slow to adopt the discounted cash flow and the shadow pricing techniques, according to the Bank's historians, Mason and Asher (1973).
10. I am grateful to Norman Girvan for this point.
11. These issues were further explored in Toye (1993).
12. For an account of these episodes, see Wade (1997).

5   Knowledge Management and the Global Agenda for Education

1. The ideas in this chapter have profited from discussions with colleagues and staff in the Japan International Cooperation Agency (JICA), Tokyo, and in the Swedish International Development Cooperation Agency (Sida) in February 2004, and in Wilton Park, United Kingdom, and the Centre of African Studies, Copenhagen, in March 2004.
2. See also Special Issue of the *Journal of International Cooperation in Education*, VII, No.1, April 2004 on 'International Education Cooperation: Toward Greater Autonomy or Dependency in Sub-Saharan Africa'.
3. 'Countries may wish to set their own targets for the 1990s in terms of the following proposed dimensions...' (WCEFA, 1990: 3).
4. Of course World Conferences have become a location for a huge number of special interest groups anxious to try and influence the final agenda. This particular World Conference possibly broke new ground by including a number of key individuals from both North and South within its International Steering Committee, by organizing a whole series of regional conferences prior to the main Conference, and by making it mandatory for the official country delegations to include national NGOs.
5. See, for example, Lockheed *et al.* (1980).
6. For an early synthesis, see Colclough (1980), and King (1991). For an example of the influence of this World Bank research without explicit references in the text, see ODA (1992). The durability of this body of work is attested by its inclusion in the lead chapter of the *EFA Global Monitoring Report* which is entitled 'Education for all is development' (UNESCO, 2002). For a detailed account of the history and influence of one component of this World Bank research, see King and Palmer (2004).
7. UNICEF had supported Colclough and Lewin's work, a first draft of which was available at Jomtien.
8. The fact that Jomtien adopted a target for universal access to, and completion of, primary education by the year 2000 was principally due to the personal intervention in Jomtien of the then Executive Director of UNICEF, Jim Grant. Several countries with large out of school populations were very reluctant to agree to this. Wadi Haddad, the Executive Secretary of the Jomtien Conference has since said 'the notion of the individual nation and its decisions was changed into a single global target [to be achieved by 2000]. This was a global mistake, as was 2015' [the target set by OECD/DAC] (Personal communication, Washington, 15 June 2004).

9. How gender disparity in the basic cycle of education could be realistically dealt with 10 years before UPE remains a mystery.
10. For a searing analysis of international targeting in education, see Jansen (2003).
11. See, however, JICA (1998).
12. Although 'the principle of shared knowledge' as a key element in development partnerships has been in DFID's policy since 1997 (DFID, 1997: 48), the many organizational changes in DFID's research architecture have made it difficult to see how knowledge from the South has contributed to DFID's overall and sectoral policies.
13. The Millennium Declaration was affirmed at the Summit – a document with a much wider set of obligations, including for the North, than the final set of MDGs.
14. It is said that the acronyms, IDTs and MDGs, are very little known or used in many developing countries.
15. The privileging of primary education through the 1990s took place despite the appearance of research-based policy papers by the World Bank on skills development and on higher education (World Bank, 1991, 1994).
16. I am indebted to Adebayo Olukoshi for this discussion of the policy terrain (personal communication, 10 March 2004, Wilton Park). See also his contribution to the UNRISD Conference *Social Knowledge and International Policy Making: Exploring the Linkages* (Geneva, 20–21 April 2004), Conference News, No. 14 (Geneva: UNRISD, 2004).
17. For instance, Smith (2003: 11) comments: 'As donor-driven decision-making moves further up the hierarchy and away from the classroom, other means need to be found which will impact positively on the quality of education in the classroom.'
18. It is evident that many donors at the country level regard their host countries as being in a situation of long-term aid dependency (see King, 2004).
19. I am indebted to Jan Waltmans of the Netherlands Foreign Ministry for this information.
20. See also World Bank, 2003a: ch. 11, and pp. 260–1.
21. Normally called Communities of Practice in the corporate literature.
22. Some groups remain identifiably similar to the old sectors.
23. For a detailed discussion of the Bank's external knowledge sharing initiatives, see World Bank (2003b: 19–32); and King and McGrath (2004: 76–92).
24. UNDP warns of the PRSPs: 'There is also a danger that without sufficient trust and open dialogue, the papers (PRSPs) can be seen as yet another donor requirement rather than a genuine shift in modalities' (UNDP, 2003b: 57).
25. For instance, the IDT on reducing infant mortality and maternal mortality could also be associated with World Bank research on the developmental impact of female education (Cochrane, 1986).
26. Though Keith Hart (1973) is routinely credited with the first use of the term 'informal sector' there can be little doubt that it was the further analysis of the concept by the World Employment Programme of the International Labour Organization (ILO) that gave the informal sector its international visibility, and also restricted its relevance to the urban rather than to rural areas (Palmer, 2004).

27. For examples of this critical engagement, see Aklilu (2001), Coraggio (2001), Mwiria (2001), Tilak (2001) and Torres (2001). See also Carlsson and Wohlgemuth (2000); and Kifle, Olukoshi, and Wohlgemuth (1997).

6 The Quest for Gender Equality

1. Paper for the Conference on Social Knowledge and International Policy Making: Exploring the Linkages, United Nations Research Institute for Social Development (UNRISD), Geneva, 20–21 April 2004.
2. In this chapter I do not get into a detailed definition or discussion of the nature or structure of international or national women's movements. I use the term here in a fairly general sense, adequate to this discussion. For a more elaborate discussion of the structure, issues, and challenges of the international women's movement, see Antrobus (2004) and Antrobus and Sen (forthcoming).
3. The term 'engendering' is used here in both its traditional dictionary meaning, and to also mean 'incorporating gender into'.
4. In India, for example, the most important event of the decade was the participatory process that led to the landmark report, *Toward Equality* (Government of India 1974) that mapped out a terrain for research, activism and policy that lasted until the 1990s.
5. For more on the DAWN network, see www.dawn.org.fj.
6. The United Nations (UN) conferences of the 1990s were an important catalyst that brought activists and researchers together. The importance of these large forums in making it possible for the women's movement to impact on discourse and policy cannot be minimized. Without these conferences, researchers and activists would have had to find other ways to come together, and that would not have been easy to do on the scale and with the frequency that the UN conferences made possible.
7. The World Bank's new president, Jim Wolfensohn, followed his promise with a series of actions to pay closer attention to gender in Bank policies.
8. The International Gender and Trade Network (IGTN) was set up explicitly to assist feminists to engage with WTO processes.
9. Annie Besant, the first president of the Indian National Congress that went on to become the main vehicle for the Indian nationalist struggle against British rule, was also a champion of women's right to birth control.
10. 'Development is the best contraceptive' was the South's slogan during the international population conference held in Bucharest in 1974.
11. This is something of an overstatement. However, though anthropologists and other social scientists have had some space, the field is largely driven by its technical aspects.
12. The Women's Global Network for Reproductive Rights (WGNRR) was the main international organization mobilizing women at this time.
13. A few women activists from the South even held demonstrations against ICPD during the actual conference.
14. The book co-edited by Sen *et al.* (1994), for example, consciously eschewed creating a book in which academic researchers would write the main chapters while women activists would provide illustrative boxes. Instead the

process of the book brought both groups together to plan and write the chapters.

15. Viewing the wife's or daughter's body as the property of the husband/family/clan and so on is common in many parts of the world; its violation is treated in the law as a property violation rather than a human rights abuse.

16. Activism has also been considerably affected by the capacity to communicate with and act at broader levels. This is true not only in the global justice movement and the WSF or anti-WTO struggles but also in particular movements, for example, the Narmada Bachao Andolan's ability to link up with anti-dam supporters in Europe and North America and even testify before the United States Congress. Other activist movements have also been able to do this.

17. The Opus Dei is a lay Catholic organization with close links to the Vatican, and that wields considerable political power in many countries of the region.

18. See footnote 13 above.

19. The congruence or otherwise between research versus activism and researcher versus activist is discussed later.

20. Some may argue that proposal and report writing are hardly research in a real sense, and at one level this is true. Increasingly, however, in my own experience organizations are expected to provide more analytical reports of their work, requiring them to have stronger information systems in place, to undertake surveys or at least focus group discussions, and to provide analytical grounds for grant renewals. It is also not very helpful in this context to have a very narrow definition of research; the definition I am using is broad enough to encompass different kinds and levels of analysis and theorizing.

21. I am using this somewhat grotesque word to indicate that the form power takes is less transparent and direct but is mediated by questions about the adequacy of reporting or monitoring and information systems (MIS) that are more difficult to perceive as the workings of power.

22. Because of the delicate nature of these internal power issues within organizations and because a fair amount of the knowledge that I have in this regard is confidential, I am not able to provide specific examples but they definitely exist and are growing.

23. Personal communication with some thoughtful leaders of organizations, and my own experience.

24. This, in turn, can depend on the tightness of the labour market for educated labour and the relationship between education and jobs.

25. India and the Philippines are probably good examples.

26. This discussion develops further the argument about personal change made in Edwards and Sen (2002).

27. To be able to fight an enemy on the terrain of one's choosing rather than on ground chosen by the enemy is a key factor in waging a successful battle, according to Sun Tsu's *Art of War* (see Giles, 1910).

28. The only (and important) exception to this was the *Human Development Report*.

29. WSF 2004 in Mumbai witnessed many more women's panels and discussions, but real integration of a feminist voice and presence has a long way to go.

7   Global Social Policy Reform

1. In terms of the actual impact of economic globalization upon social policy in more northern and more developed economies, a new scholarly consensus is emerging (Scharpf and Schmidt, 2000; Sykes *et al.*, 2001; Yeates, 2001; Swank, 2002) that argues and demonstrates that globalization does not necessarily have to lead to the residualization (and privatization) of social provision.
2. See www.gaspp.org.
3. www.ilo.org.
4. See also www.gppi.net.
5. See www.helsinkiprocess.fi.

8   Generating Knowledge in the United Nations

1. The authors are the co-directors of UNIHP. Further details about the authors and UNIHP can be found at www.unhistory.org.
2. Published by Indiana University Press, the five volumes are: Louis Emmerij, Richard Jolly and Thomas G. Weiss (2001, second printing 2003), *Ahead of the Curve? UN Ideas and Global Challenges*; Yves Berthelot (ed.) (2004), *Unity and Diversity in Development Ideas: Perspectives from the Regional Commissions*; Michael Ward (2004), *Quantifying the World: UN Ideas and Statistics*; John Toye and Richard Toye (2004), *The UN and Global Political Economy: Trade, Finance, and Development*; and Richard Jolly, Louis Emmerij, Dharam Ghai and Frédéric Lapeyre (2004), *UN Contributions to Development Thinking and Practice*.
3. Forthcoming UNIHP publications at the time of writing (2004) include: Richard Jolly, Louis Emmerij and Thomas G. Weiss (2005), *The Power of UN Ideas: Lessons from the First Sixty Years*; Thomas G. Weiss, Tatiana Carayannis, Louis Emmerij and Richard Jolly (2005), *UN Voices: The Struggle for Development and Social Justice*; Neil MacFarlane and Yuen Foong-Khong (forthcoming), *Human Security and the UN: A Critical History*; Sarah Zaidi and Roger Normand (forthcoming), *The UN and Human Rights: The Unfinished Revolution*; Devaki Jain (forthcoming), *Women, Development, and the UN: A Sixty-Year Quest for Equality and Justice*; Olav Stokke (forthcoming), *The UN and Development Cooperation*; Tagi Sagafi-nejad in collaboration with John Dunning (forthcoming), *The UN and Transnationals, from Code to Compact*; Nico Schrijver (forthcoming), *The UN and the Global Commons: Development without Destruction*; Ramesh Thakur and Thomas G. Weiss (forthcoming), *The UN and Global Governance: An Idea and Its Prospects*; and the concluding volume, Richard Jolly, Louis Emmerij and Thomas G. Weiss (forthcoming), *The United Nations: A History of Ideas and Their Future*.
4. The interviews inform all books in the series and also constitute an important product in themselves. They will be made widely available in electronic form at the conclusion of the project and a synthesis of extracts from them will be published in the volume *UN Voices: The Struggle for Development and Social Justice* (Weiss *et al.*, 2005).
5. There are two important exceptions. One is the archive of the oral history compiled by the Yale University UN project, which contains interviews of persons involved in the political and humanitarian activities of the UN. The

other is the archive of UN papers in the Bodleian library in Oxford. This is a collection of personal papers, diaries and other writings of people from Great Britain who have worked in or alongside the UN in different places and at different times.

6. One of the co-directors presses for recognition of a 'third UN' namely the core of NGOs and individuals who are closely involved with UN decision making and activities. Tempting as this seems at first sight, to recognize a 'third UN' raises extremely difficult questions as to how and where to draw the boundary around such a disparate collection of groups, though as a collective influence, there is little doubt about its growing importance.

7. This ideational approach borrows from and simplifies the analytical framework put forth by Goldstein and Keohane (1993) on how ideas influence policy. See also Checkel (1997) and Sikkink (1991).

8. Oral history transcript of the interview with Stephane Hessel, 22–23 June 2000.

9. The careful review of archival material by John and Richard Toye suggests that Singer may have been the first to identify the downward secular trend in commodity prices and its causes, while Prebisch saw its wider significance for development policy and used his position and leadership to publicize the issues and develop and promote strategies of response.

10. See chapters by Adebayo Adejeji (Africa), Gert Rosenthal (Latin America and the Caribbean), Leelanda de Silva (Asia and the Pacific) and Blandine Destremeau (West Asia).

11. See chapter by Gert Rosenthal in Berthelot (2004).

12. Quotations without citations are taken from the transcripts, all of which will be made available electronically at the end of the UNIHP.

References

Aklilu, Habte, 'Reversing the process of development: initiating the discussion'. In Wolfgang Gmelin, Kenneth King and Simon McGrath (eds), *Development Knowledge, National Research and International Cooperation* (Edinburgh: Centre of African Studies – CAS/Bonn: German Foundation for International Development – DSE/Geneva: NORRAG, 2001).

Alexander, Nancy and Tim Kessler, *The Millennium Development Goals in an Unaccountable Global Order* (Silver Spring, MD: Citizens' Network on Essential Services, 2003). http://www.servicesforall.org/html/otherpubs/MD_Goals.shtml

Althusser, Louis, *Lenin and Philosophy and Other Essays* (London: New Left Books, 1971).

Amin, Samir, *Obsolescent Capitalism* (London: Zed Books, 2003).

——, 'Regionalization in response to polarizing globalization'. In Björn Hettne, András Inotai and Osvaldo Sunkel (eds), *The New Regionalism. Vol. I: Globalism and the New Regionalism* (London: Macmillan Press, 1999), in association with the United Nations University and the World Institute of Development Economics Research.

——, *Eurocentrism* (New York: Monthly Review Press, 1989).

Anheier, Helmut, Marlies Glasius and Mary Kaldor (eds), *Global Civil Society 2001* (Oxford: Oxford University Press, 2001).

Ansari, Javed A., *The Political Economy of International Economic Organization* (Boulder, Colorado: Rienner, 1986).

Antrobus, P., *Global Women's Movement: Origins, Issues and Strategies* (London: Zed Books, 2004).

Antrobus, P. and G. Sen, 'The women's movement'. In Srilatha Batliwala and David Brown (eds), *Claiming Global Power: Transnational Civil Society and Global Governance* (Bloomfield, CT: Kumarian Press, forthcoming).

Armendariz, Beatriz and Francisco Ferreira, 'The World Bank and the analysis of the international debt crisis'. In John Harriss, Janet Hunter and Colin M. Lewis (eds), *The New Institutional Economics and Third World Development* (London: Routledge, 1995).

Arnstein, Sherry, 'A ladder of citizen participation', *Journal of the American Institute of Planners*, 35, 4, July (1971) 216–24.

Arrighi, G., 'The three hegemonies of historical capitalism'. In S. Gill (ed.), *Gramsci, Historical Materialism and International Relations*, Cambridge Studies in International Relations No. 26 (Cambridge: Cambridge University Press, 1993).

Arthur Andersen LLP, *World Bank Knowledge Management Concept Paper: A Practical Approach* (Washington: World Bank, 1996).

Asia Pacific Civil Society Forum, 'The Millennium Development Goals and the eradication of extreme poverty and hunger'. In Focus on the Global South (ed.), *Anti-Poverty or Anti-Poor? The Millennium Development Goals and the Eradication of Extreme Poverty and Hunger* (Bangkok: Focus on the Global South, 2003). http://www.focusweb.org/pdf/MDG-2003.pdf, accessed on 19 May 2004.

Barber, William J., 'Government as a laboratory for economic learning in the years of the Democratic Roosevelt'. In Mary O. Furner and Barry Supple (eds),

The State and Economic Knowledge: the American and British Experiences (Cambridge: Cambridge University Press, 1990).

Barraclough, Solon L., 'Foreword'. In Matthias Stiefel and Marshall Wolfe, *A Voice for the Excluded: Popular Participation in Development: Utopia or Necessity?* (London and New Jersey: Zed Books, 1994).

Basu, Kaushik, 'Globalization and the politics of international finance: The Stiglitz verdict', *Journal of Economic Literature*, Vol. XLI, No. 3 (2003) 885–99.

Bebbington, Anthony, Scott Guggenheim, Elizabeth Olson, Michael Woolcock, 'Exploring social capital debates at the World Bank', *Journal of Development Studies*, 40 (5) (2004) 33–64.

Bello, W., *Deglobalization: ideas for a New World Economy* (London: Zed Books, 2004).

Bendell, Jem and David F. Murphy, 'Towards civil regulation: NGOs and the politics of corporate environmentalism'. In Peter Utting (ed.), *The Greening of Business in Developing Countries: Rhetoric, Reality and Prospects* (London: Zed Books and UNRISD, 2002).

Beneria, L. and M. Roldan, *The Crossroads of Class and Gender: Industrial Homework, Subcontracting, and Household Dynamics in Mexico City*, Women in Culture and Society Series (Chicago: The University of Chicago Press, 1987).

Beneria, L. and G. Sen, 'Accumulation, reproduction, and women's role in economic development: Boserup revisited', *Signs*, 7(2) (1981) 279–98.

Berthelot, Yves (ed.), *Unity and Diversity in Development Ideas: Perspectives from the Regional Commissions* (Bloomington: Indiana University Press, 2004).

Blackburn, James, Robert Chambers and John Gaventa, 'Learning to take time and go slow: mainstreaming participation in development and the Comprehensive Development Framework (CDF)', paper presented for the Operations Evaluation Department, World Bank (Brighton: Institute of Development Studies, 1999).

Blomstrom, Magnus and Bjorn Hettne, *Development Theory and the Three Worlds: the Dependency Debate and Beyond: Third World Responses* (London: Zed Books, 1984).

Bøås, Morten and Desmond McNeill (eds), *Global Institutions and Development: Framing the World* (London and New York: Routledge, 2004).

Booth, David (ed.), *Fighting Poverty in Africa: Are PRSPs Making a Difference?* (London: Overseas Development Institute, 2004).

Boserup, E., *Women's Role in Economic Development* (London: St Martin's Press, 1970).

Boughton, James M., *Silent Revolution: The International Monetary Fund 1979–1989* (Washington, DC: IMF, 2001).

Braathen, E., 'New social corporatism: A discursive-comparative perspective on the World Development Report 2000/1, "Attacking Poverty"'. In International Social Science Council, Comparative Research Programme on Poverty, *A Critical Review of the World Bank Report: World Development Report 2000/2001. Attacking Poverty. A Group of Norwegian Researchers Have Taken a First Look at the Report* (Bergen: ISSC/CROP, 2000). www.crop.org.

Brewster, Havelock, 'CARICOM: From community to single market and economy'. In K. Hall and D. Benn (eds), *Governance in the Age of Globalisation – National, Regional and Global Dimensions* (Kingston: Ian Randle Publishers, 2003a).

——, 'Mature regionalism and the Rose Hall Declaration on Regional Governance', paper delivered at the CARICOM 30th Anniversary Conference on Regional Governance and Integrated Development, University of the West Indies, Mona Campus, October (2003b).

Brock, Karen and Rosemary McGee (eds), *Knowing Poverty: Critical Reflections on Participatory Research and Policy* (London: Earthscan, 2002).

Brock, Karen, Andrea Cornwall and John Gaventa, *Power, Knowledge and Political Spaces in the Framing of Poverty Policy*, IDS Working Paper 143 (Brighton: Institute of Development Studies, 2001).

Budlender, D. (ed.), *The Women's Budget*, Institute for Democracy in South Africa (IDASA) (Cape Town: Creda Press, 1996).

Bullard, Nicola, 'The Millennium Development Goals and the Poverty Reduction Strategy Paper: two wrongs don't make a right'. In Focus on the Global South (ed.), *Anti-Poverty or Anti-Poor?: The Millennium Development Goals and the Eradication of Extreme Poverty and Hunger* (Bangkok: Focus on the Global South, 2003). http://www.focusweb.org/pdf/MDG-2003.pdf, accessed on 19 May 2004.

Bunch, C. and C. Reilly, *Demanding Accountability: The Global Campaign and Vienna Tribunal for Women's Human Rights* (New Brunswick, NJ: Center for Women's Global Leadership; and New York; United Nations Development Fund for Women (UNIFEM), 1994).

Buvinic, M., *Projects for Women in the Third World: Explaining Their Misbehavior* (Washington, DC: International Center for Research on Women – ICRW), 1984).

Byron, Jessica, 'Rethinking international relations: Changing paradigms or more of the same? A Caribbean small state perspective'. In K. Hall and D. Benn (eds), *Governance in the Age of Globalisation – National, Regional and Global Dimensions* (Kingston: Ian Randle Publishers, 2003).

Callinicos, A., *An Anti-Capitalist Manifesto* (Cambridge: Polity Press, 2003).

Carayannis, Elias and Bruno Laporte, *By Decree or by Choice? A Case Study: Implementing Knowledge Management and Sharing at the Education Sector of the World Bank*, World Bank Institute Working Papers (Washington, DC: World Bank, 2002).

Carden, Fred, *Capacities, Contexts, Conditions: the Influence of IDRC-Supported Research on Policy Processes*, Evaluation Highlight 5, March (2005). http://www.idrc.ca/evaluation

Carlsson, J. and L. Wohlgemuth (eds), *Learning in Development Cooperation* (Stockholm: Expert Group on Development Issues, 2000).

Carnegie Commission on Preventing Deadly Conflict, *Preventing Deadly Conflict* (New York: Carnegie Corporation of New York, 1997).

Carragee, Kevin M. and Wim Roefs, 'The neglect of power in recent framing research', *Journal of Communication*, Vol. 54, No. 2, June (2004) 214–33.

Cernea, Michael, *Putting People First: Sociological Variables in Rural Development*, reprint (Washington, DC: World Bank, 1995).

Chambers, Robert, *Managing Rural Development: Ideas and Experience from East Asia* (Uppsala: Scandinavian Institute of African Studies, 1974).

Chang, Ha-Joon (ed.), *Joseph Stiglitz and the World Bank: The Rebel Within* (London: Anthem Press, 2001).

Checkel, Jeffrey T., *Ideas and International Political Change: Soviet/Russian Behavior and the End of the Cold War* (New Haven: Yale University Press, 1997).

Cichon, M., K. Pal, F. Léger and D. Vergnaud, *A Global Social Trust Network: a New Tool to Combat Poverty through Social Protection*, Financial, Actuarial and Statistical Services, Social Protection Sector of the ILO (Geneva: ILO, 2003).

Cichon, M. *et al.*, 'An interview in Geneva with Robert Holzmann, the Director of the World Bank's Social Protection Network, 11 April 2002'. In M. Cichon *et al.*, *Global Social Trust* (Geneva: ILO, 2002). http://www.ilo.org/public/english/protection/socfas/download/research/feasibility.pdf.

Cochrane, Susan, 'The effects of education on fertility and mortality', Discussion Paper No. 26, Population and Human Resources Department (Washington, DC: World Bank, 1986).

Cohen, J. and N. Uphoff, 'Participation's place in rural development: Seeking clarity through specificity', *World Development*, 8 (1980) 213–35.

Colclough, Christopher, *Primary Schooling and Economic Development: a Review of the Evidence*, World Bank Staff Working Paper No. 399 (Washington, DC: World Bank, 1980).

Colclough, Christopher and Keith Lewin, *Educating All the Children: Strategies for Primary Schooling in the South* (Oxford: Oxford University Press, 1993).

Collier, Paul, 'Conditionality, dependence and coordination: three current debates in aid policy'. In Christopher L. Gilbert and David Vines (eds), *The World Bank: Structure and Policies* (Cambridge: Cambridge University Press, 2000).

Collison, Chris and Geoff Parcell, *Learning to Fly: Practical Lessons from One of the World's Leading Knowledge Companies* (Oxford: Capstone Publishing, 2001).

Commission on Global Governance, *Our Global Neighbourhood* (Oxford: Oxford University Press, 1995).

Commission on Human Security, *Human Security Now* (New York: Commission on Human Security, 2003).

Commission on International Development, *Partners in Development* (New York: Praeger, 1969).

Commoner, Barry, *The Closing Circle: Nature, Man, and Technology* (New York: Knopf, 1971).

Cooper Andrew, and John English, 'International commissions and the mind of global governance'. In Thakur Ramesh, Andrew Cooper and John English (eds), *International Commissions and the Power of Ideas* (Tokyo/New York/Paris: United Nations University Press, 2005).

Coraggio, J.L., 'Universities as sites of local and global knowledge (re)production'. In Wolfgang Gmelin, Kenneth King and Simon McGrath (eds), *Development Knowledge, National Research and International Cooperation* (Edinburgh: Centre of African Studies – CAS/Bonn: German Foundation for International Development – DSE/Geneva: NORRAG, 2001).

Cornia, Giovanni Andrea, Richard Jolly and Frances Stewart (eds), *Adjustment with a Human Face. Vol. I: Protecting the Vulnerable and Promoting Growth* (Oxford: Oxford University Press, 1987).

Cornwall, Andrea, 'New democratic spaces?: The politics and dynamics of institutionalised participation', *IDS Bulletin*, 35(2) (2004) 1–10.

——, *Beneficiary, Consumer, Citizen: Perspectives on Participation for Poverty Reduction*, Sida Studies 2 (Stockholm: Sida, 2000).

Cornwall, Andrea and Karen Brock, 'What do buzzwords do for development policy?: a critical look at "poverty reduction", "participation" and "empowerment"', paper prepared for the UNRISD conference on Social Knowledge and Policy Making: Exploring the Linkages, Geneva, 20–21 April (2004).

Cornwall, Andrea and Garett Pratt, *Ideals in Practice: An Enquiry into Participation in Sida*, Lessons for Change Series (Brighton: Institute of Development Studies, 2004).

Cornwall, Andrea, Samuel Musyoki and Garett Pratt, *In Search of a New Impetus: Practitioners' Reflections on PRA and Participation in Kenya*, IDS Working Paper 131 (Brighton: Institute of Development Studies, 2001).

Correa, S. and R. Reichman, *Reproductive Rights and Population: Feminist Voices from the South* (London: Zed Press, 1994).

Court, David, 'Educational research environments in Kenya'. In Sheldon Shaeffer and John Nkinyangi (eds), *Educational Research Environments in the Developing World* (Ottawa: IDRC, 1983).

Court, Julius, Ingie Hovland and John Young (eds), *Bridging Research and Policy in Development: Evidence and the Change Process* (Bourton-on-Dunsmore, Rugby, Warwickshire: ITDG Publishing, 2005).

Cox, R.W., 'Civil society at the turn of the millennium: prospects for an alternative world order', *Review of International Studies*, 25 (1), January (1999) 3–28.

——, 'Introduction'. In Robert W. Cox (ed), *The New Realism: Perspectives on Multilateralism and World Order* (Tokyo, New York, Paris: United Nations University Press, 1997).

——, *Understanding Global Disorder* (London: Zed, 1995).

——, 'Structural issues of global governance: Implications for Europe'. In S. Gill (ed.), *Gramsci, Historical Materialism and International Relations*, Cambridge Studies in International Relations No. 26 (Cambridge: Cambridge University Press, 1993).

Craig, David and Doug Porter, 'Poverty Reduction Strategy Papers: A new convergence', *World Development*, Vol. 31, No. 1 (2003) 53–69.

Crewe, Emma and Elizabeth Harrison, *Whose Development?: An Ethnography of Aid* (London: Zed Books, 1999).

Crook, Richard and Alan Sverrisson, *Decentralisation and Poverty Alleviation in Developing Countries: a Comparative Analysis or, Is West Bengal Unique?*, IDS Working Paper 130 (Brighton: Institute of Development Studies, 2001).

Danida (Ministry of Foreign Affairs), *Denmark's Development Policy Strategy. Partnership 2000* (Copenhagen: Ministry of Foreign Affairs, 2000).

Deacon, Bob, *The Social Dimension of Regionalism: a Constructive Alternative to Neo-Liberal Globalisation*, Globalism and Social Policy Programme (GASPP) Occasional Paper No. 8/2001 (Helsinki: National Research and Development Centre for Welfare and Health – STAKES), 2001).

——, *Globalization and Social Policy*, Geneva 2000 Occasional Paper No. 5 (Geneva: UNRISD, 2000a).

——, 'Eastern European welfare states: the impact of the politics of globalisation', *Journal of European Social Policy*, 10(2) (2000b) 146–61.

——, 'The future for social policy in a global context: why the south now needs to take the lead', *Futura*, 4/2000 (2000c).

——, 'Towards a socially responsible globalisation: international actors and discourses', GASPP Occasional Paper No.1 (Helsinki: STAKES, 1999).

——, *Global Social Policy and Governance* (London: Sage, forthcoming).

Deacon, Bob, with M. Hulse and P. Stubbs, *Global Social Policy: International Organizations and the Future of Welfare* (London: Sage, 1997).

Deacon, Bob, E. Ollila, M. Koivusalo and P. Stubbs, *Global Social Governance: Themes and Prospects*, Elements for Discussion Series (Helsinki: Ministry for Foreign Affairs of Finland, Department for International Development Cooperation, 2003).

Department for International Development (DFID), *Policy Division Teams* (London: DFID, 2003).

——, *Eliminating World Poverty: Making Globalisation Work for the Poor*. White Paper on International Development, Cmd 5006 (London: Stationery Office, 2000a).

——, 'Doing the knowledge', unpublished paper (London: DFID, 2000b).

——, *Eliminating World Poverty: A Challenge for the 21st Century. White Paper on International Development*, Cmd. 3789 (London: Stationery Office, 1997).

Development Alternatives with Women for a New Era (DAWN), *Markers on the Way: the DAWN Debates on Alternative Development* (Suva, Fiji: DAWN, 1995).

Development Dialogue, Special Issue, 'What now? Another development' (1975).

Dixon-Mueller, R., *Population Policies and Women's Rights: Transforming Reproductive Choice* (Westport, Connecticut: Praeger, 1993).

Dollar, David and Jakob Svensson, 'What explains the success or failure of structural adjustment programmes?', *The Economic Journal*, Vol. 110, Issue 466, October (2000) 894–917.

Dryzek, John, 'The informal logic of institutional design'. In Robert Goodin (ed.), *The Theory of Institutional Design* (Cambridge: Cambridge University Press, 1996).

Dufour, Paul, *Futures of Knowledge for Development Strategies: Moving from Rhetoric to Reality*, background paper for Ad Hoc Group of Experts Meeting on Knowledge Systems for Development, 4–5 September 2003, Division for Public Administration and Development Management (DPADM) and UN Department of Economic and Social Affairs (UNDESA), New York. http://www.idrc.ca/uploads/user-S/10771245731Paul_UNDESA.pdf.

Easterly, William, 'The cartel of good intentions', *Foreign Policy*, July–August (2002).

Eaton, J. and M. Gersovitz, 'Debt with potential repudiation: theoretical and empirical analysis', *Review of Economic Studies*, 48 (1981) 289–309.

Economic Commission for Latin America and the Caribbean (ECLAC), *Globalization and Development*, LC/G.2157 (SES 29/3)/1 (Santiago: ECLAC, April, 2002).

——, *Social Equity and Changing Production Patterns: an Integrated Approach*, ECLAC Books No. 32, United Nations Sales No. E.92.II.G.5 (Santiago: ECLAC, August, 1992).

——, *Changing Production Patterns with Social Equity*, ECLAC Books No. 25, United Nations Sales No. E.90.II.G.6 (Santiago: ECLAC, March, 1990).

The Economist, 17 January (2004) p. 72.

ECOSOC (See United Nations Economic and Social Council).

Edholm, F., O. Harris and K. Young, 'Conceptualising women', *Critique of Anthropology*, 3 (9/10) (1977) 101–30.

Edwards, Michael, *Future Positive: International Co-operation in the 21st Century* (London: Earthscan, 1999).

Edwards, M. and G. Sen, 'NGOs, social change and the transformation of human relationships: A 21st-century civic agenda'. In M. Edwards and A. Fowler (eds), *The Earthscan Reader on NGO Management* (London: Earthscan, 2002).

Ehrlich, P., *The Population Bomb* (New York: Ballantine Books, 1971).

Eichner, Alfred S. (ed.), *Why Economics Is Not Yet a Science* (London: Macmillan Press, 1983).

Ellerman, David, 'Autonomy in education and development', *Journal of International Co-operation in Education*, Vol. 7, No. 1, April (2004).

Emmerij, Louis, Richard Jolly and Thomas G. Weiss, *Ahead of the Curve?: UN Ideas and Global Challenges* (Bloomington: Indiana University Press, 2001).

Escobar, Arturo, *Encountering Development: the Making and Unmaking of the Third World* (Princeton, NJ: Princeton University Press, 1995).

Eyben, Rosalind, 'The road not taken: why international development policy chose copenhagen over Beijing and the implications for Bolivia', background paper to UNRISD report on Gender and Development to mark the 10th Anniversary of the Fourth World Conference on Women (Geneva: UNRISD, 2004).

Fals-Borda, Orlando and Mohammed Anisur Rahman, *Action and Knowledge: Breaking the Monopoly with Participatory Action Research* (London: Intermediate Technology Publications, 1991).

Ferguson, J., *The Anti-Politics Machine: 'Development', Depoliticisation, and Bureaucratic Power in Lesotho* (Cambridge: Cambridge University Press, 1990).

Florini, Ann M. (ed.), *The Third Force: The Rise in Transnational Civil Society* (Washington, DC: Carnegie Endownment, 2000).

Fomerand, Jacques, 'UN conferences: media events or genuine diplomacy', *Global Governance*, Vol. 2, No. 3, September–December (1996) 361–75.

Foucault, Michel, *The History of Sexuality*, Part I (Harmondsworth: Penguin, 1979).

Frankel, Herbert, 'United Nations primer for development', *Quarterly Journal of Economics*, Vol. 67, No. 2, May (1953) 275.

Friedman, Jonathan, *Empowerment: The Politics of Alternative Development* (Oxford: Blackwell, 1992).

Fukuyama, Francis, *The End of History and the Last Man* (London and New York: Penguin, 1992).

G8 Gleneagles 2005, *The Gleneagles Communiqué*. http://www.fco.gov.uk/Files/kfile/PostG8_Gleneagles_Communique,0.pdf, accessed on 15 September 2005.

Gardner, Katy and David Lewis, 'Dominant paradigms overturned or "business as usual"?: Development discourse and the White Paper on International Development', *Critique of Anthropology*, Vol. 20, No. 1 (2000) 15–29.

——, *Anthropology and Development: the Postmodern Challenge* (London: Pluto, 1996).

Gasper, Des and Raymond Apthorpe, 'Discourse analysis and policy discourse'. In R. Apthorpe and D. Gasper (eds), *Arguing Development Policy: Frames and Discourses* (London: Frank Cass, 1996).

Gaventa, John, 'Introduction: Exploring citizenship, participation and accountability', *IDS Bulletin*, Vol. 33, No. 2 (2002) 1–11.

Gaventa, Jonathan, 'Poverty amidst plenty' rather than 'plenty amidst poverty': a discourse analysis of the construction of 'poverty' and 'the poor' in the world Development Report 2000/1 (2001) mimeo.

Gavin, M. and Dani Rodrik, 'The World Bank in historical perspective', *American Economic Review*, Papers and Proceedings, Vol. 85, Issue 2 (1995) 329–34.

George, V. and P. Wilding, *Globalization and Human Welfare* (London: Palgrave and Macmillan, 2002).

Gerth. H.H. and C. Wright Mills (eds), *From Max Weber: Essays in Sociology* (New York: Oxford University Press, 1946).

Giles, Lionel, *Sun Tzu on The Art of War*, translated from Chinese with Introduction and Critical Notes by Lionel Giles (1910). http://www.kimsoft.com/polwar.htm.

Gill, S. (ed.), *Power and Resistance in the New World Order* (Basingstoke: Palgrave, 2003).

——, (ed.), *Gramsci, Historical Materialism and International Relations* (Cambridge: Cambridge University Press, 1993).

Gill, S. and D. Law, 'Global hegemony and the structural power of capital'. In S. Gill (ed.), *Gramsci, Historical Materialism and International Relations* (Cambridge: Cambridge University Press, 1993).

Girvan, Norman, 'Reflections on the CARICOM single market and economy', Keynote Address, SALISES 5th Annual Conference, 31 March 2004, *Trinidad and Tobago Review*, 5 April (2004). Also at http://sta.uwi.edu/salises/workshop/csme/paper/ngirvan.pdf.

——, 'Regional cooperation and economic governance: the case of the Association of Caribbean States'. In K. Hall and D. Benn (eds), *Governance in the Age of Globalisation – National, Regional and Global Dimensions* (Kingston: Ian Randle Publishers, 2003).

——, 'Empowerment for development: from conditionality to partnership'. In Jo Marie Griesgraber and Bernhard G. Gunter (eds), *Promoting Development: Effective Global Institutions for the Twenty-First Century* (London: Pluto Press, 1995), with Washington, DC: Center of Concern.

The Global Fund, *Guidelines for Proposals* (Geneva: The Global Fund, 2003). www.theglobalfund.org.

Gmelin, Wolfgang, Kenneth King and Simon McGrath (eds), *Development Knowledge, National Research and International Cooperation* (Edinburgh: Centre of African Studies – CAS/Bonn: German Foundation for International Development – DSE/Geneva: NORRAG, 2001).

Goldman, Michael, 'The birth of a discipline, producing authoritative green knowledge, World Bank-style', *Ethnography*, 2.2 (2001) 191–217.

Goldstein, Judith and Robert O. Keohane (eds), *Ideas and Foreign Policy: Beliefs, Institutions, and Political Change* (Ithaca: Cornell University Press, 1993).

Goodman, Nelson, *Ways of Worldmaking* (Indianapolis, Indiana: Hackett, 1978).

Goonatilake, Susantha, *Aborted Discovery: Science and Creativity in the Third World* (London: Zed Books, 1984).

Gould, Jeremy and Julia Ojanen, *Merging in the Circle: the Politics of Tanzania's Poverty Reduction Strategy*, Institute of Development Studies Policy Paper 2003/2 (Helsinki: University of Helsinki, 2003).

Government of India, Ministry of Education and Social Welfare, *Toward Equality*, Report of the Committee on the Status of Women in India (New Delhi: Government of India, Ministry of Education and Social Welfare, 1974).

Graham, C., *Safety Nets, Politics and the Poor: Transitions to Market Economies* (Washington: Brookings Institution Press, 1994).

Gramsci, Antonio, *Selections from the Prison Notebooks* (London: Lawrence and Wishart, 1971).

Greenhill, Romilly, *What Are the Chances of Meeting the Millennium Development Goals?* Jubilee Research (2002). http://www.jubilee2000uk.org/.

Grillo, Ralph and Roderick Stirrat, *Discourses of Development: Anthropological Perspectives* (Oxford: Berg, 1997).

Haas, Peter, 'Introduction: epistemic communities and international policy co-ordination', *International Organization*, 46, 1 (1992) 1–37.

——, 'Do regimes matter?: epistemic communities and mediterranean pollution control', *International Organization*, 43, 3, summer (1989) 377–403.

Hajer, Maarten, 'Discourse coalitions and the institutionalisation of practice'. In Frank Fischer and John Forester (eds), *The Argumentative Turn in Policy Analysis and Planning* (Durham, NC: Duke University Press, 1993).

Hall, Peter, 'Policy paradigms, social learning, and the state: the case of economic policymaking in Britain', *Comparative Politics*, April (1993) 275–96.

Hardt, M. and A. Negri, *Empire* (Cambridge, Massachusetts: Harvard University Press, 2000).

Hart, Keith, 'Informal income opportunities and urban employment in Ghana', *Journal of Modern African Studies*, Vol. 2, No. 1 (1973) 61–89.

Heclo, Hugh, *Modern Social Politics in Britain and Sweden* (New Haven, CT: Yale University Press, 1974).

Held, D., *Global Covenant: The Social Democratic Alternative to the Washington Consensus* (Cambridge: Polity Press, 2004).

Held, D. and A. McGrew (eds), *Governing Globalization: Power, Authority and Global Governance* (Cambridge: Polity Press, 2002).

Henkel, Heiko and Roderick Stirrat, 'Participation as spiritual duty; empowerment as secular subjection'. In Bill Cooke and Uma Kothari (eds), *The Tyranny of Participation* (London: Zed Books, 2001).

Herrera, Amilcar O., *Catastrophe o Nueva Sociedad: Modelo Mundial Latinoamericano* (Buenos Aires: The Bariloche Foundation, 1976).

Hettne, Bjorn, *Development Theory and the Three Worlds: Towards an International Political Economy of Development* (London: Addison Wesley Longman, 1995).

Hettne, Björn, András Inotai and Osvaldo Sunkel (eds), *The New Regionalism. Vol. V: Comparing Regionalisms: Implications for Global Development* (London: Macmillan Press, 2001), in association with the United Nations University and the World Institute of Development Economics Research.

—— (eds), *The New Regionalism. Vol. I: Globalism and the New Regionalism* (London: Macmillan Press, 1999), in association with the United Nations University and the World Institute of Development Economics Research.

Hewitt, Adrian, *Evaluation of Trade Conditions in PRSPs* (London: ODI, 2003).

Hinton, R., 'Conclusion: Enabling inclusive aid'. In L. Groves and R. Hinton (eds), *Inclusive Aid: Changing Power and Relationships in International Development* (London: Earthscan Publications, 2004).

Hirschmann, Albert, *Development Projects Observed* (Washington, DC: Brookings Institution, 1967).

Hoffman, Kurt, 'Managing technology transfer'. In Norman Girvan and Kurt Hoffman (eds), *Managing International Technology Transfer: a Strategic Approach for Developing Countries* (Ottawa: International Development Research Centre, April, 1990).

Holzmann, R., M. Orenstein and M. Rutkowski (eds), *Pension Reform in Europe: Process and Progress* (Washington, DC: The World Bank, 2003).

Hopenhayn, M., *Global Approaches, Dispersed Agents: Comments on Deacon, 'The Politics of Global Social Policy Change'*, UNRISD Conference on Social Knowledge and International Policy Making: Exploring the Linkages, Geneva, 20–21 April 2004 (Geneva: UNRISD, 2004).

Independent Commission on Disarmament and Security Issues, *Common Security: a Blueprint for Survival* (New York: Simon & Schuster, 1982).

Independent Commission on International Development Issues, *Common Crisis North–South: Co-operation for World Recovery* (Cambridge: MIT Press, 1983).

——, *North–South: a Programme for Survival* (London: Pan Books, 1980).

Independent Commission on International Humanitarian Issues (ICIHI), *Winning the Human Race?* (London: Zed Books, 1988).

International Commission on Intervention and State Sovereignty (ICISS), *The Responsibility to Protect* (Ottawa: ICISS, 2001).

International Council on Human Rights Policy (ICHRP), *Duties Sans Frontières: Human Rights and Global Social Justice* (Geneva: ICHRP, 2003).

International Journal of Educational Development (IJED), Vol. 1, No. 1, April (1981) 1–64.

International Labour Organization (ILO), *A Fair Globalization: Creating Opportunities for All* (Geneva: World Commission on the Social Dimension of Globalization, ILO, 2004).

——, *Structure and Functions of Rural Workers' Organization: Participation of the Rural Poor in Development* (Geneva: ILO, 1978).

——, *Employment, Growth and Basic Needs – a One-World Problem* (Geneva: ILO, 1976).

International Labour Organization (ILO) Socio-Economic Security Programme, *Economic Security for a Better World* (Geneva: ILO, 2004).

International Monetary Fund (IMF), *IMF's Independent Evaluation Office Announces Release of Report on the Role of the IMF in Argentina*, Press Release No. 04/02 (Washington, DC: IMF, 29 July 2004). http://www.imf.org/External/NP/ieo/2004/pr/eng/pr0402.htm

Jacobs, M., A. Lent and K. Watkins, *Progressive Globalisation: Towards an International Social Democracy* (London: Fabian Society, 2003).

Jain, Devaki, *Women, Development, and the UN: a Sixty-Year Quest for Equality and Justice*, UNIHP Series (Bloomington, IN: Indiana University Press, 2005).

Jansen, Jonathan, 'The Politics of Performance and the Prospects of "Education for All" ', paper to 7th Oxford International Conference on Education and Development, 9–11 September (2003). In Special Issue of *International Journal of Educational Development*, January (2005).

Japan International Cooperation Agency (JICA), *The OECD/DAC's New Development Strategy*, 3 vols. (Tokyo: JICA, 1998).

Jolly, Richard, Louis Emmerij and Thomas G. Weiss, *The Power of UN Ideas: Lessons from the First Sixty Years*, UNIHP Series (Bloomington, IN: Indiana University Press, 2005).

——, *The United Nations: a History of Ideas and Their Future*, UNIHP Series (Bloomington, IN: Indiana University Press, forthcoming).

Jolly, Richard, Louis Emmerij, Dharam Ghai and Frédéric Lapeyre, *UN Contributions to Development Thinking and Practice* (Bloomington, IN: Indiana University Press, 2004).

Journal of International Cooperation in Education, 'International education cooperation: toward greater autonomy or dependency in sub-Saharan Africa' (Special Issue), Vol. VII, No. 1, April (2004).

Kakande, M., 'The donor–government–citizen frame as seen by a government participant'. In L. Groves and R. Hinton (eds), *Inclusive Aid: Changing Power and Relationships in International Development* (London: Earthscan Publications, 2004).

Kapur, Devesh, John P. Lewis and Richard Webb, *The World Bank: Its First Half Century* (Washington DC: Brookings Institution, 1997).

Kaul, I., I. Grunberg and M. Stern (eds), *Global Public Goods: International Cooperation in the 21st Century* (New York: Oxford University Press, 1999).

Kaul, I., P. Conceição, K. Le Goulven and R.U. Mendoza (eds), *Providing Global Public Goods: Managing Globalization* (Oxford: Oxford University Press, 2003).

Keynes, John Maynard, *The Theory of Employment, Interest, and Money* (London: MacMillan, 1936).

Kifle, H., A. Olukoshi and L. Wohlgemuth (eds), *A New Partnership for African Development* (Uppsala: Nordic Africa Institute, 1997).

Killick, Tony, 'Politics, evidence and the new aid agenda', *Development Policy Review*, Vol. 22, No. 1 (2004) 5–29.

——, *Aid and the Political Economy of Change* (London: Routledge, 1998).

King, Kenneth, 'The external agenda of educational reform?: Self-reliance versus dependency in Sub-Saharan Africa', *Journal of International Cooperation in Education*, Vol. V11 (1), April (2004) 85–96.

——, 'Towards knowledge-based aid: A new way of working or a new North–South divide?', *Journal of International Co-operation in Education* (Hiroshima), Vol. 3, No. 2 (2000) 23–48; a revised and shorter version is in D. Stone and S. Maxwell (eds), *Global Knowledge Networks and International Development: Bridges Across Boundaries* (London: Routledge, 2004).

——, *Knowledge Management, Knowledge Agency, Knowledge History: Expertise, Technical Assistance and Capacity Building in Historical Perspective*, paper presented at the Conference on Development through Knowledge? A New Look at the Global-Based Economy and Society, IUED-IRD, Geneva, 20–22 November (2002).

——, *Aid and Education in the Developing World* (Harlow: Longman, 1991).

——, 'What happened at the World Conference in Jomtien?', *NORRAG NEWS*, No. 8, June (1990) 3–24.

King, Kenneth and Simon McGrath, *Knowledge for Development?: Comparing British, Japanese, Swedish and World Bank Aid* (London: Zed Books, 2004).

King, Kenneth and Robert Palmer, *Education and Its Enabling Environments: a Review of Research and Policy, 1980–2004*, Occasional Paper No. 99 (Edinburgh: Centre of African Studies, University of Edinburgh, 2004).

Knoke, Irene and Pedro Morazan, *PRSP: Beyond the Theory – Practical Experiences and Positions of Involved Civil Society Organisations* (Berlin: Brot für die Welt, 2002).

Krueger, Anne O., *Meant Well, Tried Little, Failed Much: Policy Reforms in Emerging Market Economies*, Acting Managing Director, International Monetary Fund, Roundtable Lecture, Economic Honors Society, New York University, New York, 23 March (2004). http://www.imf.org/external/np/speeches/2004/032304a.htm

Laclau, Ernesto, 'On the death and rebirth of ideology', *Journal of Political Ideologies*, 3(1) (1996) 201–20.

Langmore, J., 'The UN Commission for Social Development, February 2001: an opportunity for international political evolution', *Global Social Policy*, 1 (3) (2001).

Leal, Pablo and Robert Opp, *Participation and Development in the Age of Globalization* (Ottawa: CIDA, 1998).

Lent, A., *Progressive Globalisation* (London: Zed Press, 2004).

Lewis, W. Arthur, *The Theory of Economic Growth* (London: George Allen and Unwin, 1955; Homewood, IL: Richard D. Irwin, 1955).

Lewis, David, Dennis Rodgers and Michael Woolcock, *The Fiction of Development: Knowledge, Authority and Representation*, LSE Working Paper No. 05–61 (London: London School of Economics and Political Science, 2005).

Lipietz, Alain, *Towards a New Economic Order: Postfordism, Ecology and Democracy* (Cambridge: Polity Press, 1992).

Lister, Sarah and Warren Nyamugasira, 'Design contradictions in the 'new architecture of aid'?: Reflections from Uganda on the roles of civil society organizations', *Development Policy Review*, Vol. 21, No. 1 (2003) 93–106.

Lockheed, Marlaine E., Dean T. Jamison and Lawrence Lau, 'Farmer education and farm efficiency', *Economic Development and Cultural Change*, Vol. 29, No.1 (1980) 37–76.

Loewenson, Rene, 'Public participation in health', *IDS Bulletin*, Vol. 31, No. 1 (2000) 14–20.

Lohmann, Larry, *Missing the Point of Development Talk: Reflections for Activists*, Corner House Briefing No. 9, August (1998a).

——, *Mekong Dams in the Drama of Development*, unpublished discussion paper (Sturminster Newton, Dorset: Corner House, 1998b).

Long, Norman, 'Conclusion'. In Norman Long and Ann Long (eds), *Battlefields of Knowledge: The Interlocking Theory and Practice of Social Research and Development* (London: Routledge, 2002).

Lovejoy, Arthur O., *The Great Chain of Being* (New York: Torchbook, 1960).

Lucas, Robert E., 'On the mechanics of economic development', *Journal of Monetary Economics*, Vol. 22, No. 1 (1988) 3–42.

MacFarlane, Neil and Yuen Foong-Khong, *Human Security and the UN: a Critical History*, UNIHP Series (Bloomington, IN: Indiana University Press, forthcoming).

Magnus, Jan R. and Mary S. Morgan, 'The ET interview: Professor J. Tinbergen', *Econometric Theory*, 3 (1987) 117–42.

Manor, James, 'User committees: a potentially damaging second wave of decentralisation?', *European Journal of Development Research*, 16(1) (2004) 192–213.

——, *The Political Economy of Decentralisation* (Washington, DC: World Bank, 1999).

Martens, J., *The Future of Multilateralism after Monterrey and Johannesburg* (Berlin: Friedrich Ebert Foundation, 2003).

Marx, Karl and Friedrich Engels, 'Manifesto of the Communist Party' (first published in 1848; translation by Samuel Moore in cooperation with Friedrich Engels in1888). In Karl Marx and Friedrich Engels, *Collected Works*, Volume Six (New York: International Publishers, 1976).

Maslow, Abraham H., 'A theory of human motivation', *Psychological Review*, Vol. 50, No. 3, March (1942) 370–96.

Mason, Edward and Robert Asher, *The World Bank Since Bretton Woods* (Washington, DC: Brookings Institution, 1973).

Mason, K., *A Feminist Perspective on Fertility Decline* (Rev.), presented at the Annual Meeting of the Population Association of America, New Orleans, Louisiana, 21–23 April 1988 (1988).

Meadows, D.H., D.L. Meadows and J. Randers, *Beyond the Limits: a Global Collapse or a Sustainable Future* (London: Earthscan, 1992).

Meadows, D.H., D.L. Meadows, Jorgen Randers and William W. Behrens III, *The Limits to Growth: a Report to the Club of Rome's Project on the Predicament of Mankind* (New York: Universe Books, 1972).

Miller-Adams, Michelle, *The World Bank: New Agendas in a Changing World* (London: Routledge, 1999).

Mittelman, James H., 'Rethinking the "new regionalism" in the context of globalization'. In Hettne, Björn, Andiás Inotai and Ôsvaldo Sunkel (eds), *The New Regionalism. Vol. I: Globalism and the New Regionalism* (London: MacMillan Press, 1999), in association with the United Nations University and the World Institute of Development Economics Research.

Mkandawire, Thandika, 'Social policy in a development context: Introduction'. In T. Mkandawire (ed.) *Social Policy in a Development Context* (Houndmills: Palgrave Macmillan, 2004).

Moore, Mick, 'Empowerment at last?', *Journal of International Development*, 13(3) (2001) 321–9.

Moscovici, Serge, 'The phenomenon of social representations'. In R.M. Farr and S. Moscovici (eds), *Social Representations* (Cambridge: Cambridge University Press, 1984).

Mosley, Paul, Jane Harrigan and John Toye, *Aid and Power: The World Bank and Policy-Based Lending*, 2 Vols, 2nd edn (London: Routledge, 1995).

Mosley, Paul, Farhad Noorbakhsh and Alberto Paloni, *Compliance with World Bank Conditionality: Implications for the Selectivity Approach to Policy-Based Lending and the Design of Conditionality*, CREDIT Research Paper No. 03/20 (Nottingham: Centre for Research in Economic Development and International Trade, University of Nottingham, 2003).

Mosse, David, 'Is good policy unimplementable?: reflections on the ethnography of aid policy and practice', *Development and Change* 35 (4) (2004a) 639–71.

——, *Cultivating Development: an Ethnography of Aid Policy and Practice* (London: Pluto Press, 2004b).

Mwiria, Kilemi, 'Education decision-making and knowledge sharing: Some lessons from the Eastern and Southern Africa region'. In Wolfgang Gmelin, Kenneth King and Simon McGrath (eds), *Development Knowledge, National Research and International Cooperation* (Edinburgh: Centre of African Studies – CAS/Bonn: German Foundation for International Development – DSE/Geneva: NORRAG, 2001).

Myrdal, Gunnar, *Objectivity in Social Research* (New York: Pantheon Books, 1969).

——, *Asian Drama: an Inquiry into the Poverty of Nations* (New York: Pantheon, 1968).

Narayan, Deepa and Patti Petesch, *Voices of the Poor: from Many Lands* (Oxford: Oxford University Press [for the World Bank], 2000).

Narayan, Deepa, Robert Chambers, Meera Kaul Shah and Patti Petesch, *Voices of the Poor: Crying Out for Change* (Oxford: Oxford University Press [for the World Bank], 2000a).

Narayan, Deepa, with Raj Patel, Kai Schafft, Anne Rademacher and Sarah Koch-Schutte, *Voices of the Poor: Can Anyone Hear Us?* (Oxford: Oxford University Press [for the World Bank], 2000b).

Nederveen Pieterse, Jan, 'Knowledge, power and development', *Courier de la Planète* No.74, *Knowledge and Power* (2005) 6–11.

Ocampo, Jose Antonio and Juan Martin (eds), *Globalization and Development: a Latin American and Caribbean Perspective* (Palo Alto: Stanford University Press, and Washington, DC: the World Bank, 2004).

O'Dell, Carla S., C. Jackson Grayson, with Nilly Essaides, *If Only We Knew What We Know: the Transfer of Internal Knowledge and Best Practice* (New York: Free Press, 1998).

Ollila, E., 'Health-related public–private partnerships and the United Nations'. In Bob Deacon, E. Ollila, M. Koivusalo and P. Stubbs (eds), *Global Social Governance: Themes and Prospects*, Elements for Discussion Series (Helsinki: Ministry for Foreign Affairs of Finland, Department for International Development Cooperation, 2003).

Olukoshi, Adebayo, *The Interactions of the United Nations with the African Research Community*. Speaking notes for a presentation at the UNRISD Conference on Social Knowledge and International Policy-Making: Can Research Make a Difference?, Geneva, 20–21 April (2004).

Orenstein, M., 'Mapping the diffusion of pension innovation'. In R. Holzmann, M. Orenstein and M. Rutkowski (eds), *Pension Reform in Europe: Process and Progress* (Washington, DC: The World Bank, 2003).

Organisation for Economic Co-operation and Development (OECD), *Harmonising Donor Practices for Effective Aid Delivery: Good Practice Papers*, DAC Reference Document (Paris: OECD, 2003).

Organization for Economic Co-operation and Development/Development Assistance Committee (OECD/DAC), *Shaping the 21st Century: the Contribution of Development Co-operation* (Paris: OECD, 1996).

Overseas Development Administration (ODA), *Aid to Education in the 90's*, Education Policy Paper, Education Division (London: ODA, 1992).

Oxfam, *Education Now: Break the Cycle of Poverty* (Oxford: Oxfam, 1999).

Oxfam International, *Gleneagles: What Really Happened at the G8 Summit?* Oxfam Briefing Note, 29 July 2005.

Øyen, Else, 'The politics of poverty reduction', *International Social Science Journal*, 162 (1999) 459–65.

Padrigu (Department of Peace and Development Research, Göteborg University), *Research on the New Regionalism at the Department of Peace and Development Research, Göteborg University* (2004). www.padrigu.gu.se/presentationer.

Palmer, Robert, *The Informal Economy Concept in Sub-Saharan Africa: Some Currently Unresolved Issues*, Occasional Paper No. 98, May (Edinburgh: Centre of African Studies, University of Edinburgh, 2004).

Patomäki, H., *Democratising Globalisation: the Leverage of the Tobin Tax* (London: Zed Press, 1999).

Patomäki, H. and T. Teivainen, *A Possible World: Democratic Transformation of Global Institutions* (London: Zed Books, 2004).

Paul, Samuel, *Community Participation in Development Projects*, World Bank Discussion Paper 6 (Washington, DC: World Bank, 1987).

Pearse, Andrew and Matthias Stiefel, *Inquiry into Participation: a Research Approach* (Geneva: UNRISD, 1979).

Pérez de Cuéllar, Javier, *Pilgrimage for Peace* (New York: St. Martin's, 1990).

Petchesky, R., *Global Prescriptions: Gendering Health and Human Rights* (London and New York: UNRISD and Zed Books, 2003).

Petrella, R., *The Water Manifesto: Arguments for a World Water Contract* (London: Zed Press, 2001).

Piron, Laure-Helene, *The Right to Development: a Review of the Current State of the Debate for the Department for International Development* (London: Overseas Development Institute, 2003).

Polanyi, Karl, *The Great Transformation* (Boston: The Beacon Press, 1957).

Pratt, Garett, *Practitioners' Critical Reflections on PRA and Participation in Nepal*, IDS Working Paper 122 (Brighton: Institute of Development Studies, 2001).

Prebisch, Raúl, *The Economic Development of Latin America and Its Principal Problems* (New York: United Nations, 1950).

Presley, Cora Ann, 'The Mau Mau rebellion, Kikuyu women, and social change', *Canadian Journal of African Studies*, Vol. 12, No. 3 (1988) 502–27.

Pretty, Jules, 'Participatory learning for sustainable agriculture', *World Development*, Vol. 23, No. 8 (1995) 1247–63.

Rahman, Mahfuzur, *World Economic Issues at the United Nations: Half a Century of Debate* (Dordrecht: Kluwer, 2002).

Rahman, Mohammed Anisur, *People's Self-Development: Perspectives on Participatory Action Research* (London: Zed Books, 1995).

Reiter, R. (ed.), *Toward an Anthropology of Women* (New York: Monthly Review Press, 1975).

Ribot, Jesse, 'Participation without representation: Chiefs, councils and forestry law in the West African Sahel', *Cultural Survival Quarterly*, Vol. 20, No. 3 (1996) 40–4.

Richter, J., *Building on Quicksand: the Global Compact, Democratic Governance and Nestlé* (Zurich: CETIM, IBFAN/GIFA and Berne Declaration, 2003).

Rischard, J.-F., *High Noon: 20 Global Problems, 20 Years to Solve Them* (Oxford: The Perseus Press, 2002).

Rist, Gilbert, *The History of Development: from Western Origins to Global Faith* (London: Zed Books, 1997).

Rodrik, Dani, 'Trading in illusions', *Foreign Policy*, March–April (2001).

Roe, Emery, 'Development narratives, or making the best of blueprint development', *World Development*, Vol. 19, No. 4 (1991) 287–300.

Room, G., 'Multi-tiered international welfare systems'. In I. Gough and G. Woods (eds), *Insecurity and Welfare Regimes in Asia, Africa and Latin America* (Cambridge: Cambridge University Press, 2004).

Rosaldo, M. and L. Lamphere (eds), *Women, Culture and Society* (Stanford: Stanford University Press, 1974).

Rosenstein-Rodan, Paul, 'Problems of industrialisation in Eastern and South-Eastern Europe', *Economic Journal*, Vol. LIII (1943) 202–11.

Rowlands, Jo, *Questioning Empowerment: Working with Women in Honduras* (Oxford: Oxfam, 1997).

Rubin, G., 'The traffic in women: notes on the "political economy" of sex'. In R. Reiter (ed.), *Toward an Anthropology of Women* (New York: Monthly Review Press, 1975).

Rudolph, Lloyd I. and Suzanne H. Rudolph, 'Authority and power in bureaucratic and patrimonial administration: a revisionist interpretation of Weber on bureaucracy', *World Politics*, 38 (1979) 195–227.

Ruggie, John Gerard, 'Taking embedded liberalism global: the corporate connection'. In David Held and Mathias Koenig-Archibugi (eds), *Taming Globalization: Frontiers of Governance* (Cambridge: Polity Press, 2003).

——, 'global governance.net: The Global Compact as learning network', *Global Governance*, Vol. 7, No. 4, October–December (2001) 371–8.

——, 'What makes the world hang together?: Neo-utilitarianism and the social constructivist challenge', *International Organization*, 52, 4, Autumn (1998) 855–85.

Sagafi-nejad, Tagi, in collaboration with John Dunning, *The UN and Transnationals, from Code to Compact*, UNIHP Series (Bloomington, IN: Indiana University Press, forthcoming).

Salole, Gerry, 'Participatory development: the taxation of the beneficiary?', *Journal of Social Development in Africa*, Vol. 6, No. 2 (1991).

Sankatsing, Glenn, 'The Caribbean: Archipelago of trailer societies', *Trinidad and Tobago Review*, December (1998). Also at http://www.crscenter.com/Trailer.html.

Scharpf, F. and V.A. Schmidt (eds), *Welfare and Work in the Open Economy*, Vol. I: *From Vulnerability to Competitiveness in Comparative Perspective*; Vol. II: *Diverse Responses to Common Challenges in Twelve Countries* (Oxford: Oxford University Press, 2000).

Schechter, Michael (ed.), *United Nations-Sponsored World Conferences: Focus on Impact and Follow-up* (Tokyo: UN University Press, 2001).

Schrijver, Nico, *The UN and the Global Commons: Development without Destruction*, UNIHP Series (Bloomington, IN: Indiana University Press, forthcoming).

Schulz, Michael, Frederick Söderbaum and Joakim Öjendal (eds), *Regionalization in a Globalizing World* (London and New York: Zed Books, 2001).

Schumpeter, J.A., *The Theory of Economic Development* (New York: Oxford University Press, 1961 – First edition in German, 1911).

Scott, J. and L. Tilly, *Women, Work and Family* (New York: Methuen, 1987).

Scott, Maurice F.G., *A New Theory of Economic Growth* (Oxford: Oxford University Press, 1989).

Seers, Dudley, *The Political Economy of Nationalism* (Oxford: Oxford University Press, 1983).

——, 'The limitations of the special case', *Bulletin of the Oxford Institute of Economics and Statistics*, 25(2) (1963).

Sen, Gita, *The Relationship of Research to Activism in the Making of Policy: Lessons from Gender and Development*, paper presented at the conference on Social Knowledge and International Policy Making: Exploring the Linkages (Geneva: UNRISD, 20–21 April 2004).

Sen, G. and S. Correa, 'Gender justice and economic justice: reflections on the Five-Year Reviews of the UN conferences of the 1990s', paper prepared for UNIFEM in preparation for the Five-Year Review of the Beijing Platform for Action, *DAWN Informs*, 1/2000 (2000).

Sen, G. and C. Grown, *Development, Crises, and Alternative Visions: Third World Women's Perspectives* (New York: Monthly Review Press, 1987).

Sen, G., A. Germain and L.C. Chen (eds), *Population Policies Reconsidered: Health, Empowerment and Rights*, Harvard Center for Population and Development Studies (Cambridge, MA: Harvard University Press, 1994).

Short, Clare, *Eliminating World Poverty: Making Globalisation Work for the Poor*, White Paper on International Development, Cm 5006 (London: Stationery Office, 2000).

Sikkink, Kathryn, *Ideas and Institutions: Developmentalism in Brazil and Argentina* (Ithaca: Cornell University Press, 1991).

Singer, Hans, 'The distribution of gains between investing and borrowing countries', *American Economic Review*, Vol. 40, No. 2 (1950) 473–85.

Singh, Ajit, 'Catching up with the West: A perspective on Asian economic development and lessons for Latin America'. In Louis Emmerij (ed.), *Economic and Social Development into the 21st Century* (Baltimore: The Johns Hopkins University Press, 1997).

Sklair, L., *The Transnational Capitalist Class* (Oxford: Blackwell, 2001).

Smith, Harvey, 'Ownership and capacity: do current donor approaches help or hinder the achievement of international and national targets for education?', paper to the Oxford International Conference on The State of Education: Quality, Quantity and Outcomes, New College, Oxford, 9–11 September (2003).

Sorel, Georges, *Reflections on Violence* (New York: Peter Smith, 1941).

South Commission, *The Challenge to the South* (Oxford: Oxford University Press, 1990).

Squire, Lyn, 'Why the World Bank should be involved in development research'. In Christopher L. Gilbert and David Vines (eds), *The World Bank: Structure and Policies* (Cambridge: Cambridge University Press, 2000).

Standing, Guy, *Globalisation: the Eight Crises of Social Protection*, mimeo (Geneva: ILO, 2001).

Stern, Nicolas and Francisco Ferreira, 'The World Bank as an "intellectual actor"'. In Devesh Kapur, John P. Lewis and Richard Webb (eds), *The World Bank: Its First Half Century. Volume 2: Perspectives* (Washington DC: Brookings Institution, 1997).

Stewart, Frances and Michael Wang, *Do PRSPs Empower Poor Countries and Disempower the World Bank, or Is It the Other Way Round?*, QEH Working Paper No. 108 (Oxford: Queen Elizabeth House, 2003).

Stiefel, Matthias and Marshall Wolfe, *A Voice for the Excluded: Popular Participation in Development: Utopia or Necessity?* (London and New Jersey: Zed Books, 1994).

Stiglitz, Joseph E., *Globalization and Its Discontents* (New York: W.W. Norton and Company; and London: Allen Lane, 2002).

——, 'More instruments and broader goals: Moving towards the post-Washington Consensus'. In Ha-Joon Chang (ed.), *Joseph Stiglitz and the World Bank: the Rebel Within* (London: Anthem Press, 2001).

Stokke, Olav, *The UN and Development Cooperation*, UNIHP Series (Bloomington, IN: Indiana University Press, forthcoming).

Stone, D., *Banking on Knowledge: the Genesis of the Global Development Net* (London: Routledge, 2000).

——, *Capturing the Political Imagination: Think Tanks and the Policy Process* (London: Frank Cass, 1996).

Stone, Diane and Simon Maxwell (eds), *Bridges across Boundaries: Global Knowledge Networks and International Development* (London: Routledge, 2004).

Streck, C., 'Global public policy networks as coalitions for change'. In D. Esty and M.H. Ivanova (eds), *Global Environmental Governance: Options and Opportunities* (New Haven, CT: Yale University, 2002).

The Structural Adjustment Participatory Review International Network (SAPRIN), *Structural Adjustment: The SAPRI Report, The Policy Roots of Economic Crisis, Poverty and Inequality* (London and New York: Zed Books, 2004).

Swank, D., *Global Capital, Political Institutions and Policy Change in Developed Welfare States* (Cambridge: Cambridge University Press, 2002).

Swedish International Development Cooperation Agency (Sida), *Sida at Work: a Guide to Principles, Procedures and Working Methods* (Stockholm: Sida, 2003).

——, *Sida's Policy for Capacity Development* (Stockholm: Sida, 2000a).

——, *Sida's Policy for Sector Programme Support and Provisional Guidelines* (Stockholm: Sida, 2000b).

——, *Sida Looks Forward* (Stockholm: Sida, 1997).

Sykes, R., B. Palier and P. Prior, *Globalization and the European Welfare States: Challenges and Change* (Aldershot: MacMillan, 2001).

Taylor, Lucy, *Citizenship, Participation and Democracy: Changing Dynamics in Chile and Argentina* (London: Macmillan, 1998).

Taylor, Marilyn, with Gary Craig, Surya Monro, Tessa Parkes, Diane Warburton and Mick Wilkinson, 'A sea-change or a swamp? New spaces for voluntary sector engagement in governance in the UK', *IDS Bulletin*, Vol. 35, No. 2 (2004).

Tendler, J., 'Why social policy is condemned to a residual category of safety nets and what to do about it', Mimeo, paper prepared for the UNRISD project on Social Policy in a Development Context in the UNRISD programme on Social Policy and Development (Geneva: UNRISD, 2002).

Thakur, Ramesh and Thomas G. Weiss, *The UN and Global Governance: an Idea and its Prospects*, UNIHP Series (Bloomington, IN: Indiana University Press, forthcoming).

Thompson, John, 'Participatory approaches in government bureaucracies: facilitating the process of institutional change', *World Development*, Vol. 23, No. 9 (1995) 1521–54.

Tilak, J.B., 'International aid and knowledge societies'. In Wolfgang Gmelin, Kenneth King and Simon McGrath (eds), *Development Knowledge, National Research and International Cooperation* (Edinburgh: Centre of African Studies – CAS/Bonn: German Foundation for International Development – DSE/Geneva: NORRAG, 2001).

Tinbergen, Jan, *The Design of Development* (Baltimore: Johns Hopkins Press for IBRD, 1958).

Tinker, I., 'The adverse impact of development on women'. In I. Tinker and M.B. Bramsen (eds), *Women and World Development* (Washington, DC: Overseas Development Council, 1976).

Tooze, J. Adam, *Statistics and the German State, 1900–1945: The Making of Modern Economic Knowledge* (Cambridge: Cambridge University Press, 2001).

Torres, Rosa Maria, 'Development, knowledge, research and international cooperation. A view from the "Critical South" '. In Wolfgang Gmelin, Kenneth King and Simon McGrath (eds), *Development Knowledge, National Research and International Cooperation* (Edinburgh: Centre of African Studies – CAS/Bonn: German Foundation for International Development – DSE/Geneva: NORRAG, 2001).

Townsend, P., 'The restoration of 'universalism': the rise and fall of Keynesian influence on social development policies', paper prepared for the UNRISD project on Social Policy in a Development Context in the UNRISD programme on Social Policy and Development (Geneva: UNRISD, 2002).

Townsend, P. and D. Gordon (eds), *World Poverty: New Policies to Defeat an Old Enemy* (Bristol: Policy Press, 2002).

Toye, John, 'Social knowledge and international policy making: the Bretton Woods institutions', paper prepared for the UNRISD conference on Social Knowledge and Policy Making: Exploring the Linkages, Geneva, 20–21 April (2004).

——, *Dilemmas of Development: Reflections on the Counter-Revolution in Development Theory and Policy* (Oxford: Basil Blackwell, 1993, 1987).

Toye, John and Richard Toye, *The UN and Global Political Economy: Trade, Finance and Development* (Bloomington, IN: Indiana University Press, 2004).

United Nations, *2005 World Summit Outcome*, Sixtieth session of the General Assembly, A/60/L.1 (New York: United Nations, 2005). http://www.globalpolicy. org/msummit/millenni/2005/0913thirteenth.pdf, accessed on 26 September 2005.

——, *Resolution Adopted by the General Assembly. 55/2. United Nations Millennium Declaration*, A/RES/55/2, Fifty-fifth Session, Agenda item 60 (b), 18 September (New York: United Nations, 2000). http://www.worldvolunteerweb.org/ development/mdg/background/ares552e_mill_dec.pdf.

——, *The World Conferences: Developing Priorities for the 21st Century* (New York: United Nations, 1997).

——, *Charter on Economic Rights and Duties of States*, Resolution 3281 (XXIX) adopted by the Twenty-ninth session of the General Assembly, 12 December (1974). http://www.un.org/documents/ga/res/29/ares29.htm.

——, *Measures for the Economic Development of Under-Developed Countries* (New York: United Nations, 1951a).

——, *Measures for International Economic Stability* (New York: United Nations, 1951b).

——, *National and International Measures for Full Employment* (New York: United Nations, 1949).

United Nations Department of Economic and Social Affairs (UNDESA), *Report on the World Social Situation: the Inequality Predicament* (New York: United Nations, 2005).

United Nations Conference on Trade and Development (UNCTAD), *Economic Development in Africa: Rethinking the Role of Foreign Direct Investment* (New York and Geneva: United Nations, 2005).

——, *São Paolo Consensus Adopted by UNCTAD XI*, 18 June (2004). www.unctad.org.

United Nations Development Programme (UNDP), *Human Development Report 2005: International Cooperation at a Crossroads: Aid, Trade and Security in an Unequal World* (New York: UNDP, 2005).

——, *Human Development Report 2003: Millennium Development Goals: a Compact among Nations to End Human Poverty* (Oxford and New York: Oxford University Press, 2003a).

——, *Ownership, Leadership and Transformation: Can We Do Better for Capacity Development?* (New York: UNDP, 2003b).

——, *Developing Capacity through Technical Co-operation* (New York: UNDP, 2002).

——, *Capacity for Development. New Solutions to Old Problems* (New York: UNDP, 2001).

——, *Human Development Report 1999* (New York: Oxford University Press, 1999).

United Nations Economic Commission for Europe (ECE), *Economic Survey of Europe 1990–1991: The Hard Road to the Market Economy* (Geneva: United Nations, 1991).

——, 'Economic reform in the East: a framework for Western support', *Economic Survey of Europe 1989–1990* (Geneva: United Nations, 1990).

United Nations Economic and Social Commission for Asia and the Pacific (UNESCAP), *Restructuring the Developing Economies of Asia and Pacific* (Bangkok: UNESCAP, 1990).

United Nations Economic and Social Council (ECOSOC), *Improving Public Service Effectiveness*, Report of the Secretary-General to the Commission for Social Development, Forty-second session, 4–13 February 2004, UN Doc. E/CN.5/2004/5 (New York: United Nations, 2003).

——, *Enhancing Social Protection and Reducing Vulnerability in a Globalizing World*, Report of the Secretary-General to the Commission for Social Development, Thirty-ninth session, 13–23 February 2001, UN Doc. E/CN.5/2001/2 (New York: United Nations, 2000).

United Nations Educational, Scientific and Cultural Organization (UNESCO), *Education for All: Is the World on Track?*, EFA Global Monitoring Report (Paris: UNESCO, 2002).

United Nations Research Institute for Social Development (UNRISD), *Gender Equality: Striving for Justice in an Unequal World* (Geneva: UNRISD, 2005).

——, *Social Knowledge and International Policy Making: Exploring the Linkages*, Geneva, 20–21 April 2004, Conference News, No. 14 (Geneva: UNRISD, 2004).

——, *The Need to Rethink Development Economics*, Conference News, Report of the UNRISD Conference, Cape Town, South Africa, 7–8 September 2001 (Geneva: UNRISD, 2003).

Utting, Peter, 'Corporate responsibility and the movement of business', *Development in Practice*, Volume 15, Issues 3 and 4, June (2005a) 375–88.

Utting, Peter, *Rethinking Business Regulation: from Self-Regulation to Social Control*, Programme Paper on Technology, Business and Society, Paper No. 15 (Geneva: UNRISD, 2005b).

Vandemoortele, Jan, 'Are the Millennium Development Goals feasible?'. In R. Black and H. White (eds), *Targeting Development* (London: Routledge, 2004).

Vengroff, Richard, 'Popular participation and the administration of rural development: the case of Botswana', *Human Organisation*, Vol. 33, No. 3 (1974) 303–9.

de Vibe, Maja, Ingeborg Hovland and John Young, *Bridging Research and Policy: an Annotated Bibliography*, Working Paper 174 (London: Overseas Development Institute, 2002).

Wade, Robert, 'Showdown at the World Bank', *New Left Review*, 2nd Series, No. 7 (2001) 124–37.

——, 'Greening the Bank: The struggle over the environment 1970–1995'. In D. Kapur, J. Lewis and R. Webb (eds), *The World Bank: Its First Half Century*, Vol. II (Washington, DC: Brookings Institution, 1997).

——, 'Japan, the World Bank and the art of paradigm maintenance: The East Asian miracle in political perspective', *New Left Review*, No. 217, May–June (1996) 3–36.

Ward, Michael, *Quantifying the World: UN Ideas and Statistics* (Bloomington, IN: Indiana University Press, 2004).

Watson, Peter, *A Terrible Beauty: the People and Ideas that Have Shaped the Modern Mind: a History* (London: Phoenix Press, 2001).

Weisbrot, Mark, 'The IMF has lost its influence', *International Herald Tribune*, 23 September 2005.

Weisbrot, Mark, Dean Baker, Robert Naiman and Gila Neta, *Growth May Be Good for the Poor – But Are IMF and World Bank Policies Good for Growth?: A Closer Look at the World Bank's Recent Defense of Its Policies* (Washington, DC: Center for Economic and Policy Research, May 2001).

Weiss, C., 'Research for policy's sake: The enlightenment function of social research', *Policy Analysis* 3(4) (1977) 531–45.

Weiss, Thomas G. and Tatiana Carayannis, 'Whither United Nations economic and social ideas? A research agenda', *Global Social Policy*, vol. 1(1) (2001) 25–47.

Weiss, Thomas G., David P. Forsythe and Roger A. Coate, *The United Nations and Changing World Politics*, 4th ed. (Boulder: Westview, 2004).

Weiss, Thomas G., Tatiana Carayannis, Louis Emmerij and Richard Jolly, *UN Voices: the Struggle for Development and Social Justice*, UNIHP Series (Bloomington, IN: Indiana University Press, 2005).

West Indian Commission (WICOM), *Time for Action: Report of the Independent West Indian Commission* (Black Rock, Barbados: The West Indian Commission, 1992).

Whaites, Alan (ed.), *Masters of Their Own Development? PRSPs and the Prospects for the Poor* (Geneva: World Vision Publications, 2002).

Whitehead, Ann, *Failing Women, Sustaining Poverty: Gender in Poverty Reduction Strategy Papers*, Report for the UK Gender and Development Network (London: Christian Aid, 2003).

Wilks, Alex and Fabien Lefrancoise, *Blinding with Science or Encouraging Debate? How World Bank Analysis Determines PRSP Policies* (London: Bretton Woods Project and California: World Vision International, 2002).

Williams, F., *Social Policy: a Critical Introduction* (London: Sage, 1987).

Williams, Raymond, *Keywords* (London: Picador, 1976).

Williamson, John, 'What Washington means by policy reform'. In John Williamson (ed.), *Latin American Adjustment: How Much Has Happened?* (Washington, DC: Institute for International Economics, 1990).

Witte, Jan Martin, Wolfgang H. Reinicke and Thorsten Benner, 'Beyond multilateralism: Global public policy networks', *International Politics and Society*, 2/2000 (2000).

Wolf, Eric R., *Europe and the People Without History* (Berkeley: University of California Press, 1982).

Wolfensohn, James, *People and Development*, Annual Meetings Address, 1 October (Washington, DC: World Bank, 1996).

Wood, Geof (ed.), *Labelling in Development Policy* (London: Sage, 1985).

Woods, Ngaire, 'Order, justice, the IMF and the World Bank'. In Rosemary Foot, John Lewis Gaddis and Andrew Hurrell (eds), *Order and Justice in International Relations* (Oxford: Oxford University Press, 2003).

——, 'Global governance and the role of institutions'. In D. Held and A. McGrew (eds), *Governing Globalization* (Cambridge: Polity Press, 2002).

——, 'Economic ideas and international relations: Beyond rational neglect', *International Studies Quarterly*, Vol. 39 (1995) 161–80.

World Bank, *World Development Report 2006: Equity and Development* (New York, Oxford University Press, 2005).

——, *World Development Report 2004: Making Services Work for Poor People* (Washington, DC: World Bank, 2003a).

——, *Sharing Knowledge: Innovations and Remaining Challenges: an OED Evaluation*, Operations Evaluation Department (Washington, DC: World Bank, 2003b).

——, *World Development Report 2003: Sustainable Development in a Dynamic World: Transforming Institutions, Growth, and Quality of Life* (New York, Oxford University Press, 2002a).

——, *Constructing Knowledge Societies: New Challenges for Tertiary Education* (Washington, DC: World Bank, 2002b).

——, *Remarks to the Plenary Meeting*, speech by James Wolfensohn at the International Conference on Financing for Development, Monterrey, Mexico, 18–22 March 2002c, available online at www.worldbank.org (News & Broadcast, speeches).

——, *World Development Report 2002: Building Institutions for Markets* (New York, Oxford University Press, 2001a).

——, *Enhancing the Use of Knowledge for Growth and Poverty Reduction* (Washington, DC: World Bank, 2001b).

——, *World Development Report 2000/2001: Attacking Poverty* (New York, Oxford University Press, 2000a).

——, *Engendering Development through Gender Equality in Rights, Resources, and Voice*, a World Bank Policy Research Report (New York: Oxford University Press, 2000b).

——, *World Development Report 1998/1999: Knowledge for Development* (New York, Oxford University Press, 1999).

——, *Higher Education: the Lessons of Experience* (Washington, DC: World Bank, 1994).

——, *Vocational and Technical Education and Training: a World Bank Policy Paper* (Washington, DC: World Bank, 1991).

——, *World Development Report 1990*, A World Bank Publication (New York: Oxford University Press, 1990a).

——, *Primary Education: a World Bank Policy Paper* (Washington, DC: World Bank, 1990b).

——, *Poverty Reduction Strategy Sourcebook* (No date). http://www.worldbank.org/poverty/strategies/sourcons.htm, accessed on 19 May 2004.

World Commission on Environment and Development, *Our Common Future* (Oxford: Oxford University Press, 1987).

World Conference on Education for All (WCEFA) (5–9 March 1990, Jomtien, Thailand), *World Declaration on Education for All and Framework for Action to Meet Basic Learning Needs*, Inter-Agency Commission, April (New York: UNICEF House, 1990).

World Education Forum, *The Dakar Framework for Action* (Paris: UNESCO, 2000).

Yeates, N., *Globalization and Social Policy: the Regional Dimension* (Geneva: UNRISD, 2004).

——, *Globalization and Social Policy* (London: Sage Publications, 2001).

Yee, Albert, 'The causal effects of ideas on policies', *International Organization*, Vol. 50 (1996) 59–108.

Zaidi, Sarah and Roger Normand, *The UN and Human Rights: the Unfinished Revolution*, UNIHP Series (Bloomington, IN: Indiana University Press, forthcoming – 2005).

Zammit, Ann, *Development at Risk: Rethinking UN–Business Partnerships* (Geneva: South Centre/UNRISD, 2003).

Index